PUBLIC ENEMIES

PUBLIC ENEMIES

MICHEL HOUELLEBECQ

— AND —

BERNARD-HENRI LÉVY

Atlantic Books

LONDON

First published in France as *Enemis Publics* by Flamarrion /
Grasset & Fasquelle, 2008

First published in Great Britain in 2011 by Atlantic Books, an
imprint of Atlantic Books Ltd

123456789

A CIP catalogue record for this book is available from the British
Library.

Hardback ISBN: 978 1 84887 158 8
Airport and Trade Paperback ISBN: 978 1 84887 159 5

Design by Liz Cosgrove
Printed and bound by TJ International Ltd, Padstow, Cornwall

Atlantic Books
An imprint of Atlantic Books Ltd
Ormond House
26–27 Boswell Street
London
WC1N 3JZ

www.atlantic-books.co.uk

PUBLIC ENEMIES

Dear Bernard-Henri Lévy,

We have, as they say, nothing in common—except for one essential trait: we are both rather contemptible individuals.

A specialist in farcical media stunts, you dishonor even the white shirts you always wear. An intimate of the powerful who, since childhood, has wallowed in obscene wealth, you are the epitome of what certain slightly tawdry magazines like *Marianne* still call "champagne socialism" and what German journalists more astutely refer to as the Toskana-Fraktion. A philosopher without an original idea but with excellent contacts, you are, in addition, the creator behind the most preposterous film in the history of cinema.

Nihilist, reactionary, cynic, racist, shameless misogynist: to lump me in with the rather unsavory family of "right-wing anarchists" would be to give me too much credit; basically, I'm just a *redneck*. An unremarkable author with no style, I achieved literary notoriety some years ago as the result of an uncharacteristic error in judgment by critics who had lost the plot. Happily, my heavy-handed provocations have since fallen from favor.

Together, we perfectly exemplify the shocking dumbing-down of French culture and intellect as was recently pointed out, sternly but fairly, by *Time* magazine.

We have contributed nothing to the electro-pop revival in France. We're not even mentioned in the credits of *Rata-touille.*

These then are the terms of the debate.

The debate?

There are three possible approaches, dear Michel Houelle-becq.

Approach 1. Well done. You've said it all. You're mediocre, I'm a nonentity, and in our heads there's nothing but a resounding void. We both have a taste for playacting, we could even be called impostors. For thirty years I've been wondering how I've managed to take people in and continue to do so. For thirty years, tired of waiting for the right reader to come along and unmask me, I've been stepping up my lame, dull, halfhearted self-criticisms. But here we are. Thanks to you, with your help, maybe I'll get there. Your vanity and mine, my immorality and yours . . . As another contemptible fellow—and he was of the highest order—once said, you lay down your cards and I'll lay down mine. What a relief!

Approach 2. Maybe you. But why me? Why should I walk into this exercise of self-denigration? Why should I follow you into this explosive, raging, humiliated self-destruction you seem to have a taste for? I don't like nihilism. I loathe the resentment and melancholy that go with it. I believe that the sole value of literature is to take up arms against this *depres-*

sionism, which, more than ever, is the password of our era. In that case, I could go out of my way to explain that there are also happy beings, successful works, lives more harmonious than the killjoys who detest us appear to believe. I would take the villain's role, the true villain, Philinte versus Alceste,* and wax lyrical in a heartfelt eulogy of your books and, while I'm about it, my own.

Then there's approach number 3. To answer the question you raised the other night at the restaurant, when we came up with the idea of this dialogue: Why is there so much hatred? Where does it come from? And why, when the targets are writers, is it so extreme in its tone and virulence? Look at yourself. Look at me. And there are other, more serious cases: Sartre, who was spat on by his contemporaries; Cocteau, who could never watch a film to the end because there was always someone waiting to take a crack at him; Pound in his cage; Camus in his box; Baudelaire describing in a tremendous letter how the "human race" is in league against him. And the list goes on. Indeed, we would need to look at the whole history of literature. And perhaps we would also need to try and explore writers' own desire. Which is? The desire to displease, to be repudiated. The giddiness and pleasure of disgrace.

You choose.

---

*Philinte and Alceste: characters in Molière's play *The Misanthrope.* Alceste is the hypercritical misanthrope of the title, while Philinte is a social hypocrite.

Dear Bernard-Henri,

I will forgo, for the moment, the pleasures of the delicious debate we could have (we *will have*) about "depressionism," a subject on which I am, as you say, one of the undisputed authorities. It's just that I'm in Brussels, where I have none of my books to hand, and so might make a slip in this or that quotation from Schopenhauer, whereas Baudelaire is about the only author I can quote more or less from memory. Besides, talking about Baudelaire in Brussels is always nice.

In a passage that probably predates the one you mention (in that he hasn't yet started laying into the human race as a whole, only France), Baudelaire states that a great man is what he is only *in spite of* his compatriots and that he must therefore develop an aggressive force equal to or greater than the collective defensive forces of his compatriots.

The first thought that occurs to me is that this must be extraordinarily exhausting. The second thought is that Baudelaire died at the age of forty-six.

Baudelaire, Lovecraft, Musset, Nerval—so many of the authors who have mattered to me in my life, for different reasons—died in their forty-seventh year. I clearly remember my forty-seventh birthday. In midmorning, I completed the work I was doing on *The Possibility of an Island* and sent the novel to the publisher. A couple of days earlier, I had gathered together unfinished texts lying around on CD-ROMs and floppy disks and, before throwing out the disks, collected all the files together on a hard drive from an old computer; then, completely accidentally, I formatted the hard drive, permanently erasing all of the texts. I was still a few meters from the brow of the hill and I had a fair idea of what the long downhill slope that is the second half of life would be like: the successive humiliations of old age and then death. The idea occurred to me more than once, in brief, insistent thoughts, that nothing was forcing me to live out this second half; that I had a perfect right to *play hooky.*

I did nothing about it and I began my descent. After a few months I realized that I was venturing into an uncertain, viscous territory and that I would have to fill in time before I could get out. I felt something like a falling-off (sometimes brief, sometimes long) in the will to be disliked that was my way of facing the world. More and more frequently, and it pains me to admit it, I felt a *desire to be liked.* Simply to be liked, by everyone, to enter into a magical space where there was no finger-pointing, no dirty tricks, no polemics. Needless to say, on each occasion a little thought convinced me of the absurdity of this dream; life is limited and forgiveness impossible. But thought was powerless, the desire persisted—and, I have to admit, persists to this day.

Both of us have doggedly sought out the delights of abjection, of humiliation, of ridicule; and in this we have succeeded, to say the least. The fact remains that such pleasures are neither immediate nor natural and that our true, our primitive desire (excuse me for speaking for you), like that of everyone else, is to be admired, or loved, or both.

How can we explain the strange detour that, unbeknownst

to each other, we both took? I was struck the last time we met by the fact that you still Google yourself, in fact you even have a Google alert so you know every time a new story appears. I've turned off my Google alerts, in fact I've even stopped Googling myself.

You wanted, you explained to me, to know your adversary's position so that you might be better able to respond. I don't know whether you genuinely enjoy war, or rather I don't know how much of the time you enjoy it, how many years' training it took to find an interest and a charm in it; but what is undeniable is that, like Voltaire, you believe that ours is a world where one lives or dies *"les armes à la main."*

The fact that you are not *battle weary* is a powerful force. It prevents you and will go on preventing you from succumbing to misanthropic apathy, which, to me, is the greatest danger; that bleating, sterile sulkiness that makes one hole up in a corner constantly muttering "arseholes, the lot of them" and, quite literally, do nothing else.

The force in me that might play this socializing role is rather different: my *desire to displease* masks an insane *desire to please*. But I want people to like me "for myself," without trying to seduce, without hiding whatever is shameful about me. I have been known to resort to provocation; I regret that, for it is not in my innermost nature. By provocateur I refer to anyone who, independently of what he thinks or what he is (and by constantly resorting to provocation, the provocateur no longer thinks, no longer is), calculates his words, his attitude to provoke maximum annoyance or discomfiture in his interlocutor. Many humorists in recent decades have been remarkably provocative.

I, on the other hand, suffer from a form of perverse sincerity: I doggedly, relentlessly seek out that which is worst in me so that I can set it, still quivering, at the public's feet—exactly the way a terrier brings his master a rabbit or a slipper. And this is not something I do in order to achieve some form of redemption, the very idea of which is alien to me. I don't want to be loved *in spite of* what is worst in me, but *because of* what is worst in me. I even go so far as to hope that what is worst in me is *what people like best about me.*

The fact remains that I am uncomfortable and helpless in the face of outright hostility. Every time I did one of those famous Google searches, I had the same feeling as, when suffering from a particularly painful bout of eczema, I end up scratching myself until I bleed. My eczema is called Pierre Assouline,* Didier Jacob, François Busnel, Pierre Mérot, Denis Demonpion[†], Éric Naulleau[‡], and so many others—I forget the name of the guy at *Le Figaro*—I don't really know anymore. In the end, I stopped counting my enemies although, in spite of my doctor's repeated advice, I still haven't given up scratching.

Nor have I given up trying to beat my eczema, but I believe I have finally realized that for the rest of my life I will have to suffer the microparasites who can—literally—no longer survive without me, whom I provide with a reason for existing, who will go so far, as in the recent Assouline case, for example, as to rummage through notes for a conference in Chile (where I felt I might be somewhat sheltered), anything they can dig out, cutting and remixing it a little to present me as ridiculous or odious.

And yet I don't want to have enemies, sworn, self-

---

*Pierre Assouline (born 1953) is a French journalist, novelist, and influential literary critic who has written widely for—among other publications—*Le Monde* and *Le Nouvel Observateur*.

[†]Denis Demonpion (born 1954) is a French journalist who wrote *Houellebecq non autorisé: Enquête sur un phénomène"* (2005), an unauthorized biography of Michel Houellebecq.

[‡]Éric Naulleau (born 1961) is a French publisher, translator, writer, polemicist, and literary critic.

confessed enemies, it simply does not interest me. While I have in me a desire to please and a desire to displease, I have never felt the least *desire to vanquish,* and it is in this, I believe, that we differ.

By this I do not mean that you do not also feel a desire to please, but that you *also* feel a desire to vanquish; in this you walk with both feet (which, according to president Mao Zedong, is preferable). And it's true that if you want to go far, go fast, it is preferable. On the other hand, the movements of a one-legged man have something whimsical, unpredictable about them; he is to the ordinary walker what a rugby ball is to a soccer ball; it's not impossible that a healthy one-legged man might more easily escape a sniper.

Enough of these dubious metaphors, which are simply a way of evading the question you were asking: "Why so much hatred?" Or more exactly, *"Why us?"* Even if we admit that *we were asking for it,* we still need to understand how we so consummately succeeded. It might be thought that I am senselessly wasting my energy on individuals as insignificant as Assouline or Busnel. The fact remains that my personal parasites (and, in the same way, yours) have, in their relentlessness, had certain results. On several occasions I have received e-mails from secondary-school students telling me that their teachers *warned them against* reading my books. By the same token, there has always been a scent of the lynch mob around you. Often, when your name comes up in conversation, I will notice an evil grin I know all too well, a rictus of petty, despicable pleasure at the prospect of being able to *insult without risk.* Many times, as a child (every time I found myself in a group of young men, in fact), I witnessed this vile process, the singling out of a victim that the group will then be able to humiliate and insult to their heart's content—and I have never for a moment doubted that, in the absence of a higher author-ity, specifically of their teachers or the cops, things would have gone much further, would have resulted in torture and mur-der. I never had the physical courage to side with the victim; but at least I never felt the desire to join the executioners' camp. We are perhaps, neither of us, particularly morally admirable, but we have nothing of the *pack animal* about us, this is one thing at least that can be said in our favor. As a child, when confronted by such painful scenes, I simply turned away, happy at the thought that I had been spared *this time.* And now that I am one of the victims, I can still turn away, more or less convinced that things will not go beyond the verbal, at least, as long as we live in a reasonably well-policed state.

Or I might try to understand, to contemplate this unpleas-ant phenomenon—although I have never really been convinced by the essentially symbolic explanations given for it, based on the history of religions. The phenomenon existed in rural civi-lizations, it exists today in our cities, it would continue to exist if cities ceased to exist and all communication were virtual. It seems to me to be entirely independent of the political or spiri-tual order of the times. Revealed religions could, I believe, dis-appear without the phenomenon being markedly affected.

A number of passages in *Comédie,** which I've just finished, make me think that you have had occasion to ponder the question in your own case. So . . . I pass the baton to you.

And I cordially salute you.

**Comédie (Grasset)* is an intensely personal book by Bernard-Henri Lévy in which he mocks his public persona—a "puppet" serving up biting self-criticism of "BHL."

Oh yes, eczema . . .

Are you familiar with those tremendous pages in Cocteau about just that, eczema?

They're in that marvelous little book, his journal of the making of *La Belle et la bête* [*Beauty and the Beast*], which Truffaut recommends that all budding filmmakers should read.*

It has some interesting pages about the adventure of shooting a film, his relations with Bérard, the disagreements with Alekan about lighting, the discovery of the tracking shot, special effects, style, the patience of the extras, living statues, Jean Marais.

But it also contains (and I'm tempted to say that this is the book's obsession, its leitmotif) astounding pages, almost physically painful for the reader, about what he calls his "carapace of cracks, ravines and itches," his "coral of fire," or the "burning bush" of nerves that have replaced his features, his "boils," "abscesses," red "gashes," his "blisters," and his

---

*Jean Cocteau, *Journal d'un film*, published 1947 (shooting diary).

oozing "wounds." The entire book is one long moan, a cry of pain on paper, the display of a face eaten up by unbearable pain, so that there are mornings when he can only appear on the shoot with layers of fresh lard that his chief electrician has spread over his cheeks and nose.

Poor Cocteau . . .

Poor "prince of poets." Despite Arno Breker,* despite that phony style of his, his emphatic, bombastic side, I've never been able to think badly of him.

And of course, poor Baudelaire—member of the human race, of France, of Belgium, as you say. He had everyone breathing down his neck. They were baying for his blood from the word go. Reproof at first sight! At first the pack was cautious, intimidated by the dandy airs of this son of Caroline and her first husband, the defrocked priest, but very soon, in the second part of his life, during his stay in Brussels at the Grand Miroir Hotel, their howling got louder and louder! Few writers before Sartre—and it's no coincidence that he wrote a good life of Baudelaire—have been so loathed. Few of them, particularly during their years of exile, had to deal with rejection on this scale. Dear Michel, I envy you for being in Brussels. I stayed there to write my novel on his last days (Baudelaire's, I mean). It was a few months after the Grand Miroir had been torn down and replaced by a sex shop. And what a wonderful name—the Grand Miroir—for a man who made a profession out of "living and dying in a mirror" in order to be "continually sublime." The fact that I got there too late, that I just missed the Grand Miroir and its mysteries, is one of my true literary regrets in life. I envy you for being there, because—if any of this appeals to you—the cobble-

---

*German neoclassicist sculptor, beloved of Nazis (and one himself).

stones of the rue Ducale remain, with girls still twisting their ankles on the footprints of the author of *Fusées*.* There's Petit Sablon Square, where, in my day, a brothel he used to like still survived, and the Augustine convent where he was locked up after his aphasia. And then, of course, there's Namur, Église Saint-Loup de Namur, where for the first time he was touched by "the breeze of imbecility flapping its wing."

But back to your question—whether I have, as you put it, had occasion to reflect on "the" question based on my own experience.

Well, yes and no.

Naturally, yes, insofar as, even when I'm not there, I have eyes to see and ears to hear the nasty rumblings in response to any mention of me in a public place.

And yet, at the same time, no, because through a rather strange phenomenon, I—unlike you, apparently—have never managed to think of myself as or feel like the "victim" of real "persecution."

Few other writers are abused as much as I am.

For each of my books I receive a volley of insults that plenty of other people would find demoralizing.

As for eczema, well, if that were a criterion, I have to admit that I'm something of an expert on that as well.

The fact is that I find it terribly difficult not so much to take note of these attacks but to relate to the image of me they contain, to make it my own, to associate this reflection, hardly flattering, sometimes appalling, with my deep self or even simply my social self.

Let's take for example the film I shot twelve years ago and which got me reading the journal of *La Belle et la bête* so

Fusées: Charles Baudelaire's journals.

closely. I know what has been and what continues to be said about it. When it isn't entirely annihilated by the wags, I know that it's said to be "trash," an officially "impoverished" work and, according to Serge Toubiana, at the time the editor of *Cahiers* [*du cinéma*], "the worst film in the history of cinema." I know that when it's scheduled to be shown on television there are people who arrange a "dinner for idiots," where the idiots are the film and its author. But how can I explain this to you? I know it but without living it. I'm aware of it but don't ingest it. I know all about the avalanche of mud that was hurled at it when it was released, but I can't think of myself as the maker of the most impoverished and mud-covered film in the history of cinema and I am quite capable of ending up in a situation, a debate, a meeting with friends, a business meeting where, without noticing the sneers around me, oblivious to the ridicule I'm heaping on myself through the polite embarrassment I'm provoking, I talk about it as a normal film, in fact a rather good one, almost important, and which I am proud of.

Another example, more meaningful and with greater implications, is my being Jewish. As a rule, being Jewish means having a special relationship with this subject of persecution. For most Jews, being Jewish is an automatic passport to a perception of oneself as vulnerable, at risk, never completely at home, at the mercy of anti-Semitism. I know very few Jews who don't have in their memory some family or personal anecdote, sometimes a primal scene, that smacks of this innate familiarity with offense. But there again, that's not the case for me. I certainly do struggle against anti-Semitism. As you know, I'm one of those people who will let nothing get through on that subject, absolutely nothing. But perhaps that's a form of denial. Perhaps it's a symptom of my fundamental neurosis. Perhaps it's due to the fact that I was born in a part of the world where Jews were relatively spared. The fact is that when I'm fighting on behalf of Jews, I never have the feeling that I'm fighting for my own safety. The fact is—and please believe me—that I don't remember, either as a child or later on, suffering either physically or mentally from the discrimination, the insults against which I protest and rebel. There are Jews who suffer; I'm a Jew who fights. There are Jews who experience their Jewishness as a voyage into the depths of desolation, a voyage to the end of the night. I'm a happy Jew, what Jean-Claude Milner* would call an "affirmative" Jew, a "Solal,"† like Albert Cohen's, which in his vocabulary means "solar" and almost "Greek," one who sees only glory, splendor, and light in the biblical and Talmudic memory they have inherited.

And since we're on the subject of childhood memories, I'll tell you one too. Like you, I've known those classes of polymorphous perverts that find someone to pick on, stealing his satchel, emptying his wallet, or splashing ink on his face. At Pasteur de Neuilly, where I attended secondary school, the official whipping-boy was named Mallah. I can't remember his first name. But I can still see his pale face, his clumsy, frightened gestures, the beseeching way he looked at his tormentors. And his name came back to me when I read in the papers recently that President Sarkozy's mother came from a Jewish family in Salonica, whose name was none other than Mallah. Was he a relative? A cousin? A sort of older Sarkozy? I don't know. Nor do I know what became of him or even if

---

*French linguist and philosopher.

†*Solal:* Albert Cohen's first in a cycle of four autobiographical novels, published in 1930. Solal is Cohen's handsome and successful but permanently discontented alter ego, who struggles to reconcile his Jewish roots with his social position.

he's still alive. What I know is that, like you, I kept my distance from the pack of little hyenas who sought him out to humiliate him, even going as far as the metro to "look for" him. But not taking part in the posse after Mallah, keeping away from the squad of junior lynchers, was not enough. I took that boy under my wing and for several consecutive years made him my best friend. I don't deserve to be praised for this, any more than you do. But I note the psychological trait that, after all, was not an obvious one for the little Jewish boy I was at the end of the 1950s. It was so inconceivable to me that I myself might end up as a prey for this sort of pack, I was so far from fearing that I could be another possible target for the same horde of bastards, or, if you want to phrase it differently, the nightmare of persecution was so profoundly alien to me, that I had no problem at all with his being seen to be associated with me; indeed I flaunted my friendship with him.

By the way, some time later I made an extremely disturbing discovery. I had a literature teacher in the first year of prep at the École Normale Supérieure named Jean Deprun. Although he was thirty years older, he was like a clone of this little Mallah (with the same sort of feverish intelligence, the same large head on a deformed body, the same pale complexion with surprisingly fresh flesh, still looking unworn). I found his manner toward me strange, almost hostile. Without understanding why, I noticed that he avoided making eye contact when he called me up to the board to comment on a poem by Maurice Scève* or a page of *Salammbô*.† Then one day I mentioned his name at a family meal and my father

---

*Sixteenth-century French poet, leader of the Lyonese school, who "discovered" the tomb of Petrarch's Laura.

†Historical novel by Gustave Flaubert.

exclaimed, "Deprun? But I knew him very well." He told me that during the war, at the Cherchell Military Academy, this eminent scholar, a specialist in the philosophy of anxiety among eighteenth-century writers, had been a sort of fore-runner of Mallah, tormented by a league of young males, hounded, bullied, and my father had given him his protec-tion, just as I was to do thirty years later for his reincarnation in Neuilly.

My reason for telling you about this episode, the reason why I'm remembering and telling it, is that I'm always fascinated by the mystery of these ancient gestures that bewitch us, and which we unknowingly repeat.

But even more so, I wanted to tell you that I know all about this merging, potentially criminal group, the lynch mob, avid, bloodthirsty, the "hairless, malignant beast" of which Frantz speaks in [Sartre's play] *Les Séquestrés d'Altona* [*The Con-demned of Altona*],* the "carnivorous species that has sworn [our] destruction," in a word the great animal "lurking in the familiar eyes of our neighbors," which is rearing to be "released." In a sense I know it doubly. I am almost genealog-ically familiar with its characteristic breath, the quickened step, the warning signs, the war cry, the treachery. But I've never really felt that it was targeting me in particular or that I had it coming, that sooner or later my turn would come.

Let's put it differently.

Having reflected on your question, yes, of course.

Yes, it's quite clear that this is "the" phenomenon par excellence, that this phenomenon is the basis of social

---

*A family psychodrama, first produced in 1959, addressing Holocaust and German guilt and responsibility.

relations, far more than, say, love, the social contract, or universal affection among mankind. That's clear.

It's clear too that inclusion implies exclusion, and that generally whenever two men meet they have agreed to reject and banish a third . . . In other words, we must be suspicious of what the Greeks called *syncretism*—I've always thought that its deeper meaning was not the one claimed by etymology, a "union of several Cretans," but rather "everyone united against the Cretans" (they were, after all, the least favorably viewed, the most disreputable people in the ancient world). Doesn't that fit perfectly?

Yet, the more I have gained this knowledge applied to others, the more prolifically I've written about its underlying logic, the more I believe, for example—and to reply to one of your other remarks, the more I've helped, following the path opened up by René Girard,* to show that revealed religions are not responsible for producing scapegoats but rather help to subdue savagery—the more I feel that my personal case, my experience as a young man or as a man, hardly helped me to reach these conclusions.

It's odd but that's how it is.

It doesn't square with the idea that was our starting point, of the writer who has been disowned, insulted, dragged into the mud, et cetera. But it's the truth.

One last thing.

You seem skeptical when I say that the things written about me and that I discover from time to time on diabolical Google are significant for me only insofar as they keep me

---

*French historian, literary critic, philosopher, and anthropologist.

informed of the state of play, what my adversary is up to, his weaknesses if any, and how to react appropriately.

You're wrong.

I can assure you that this is also true.

As soon as I've read them and immediately drawn the obvious tactical or strategic conclusions, I forget the articles by those people.

They have no effect on my narcissism.

In the face of assaults, my ego is fireproof, shatterproof.

And there's a magic slate aspect, so that the malevolence spread in this way evaporates as soon as it stops scattering its effluents and informing me of the position of what Flaubert in a letter to Baudelaire called the adversary's "batteries" and "carriages."

In other words—and you were right there—there's nothing to equal the drive to conquer as an antidote to these two twin poisons, the desire to please and the desire to displease.

There's nothing to equal a *sense of war*, not only to protect a work, shelter it, give it sanctuary but also to see it through and to hang on to the desire to continue, unshaken by winds, tides, and the ravening pack.

I'd forgotten that phrase of Voltaire's.

But I have to say that I like it a lot and that's how I like to think of the writers I admire: living and dying bearing their weapons, making the best of it, like the great Valmont,* that "painter of battles." That's how I like to think of myself too, but my battles are like the ones in that book by Pérez-Reverte† that you recommended to me, and which I found gripping . . .

---

*"Valmont" presumably refers to the vicomte de Valmont, a character in *Les Liaisons dangereuses* (*Dangerous Liaisons*) by Pierre Choderlos de Laclos. He dies in a duel.

†Arturo Pérez-Reverte Gutiérrez, Spanish novelist and journalist.

But I'll stop here, dear Michel.

Because otherwise we'll have to come back to this art of warfare.

I mean the battlefield that is specifically the literary or philosophical scene.

And that state of continual battle dress, which according to the greatest too, sums up the life of a writer.

Kafka, for example . . .

Kafka, who, as you know, was an admirer of Napoleon and saw in the hesitations of the emperor at the Battle of Borodino or the scene of the withdrawal from Russia, the encrypted truth of those "campaigns" and "maneuvers" that made up his own everyday existence as a novelist . . .

Believe me—we'll save time this way.

Dear Bernard-Henri,

I believe you. Initially, your letter produced a sense of shock, but I chose to believe you—and I deserve a certain amount of credit for doing so, because an ego as robust as yours amounts to a mystery, even an anomaly.

The last time I felt so shocked goes back—the comparison is unfortunate, but I can't help that—to an interview with Yasmina Reza in which she related how Nicolas Sarkozy had greeted the prospect of her book about him. Our president, apparently, accepted with the words "Even if you demolish me, you will make me greater." I had to read the sentence three times before I accepted the fact: there truly are people whose ego has such power. In moments of rare good humor, I have subscribed to Nietzsche's famous dictum: That which does not kill me makes me stronger (most of the time I would be tempted, more prosaically, to think, That which does not kill me hurts me, and eventually weakens me). But I think Nicolas Sarkozy has gone one better.

You are not quite there, but then you are not a warrior or a politician but a writer. And such small fry are not noted for their invulnerability to wounded pride. How does a writer usually react when someone tries to hurt him? Quite simply, he suffers.

Incidentally, it is remarkable to note quite how powerful the writer's identity is. I don't know how many films Cocteau, Guitry, and Robbe-Grillet* and Pagnol made, but when we think of them we see them first and foremost as writer. There are, *a contrario*, some people who remember that Malraux was minister of culture. But I have no doubt that a few decades from now, that will be completely forgotten—you only have to think of the faint astonishment we feel now when we remember that Lamartine *really* stood as a candidate for president of the Republic.

The fact remains that you have developed a sort of magic potion that diminishes your vulnerability, and I would be interested in the recipe, especially as I am releasing a film this year and can therefore look forward to a screening of copious insults and spitting—from my traditional enemies and from others I have yet to discover: that about sums up my calendar for 2008.

There is, of course, the Obélix solution—fall into the cauldron as a baby—and the worst thing is that, in your case, that's probably the right answer, the trouble is, it doesn't help me much. We all end up becoming like our fathers, more or less; this is a penny that has long since dropped on me with the elegance of a concrete block, and it's possible that, from your time with your father, you have drawn only powerful, luminous images; in my case, the results are more mixed.

But, then again, the disturbing Chapter 5 of *Comédie* sug-

*Alain Robbe-Grillet was a French writer and filmmaker who died in 2008. He was associated with the *nouveau roman. C'est Gradiva qui vous appelle* is one of his so-called cine-novels.

gests that your secret may lie in a careful utilization of the *social self*. My first real contact with such realities dates back to 1998, when the ubiquitous Jérôme Garcin, flanked by his sinuous acolyte Fabrice Pliskin, contacted me to invite me, together with Philippe Sollers,* to debate in the columns of their magazine. I can still see their irritated faces when they found out that we had had dinner together the night before. "You've met each other before . . . ?" Jaws dropped. Of course we have, arsehole, is that against the law? The two cronies obviously wanted to goad the man with the cigarette holder through the "vitriolic portrait" of him I give in *The Elementary Particles*. The problem was that, at the time, Philippe was completely prepared to forgive me. First and foremost, it must be admitted, because I was in a *position of strength*. That's the trouble with Philippe, he is a barometer: he attacks me when I'm weak, supports me when I'm strong, he's a more accurate barometer than an army of frogs.

But I had also spun him a line in suggesting (quite honestly, in fact) that I had had no intention of painting a portrait of the *real Philippe Sollers*, because I didn't know the *real Philippe Sollers*, only the *media-friendly Philippe Sollers*—someone I knew only too well (and it's true that *ce cher Philippe* sometimes went too far in his omnipresence in the media; I think things have improved since then—unless it's simply that I've stopped watching TV). Anyway, Philippe immediately got the point: the idea of the *media-friendly Philippe Sollers* spoke to him. Here was a man who had truly integrated the distinction between the *innermost self* and the *social self*.

*Philippe Sollers (born 1936) is an influential French writer and critic who founded the avant-garde journal *Tel Quel* (1960–1982) and subsequently a journal called *L'Infini*, which is also the name of an imprint he directs for the prestigious French publisher Gallimard.

Since then I've occasionally been beset by a nagging, vaguely metaphysical doubt: Is there still a *real Philippe Sollers* beneath the *social Philippe Sollers*? I'm not entirely joking; Cioran notes with some amusement that when the libertine aristocrats of the eighteenth century died in public, crowds flocked to see it, just like to the theater, in the hope that the dying man might produce one last witticism—and in the fear that, whimpering and weeping, he might at the last moment beg to take communion. Staging one's own death, worrying that it might turn out to be a *flop*? You can see just how far man has been prepared to go in the service of art.

Philippe Sollers is not at that level, because this is not the eighteenth century, and because the Bordeaux bourgeoisie are not quite the aristocrats of the *ancien régime*. All the same, Philippe Sollers on television is about as unpredictable as Jean-Pierre Coffe; but that's probably the only sensible way to appear on TV: first, consider yourself to be a *permanent guest*; then put together a little schtick, with a few gimmicks, and wheel it out whenever you need to. And carefully bury your *innermost self,* make it all but inaccessible (at the risk, I repeat, of losing it).

Except that this is not what you do either: you appear on television, it seems to me, when you have *something to say*— you've written a book, you have some cause to champion, it varies. Your *innermost self* is not kept on a leash and, cher Bernard-Henri, it comes through at times almost violently, and it is doubtless modesty that prevents you from citing among your strengths the capacity for *conviction* and *indignation*.

This, please note, is of no use to me either. In my life, I have never really interested myself in anything beyond the field of literature, and there is little in that to get truly indignant about. And yet I have known intelligent, sensitive, remarkably cultured people (some of whom occasionally wrote reviews, conducted interviews) who never truly achieved a *position of strength*. It is Jérôme Garcin, not Michka Assayas, who edits the culture section of *Le Nouvel Obs[ervateur]*. So what? Who gives a fuck who edits the culture section of *Le Nouvel Obs*? It's clearly not as important as Bosnia.

To tell the truth, even if Michka Assayas were appointed to run the culture section of *Le Nouvel Obs*, I'm pretty sure he would resign after a couple of months; he would barely manage to deliver his weekly roundup for *VSD*. It's not about laziness (his *Dictionnaire du rock*, for example, was a mammoth undertaking), it's something more pernicious, a mixture of indifference and independence, something that, whatever it is, keeps you firmly *on the margins*.

There are, of course, exceptions; for example, I have a lot of admiration for Sylvain Bourmeau,* a hard worker if ever there was one. And I think that, thanks to my regular admonitions, Frédéric Beigbeder[†] has decided to keep his next job for more than a year. Even so, there is in those I admire a tendency toward irresponsibility that I find only too easy to understand. I am, after all, the son of a man who has (and I'm not up-to-date on everything he's done) launched three companies, only to get bored as soon as they became vaguely successful; who built five houses (actually built, poured the concrete, planed the wood, et cetera), only to give up on the idea of living in them almost as soon as they were built.

---

*Sylvain Bourmeau (born 1965) is a French journalist and former editor of the influential magazine *Les Inrockuptibles*.

[†]Frédéric Beigbeder (born 1965) is a French novelist, commentator, and literary critic.

.   .   .

Here we go again. We can't escape it. My role in your destiny may well be to have dragged you down to *confessional writing*—and that may not be altogether a bad thing. Schopenhauer notes with surprise that it is quite difficult to lie in one's letters (current thinking has not progressed on the subject and, for my part, I cannot help but *note with surprise:* there is something in an exchange of letters that fosters truth, participation—what?).

I don't have a particular affinity with confessional literature; my problem is that I like almost *all* forms of literature. I have happily wallowed in the writings of Montaigne and Rousseau, but I still feel a delicious visceral shock when reading Pascal's verdict on Montaigne, the extraordinary insolence like a slash of a whip full in the face: "The stupid plan he has to depict himself." I have also taken inordinate delight in the absolute antithesis of confessional literature that is fantasy and science fiction; my panegyrics on Lovecraft may at times be over the top, it doesn't matter, I stand by them.

And above all I have loved, and finally made my own, the *middle way*, which is that of the classic novelists. Who borrow from their own lives, or the lives of others, it doesn't matter, or who invent, it's all the same, in order to create their characters. The novelists, those consummate omnivores.

All the same, a little confessional writing might not be so bad. What do I know, I've never really tried it, and I don't think you know anything about it either. We are so often misinformed about our own vocation (it's surprising, for example, to think that Sartre may have attached greater importance to his works on theoretical philosophy than he did to *Nausea* or *The Words*).

Feel up to it?

For almost a week, dear Michel, I haven't managed to reply to you.

There was my day for writing my "Bloc-Notes" article.

Then there was the gathering we organized with Philippe Val, Laurent Joffrin, and Caroline Fourest around Ayaan Hirsi Ali,* that radiant young woman who's been condemned to death in the Netherlands for having dared to make some statements about Islam, of the kind that seven or eight years ago got you yourself dragged into court. (I don't agree with those statements: I don't believe for a minute that Islam is intrinsically hostile to democracy and human rights, but I'm struggling for her and for you to be entitled to express that opinion.)

There was the jury of the French Golden Globes equivalent, which I agreed to chair as a favor to a friend—that took up another day.

There have been the thousand concerns that I found or

*Ayaan Hirsi Ali (born 1969) is a Dutch intellectual, feminist activist, writer, and politician. Her screenplay for Theo van Gogh's movie *Submission* led to death threats. After van Gogh's assassination in 2004, she lived in seclusion under the protection of Dutch authorities. She now lives in the United States.

invented and that, caught up as I was in the madness and bustle of the day, caused me to put off replying to you.

But more than anything, there was the word *confession* that you ended with. Despite the passing years, I see that it still has the same ability to paralyze me . . .

Dear Michel, you have to understand that I am one of the few writers of my generation to have written novels (twenty years ago, you'll say, but in that respect I haven't changed) in which I consciously sought to create characters who were nothing like me.

You have to understand that in *Comédie,* which you quote (and which I published in the—oh so dramatic—aftermath of my own film's release; welcome to the club, by the way, and good luck!), everything was organized, literally everything, up to and including setting up the Great Confession, to give away as little as possible, to hide while appearing to open up and certainly not to yield to that illusion of transparency, of baring your heart, and so on, for which I feel an almost phobic aversion. False confessions, then . . . "screen confessions," the way psychoanalysts talk about screen memories . . . cunning, clever confessions whose entire purpose was to stand in the way of the big, juicy confessions I promised, even though I knew that I would have to shirk them. More than ever, when writing that book, I felt how patently true it is that turning your back on ambiguity can only be to your detriment.

You speak of Philippe Sollers, about whom, by the way, I think you're being unjust (the same goes for Garcin, who has the merit—rare nowadays—of keeping the proper distance in talking about both actresses and dead friends). I'd like you to know that the only serious disagreement Sollers and I have ever had over thirty years of real friendship is when he says (although, in passing, I'm not sure whether he applies the rule to himself) that writers are there to "tell how they live." The formula itself petrifies me. When he pronounces it, it plunges me into an abyss of perplexity, and I always feel like replying that I believe exactly the opposite—that writers have every right and can talk about whatever they like but not how they live, not their inalienable secret life!

As for television and the way you think you should behave there, I agree with your recommendations. I concur with your analysis of the need to perfect an "act" that allows us to hide and protect our "deep self." I also agree about the risk that, in doing so, like the "man who lost his shadow," you can lose the trace of the "deep self," let it lie fallow, forget it. Where you're wrong, or where I fear you rate me too highly, is when you attribute to me a capacity for indignation that shields me from that risk so that, fired up in a polemic, a political battle or a rage, I supposedly let the "real" me rise up to the surface. Sadly, indignation has no role in this. You can be indignant and yet take a strategic tack. You can be scandalized or enraged, but precisely because you're at war you manage to keep control of the impression you make. In my case, that's a fact. It's even, if I dare say so, an obligation. Even in extreme situations, when I return from Darfur or Sarajevo, when I rail against the indifference of the well-off toward this or that forgotten war, which I've taken the trouble to go and see and from where I bring back my distressed accounts, my phobia for these confessional stories is such that even there—I almost wrote *especially there*—I do whatever I can to stay in control of my emotions, reflexes, language, and facial expressions. (The face, oh dear . . . its shameful turmoil, its minuscule rages, which give away so much . . . it's the reason why I leave those [television interview] programs in a state of nervous exhaustion, which those who take me at my word when, quoting Bataille,* I trumpet that the principle to follow on television is to think "the way a girl takes her dress off" could hardly imagine.)

In my last letter I spoke to you about my indifference to the horrors they may write about me and which, I know, weaken me in my struggles.

There was a claim that my father made his fortune in a vile way, which I didn't contradict.

I let it pass when it was written that I hardly knew Massoud† and that giving him as a reference, laying claim to both his values and his friendship, was a fabrication.

I've allowed books to appear and be disseminated on the Internet that I obviously did look through, even if at the time I claimed I didn't, and whose basic message was always to make me out to be a bastard.

The reason I've put up with all this wasn't simply negligence, indifference, or contempt. It's not because I have a shatterproof, armor-plated ego or that I'm beyond reach. It's not even that I take that pleasure in being disliked, which we spoke of in our first exchange and which for me, as for you too perhaps, is another form of posing. No, what I now think is that if I have never refuted their claims and naturally never sued that evil lot, it's because part of me gets something out of it. That part of me prefers even disinformation and the supreme, Gidian art of the counterfeiter, an expert on false clues and ruses, to the obscenity of giving in to the universal

*Georges Bataille (1897–1962): highly influential French author and intellectual who developed the concept of base materialism.

†Ahmad Shah Massoud, Afghan rebel and anti-Soviet resistance leader, considered a moderate, who was assassinated two days before September 11, 2001.

exhortation, be yourself (i.e., love yourself), which is the commandment of our age.

Of course, the question is why.

What's behind this refusal, this phobia, this tendency to tell as little as possible, not to confess?

Where does it come from and what does it conceal—this desire to hide your cards, to be the champion of false confessions, an artist of trompe-l'oeil and deception, at the risk, I must repeat, of having highly offensive claims made about you without reacting?

I could tell you, and it would be true that there is a literary conception behind it: when I was writing the *Les Derniers Jours de Charles Baudelaire* [*The Last Days of Charles Baudelaire*], I was obsessed with the opposition between the good "Flaubertian model" and the bad "Stendhalian model": a cold, cold-blooded, possibly rigid, even stuffy literature versus the exquisite but to my mind antiliterary stylistic freedom of the literature of "release." Even today, I haven't changed that much. The experiments that fascinate me are still those where the "I" is withheld or even—and I hope we'll come back to this—where, as in Gary or Pessoa,* it is a minotaur lurking in the depths of a labyrinth of words, a clandestine orchestral director manipulating his clones like puppets on strings.

I could tell you, and it would be no less accurate, that this attitude derives from the idea I have—and which was also Michel Foucault's in his very last texts—as to why anyone

*Romain Gary (French author) and Fernando Pessoa (Portuguese author). Both were remarkable for their use of pseudonyms as alter egos, or, to use Pessoa's term, "heteronyms," suggesting that these personae took on a life of their own. In his letter of June 30, Lévy describes how Gary's identity was ultimately engulfed by his "creation," Paul Pavlowitch. Pavlowitch was Gary's cousin, who posed as Émile Ajar, Gary's alter ego.

embarks on the adventure of writing, which is that you write in order to find out not so much who you are as who you're becoming. I believe that what is at stake in a book is not being yourself, finding yourself, coinciding with your truth, your shadows, the eternal child within, or any of that other idiotic stuff, but rather changing, becoming other than the person you were before beginning and whom the book's own growth has rendered obsolete and uninteresting. Do we write to retreat into ourselves or to escape; to disappear or to make an appearance; to occupy a territory or to mine it and, having mined it, to change it and lose ourselves in the maze of an unreachable identity? For me, the answer is obvious and in itself explains why I couldn't care less about the nonsense written about the "truth" of my relations with money, media, power, or the Commander Massoud.

I could tell you—and it would also be true—that this mode of action, this repugnance for confession and for staging the inner self, reflects my metaphysical makeup, for better or for worse. In general, this derives from phenomenology, which reached its pinnacle in Sartre, then in the antihumanism of Althusser, Lacan, and once again Foucault, and whose fundamental principle is to view the subject as an empty form, with no real content, almost abstract, consisting entirely of the contact it establishes with the world and the content bestowed on it by that contact, this content being each time new, never substantial.

But the question of questions (and I don't need to explain this to Michel Houellebecq, the Nietzschean) is naturally what is behind the metaphysics, poetical arts, conceptions of the literary adventure. The real question is to ask ourselves what this type of argument—this reasoning too straightforward to be honest; this choice, for example, between the Flaubertian and Stendhalian models, which may exist only in

my imagination—may hide in my personal history, in terms
of subjective denials and fears, badly healed wounds, and the
unconfessed family saga.

You spoke to me of your father (and I would be happy to hear
more about the whimsical, poetical character he seems to be).

I should tell you a little about my own (because "concrete
block" or not, this is probably the key for me as well).

I come from a family that elevated to the status of an imperative its sense of propriety, a horror of bombast, and a revul-
sion for anything resembling emotional excess or indiscretion.

My father was melancholic and powerful, silent and war-
like, a chess player, unfathomable, clearheaded and skeptical, solitary and independent. For him secrecy was not only
an intellectual experience but also—I'm convinced of this
today—a way of being and living.

He had another peculiarity, unusual for a man who, in
conventional terms, would not be thought of as an intellectual, which was his strange, almost superstitious relationship
with the words of everyday language. There were those he
used and handled very delicately, with infinite caution, as you
would move a chess piece. Then there were those addressed
to him that had the power (we didn't always know which
ones, we never knew exactly why; they were ordinary words
belonging to everyday life) to catapult him into sudden rages,
cold but dreadful, as if they'd reached some obscure place in
him and set fire to it.

A scrap of mystery, blown down by a distant storm.

A biographical enigma, resisting any explanation.

And that way he had of dismissing other people's idle chat-
ter with phrases like "as futile as if you'd said nothing," "like
ghosts," "a waste of breath . . ."

He died on my birthday, which, when I think about it, seems part of a plan.

He bequeathed me this taste for and practice of secrecy, which I sometimes take too far.

He passed on to me this fear of words and of their terrifying power, as well as—naturally—a love of them.

He left me this dream I have at times of writing in a dead language, which would discourage any risk of confidences, being addressed directly to the dead.

But I have already said too much. He would have hated that.

Dear Bernard-Henri,

Several times over the past weeks I have thought about the case of Ayaan Hirsi Ali. Thought about it in precisely these terms: I asked myself what I would have done in her place.

Some years ago, I remember enormously appreciating the letter Philippe Sollers wrote (and later published) to Taslima Nasrin*—you see, I don't just see flaws in good old Philippe . . . His message might be summed up: Flee. Don't play their game; don't allow yourself to succumb to the temptation of heroism. Liberty has no need of martyrs.

But, that said, in concrete terms, *flee to where*? To be brutally honest, I don't believe that the French police could effectively ensure Ayaan Hirsi Ali's safety. It is not easy to prevent a public figure from being assassinated—especially when the assassins are prepared to risk their own lives and would not balk at taking a few dozen other victims with them. The Israelis are well trained—and even they fail sometimes. The

*Taslima Nasrin (born 1962) is a Bengali author whose radical feminist views and criticism of Islam have forced her to live in exile since 1994.

English have a certain practical experience. But the French police? To be honest, I have my doubts.

The vast majority of immigrants of Muslim origin in Western Europe are peaceable people. The corollary is that in any country with a large Muslim community, the chances are good that you can enlist enough thugs to mount a serious assassination attempt against someone who is moderately careful (you have to study the victim's movements, buy the weapons, I mean, there's a ton of work involved). It is an unpleasant corollary, I know; but I am not trying to suggest what is desirable, I am simply giving my opinion about a pressing, practical problem.

In practice, therefore, this is what I would do in her shoes: I would move to a country where there is a small Muslim population—Prague or Warsaw, for example. I would avoid all public appearances, obviously; I would go on working via the Internet, though only after getting help from an IT expert (it's perfectly possible, using a proxy, to hide your real IP address). And I would wait for Europe to have the good sense to provide me with decent police protection.

Okay, I'm sorry for reducing the issue to the specific, but there are some questions on which I tend to think pragmatically, though I'm embarrassed to admit it.

I didn't know (though I can't say I'm surprised) that people had written so many unpleasant things about you; I haven't read any of the biographies dedicated to you. Nor have I read the biography of which I was the unwilling subject. To tell the truth, I can't remember ever finishing a single biography. Those I started reading made me think of bad spy novels (or mystery novels) in which the author's sympathies are clear from the outset, in which only the most obvious schemes and motives are explored, the sort of novel where you can work out whodunit in the first twenty pages. To put it another way, I have never been able to imagine a biography that is exempt from a certain *vulgarity*.

Confessional literature, on the other hand, is like a good spy novel (there are some, though they are rare) or mystery novel (of which there are considerably more; there is nothing tongue-in-cheek about my praise for the works of Agatha Christie and Arthur Conan Doyle) in which each new revelation merely adds another layer to the mystery, in which the accretion of information leads one to a generalized, paroxysmal sense of puzzlement that is poetic in its paroxysm, in the universal atmosphere of mystery that eventually engulfs the whole narrative.

Let me go back to my own biography for a moment. At the time it was published—back then I still Googled myself—I simply glanced through the advance sheets that appeared on *L'Express*'s Internet site, from which I could clearly work out that my father and my mother were the indisputable stars of the book and consequently that the book would necessarily be of no interest whatever. How could any journalist—always assuming he is conscientious and very shrewd (though the few e-mails I exchanged with Demonpion offer little evidence of his shrewdness)—in the space of a few short interviews, glean from my father and my mother (two people, in their different ways, of terrifying subtlety and an intelligence bordering on perversity) anything approaching the *truth*?

It was obvious that both of them would jump at the chance to make a grand production of their usual shtick, that each in their own way would retrace the story of their relationship. Though not necessarily to show themselves in the best light.

My father, it's true, usually likes to play the *good little guy*, the honest, decent, working-class boy taken in by a dangerously unbalanced woman. My mother, on the other hand, often finds it entertaining to give a certain *rock and roll* edge to her story, for example by exaggerating the quantity of drugs she consumed. I must have heard the story, of how they met, their lives together, how they split up, at least a dozen times as a child, from both protagonists and from direct and indirect witnesses. Every time, my mother and my father would embellish their version a little more, contextualize it, make up some *period detail*, some *local color*. The only reasonable conclusion I can come to now is that they shared a great love affair—one of the greatest of their lives—so much so that twenty years later, it is still the most fascinating topic of conversation either of them could think of.

In the end, the two of them would have made a great subject for a novel—which would also have been a fine novel about *Les Trentes Glorieuses*,* that most astonishing period of recent French history. *The Elementary Particles* is not that novel. It's just possible to find in it some similarities to my mother, but I entirely evaded the subject of my father. As a character, Michel's father is flimsy; Bruno's father is more successful, but is utterly unlike my own father. All this simply serves to confirm an idea that I find increasingly more striking: in literature, the amount of truth, perhaps of autobiographical truth, you invest in a character is of no importance. The corollary of this is that you can confess everything, can say anything and everything, true or false, and none of it will have the slightest bearing on its eventual success.

Basically, the only important thing you need to know is

Les Trentes Glorieuses refers to the thirty years of uninterrupted growth in France after World War II.

whether confessional literature is appropriate for you, Bernard-Henri Lévy, whether it will allow you to write something you can be proud of. In my opinion it is impossible to tell until you have tried it. In my case, I am not too sure. In 2005, taking a break from *The Possibility of an Island,* I began to recount some memories on the Internet. The fact is, I gave up quite quickly and, though I later agreed to publish these pieces in a magazine, I have been reluctant, and thus far have refused whenever anyone has suggested collecting them as a book. The great autobiographical undertaking—that of a Rousseau or a Tolstoy—is, I fear, *not quite my style.* And yet I think perhaps a few scattered memories, sprinkled through a manuscript whose goal is something different, can have a certain aesthetic interest (sorry, all this is a little Stendhalian). Actually, I don't know, I'm experimenting. There remains the question you posed: *Why?* (Why not in your case and why so in mine?)

Well, the *propensity to confess* that I manifest from time to time comes, it seems to me, from two very different sources. The first, as I have already said, is my deep-rooted conviction that no confession can change anything about one's personality, cannot make good or make worse whatever flaws we have; in short an antipsychoanalytical conviction—one of the few that I have always held to, that and the nonexistence of God. The second is my extraordinary overestimation of myself, something that I occasionally fall victim to, which leads me to believe that no confession can ever exhaust the indefinite richness of my personality, that one could draw endlessly on the ocean of my possibilities—and that if someone believes they know me, they are simply lacking information.

I sometimes feel like Nietzsche in *Ecce Homo,* feeling it appropriate to give an account of his dietary habits, like his taste for "*thick oil-free cocoa,*" convinced that nothing that concerns him could be entirely without interest (and what is worse, one does read these pages with a certain pleasure; pages that may well outlive *Thus Spake Zarathustra*). I do, however, realize that this Stendhalian, aristocratic, flippant approach can be irritating (less with Nietzsche, in fact, since he never quite gets there; he preaches flippancy rather more than he practices it).

A modern variation, one from the era of the mass media: face-to-face with certain journalists I had sometimes felt like Kurt Cobain telling a tactless interviewer, "I'm homosexual, I'm a pagan, I'm a drug abuser, and I like to fuck pot-bellied pigs! Is that enough?"

I now have the well-established reputation of *hating journalists*; this is, at best, approximate. I can truly say I have encountered the worst and the best in the profession. I don't think I have been remotely unfair to Jérôme Garcin. Everything about the man rings false, his every sentence oozes speciousness and affectation. The restrained emotion, the walks across the moors "lashed by the bitter wind" . . . you feel like you're in a BMW commercial. But I have a powerful memory of Harriet Wolff, the very strange German journalist I allude to in the first page of *The Possibility of an Island*. (Was she really a journalist, in fact? I'm fairly sure she mentioned the name of a newspaper, but I never did ask to see her press card.) I am sorry that at my age I have come to the sad but trite conclusion that there are some people who are worth talking to, and others who aren't.

We're up to our necks in *contempt*, and I hate that. Because contempt, which is so difficult to avoid as you get older, is anything but a strength. When you are contemptuous of your adversary, you can be almost certain you are beaten. For example, how effective is contempt when you are attacked by a tapeworm (it must be thinking figuratively about Pierre Assouline that prompted this image)? Clearly the temptations of contempt are dangerous; I have known this for years and yet I succumb to them more and more.

It will be the death of me, in the end. I can still remember watching my father (you wanted more information; you don't have to ask twice . . .) pulling his camper van into a truck stop when we were going on holiday. I saw the same scene many times. In a few short minutes, a number of emotions played across his face. Gloomy puzzlement, usually; amusement, sometimes, fleeting; something like envy; but more often than not, infinite, unfathomable contempt. In any case I never saw him jump out of the van as soon as he pulled up and mingle with the other families, the groups of teenagers on holiday, queuing up to buy their *jambon-fromage*. On every occasion, I saw him pause for several minutes before going to join the throng of his *fellow men;* and how long those minutes seemed to me! Few adults, very few, are aware to what extent children watch their parents, constantly on the lookout for some sign of how they should approach the world; how sharp and vibrant their intelligence is in the years leading up to the disaster of puberty, how quick to summarize, to draw broad conclusions. Very few adults realize that every child, naturally, instinctively, is a *philosopher*. It sometimes seems to me that, as a man, all I have done is to give aesthetic expression to the *withdrawal* that as I child I witnessed in my father.

That, it has to be said, would not be so bad. For what would remain, if I were not here, of the subtle, significant, insidiously tactful gestures of my father? Of the ludicrous, almost offensive *courtesy* whose sole purpose was to prove, against all expectations, against all reason, that he was prepared to *make a gesture,* to offer the other person one last

chance to come to terms with his own vulgarity, his emptiness? I later discovered (during a cleanup, God knows he
would have hated to acknowledge it, so much so that I never
mentioned seeing the document) that in his youth, my father
had performed *acts of bravery*—specifically in the domain of
mountain rescue. Strange destiny, to save the lives of human
beings for whom you feel nothing but contempt. Strange destiny to have been (and for many years this was the case, in his
career as a mountain guide) at the service of a bourgeoisie for
whom he had no respect. My own choice, all in all, seems to
me more consistent: I have always loved books, I write books;
it's astoundingly simple.

Dear Michel,

Be careful with your "tapeworm."

It's what Céline calls Sartre in "À l'agité du bocal."*

Using it again is a mistake in two ways. First, it does too much credit to the person you implicitly compare to Sartre and who, when these letters are published, will use it as an excuse to puff himself up. Moreover, you sell yourself short by contravening the healthy law of rhetorical and political diet (drawn up, incidentally, by Sartre himself in the preface to *The Wretched of the Earth*), according to which you should never characterize your opponents in animal, zoological, or physiological terms. It's a golden rule . . .

On the other hand, I like what you wrote about your father.

Our fathers were clearly very unalike.

And our relations with them were also, clearly, very different. I adored mine and had nothing but respect for him. Unlike yours, mine impressed me to the end.

---

*"À l'agité du bocal": essay by Louis-Ferdinand Céline, considered to be inflammatory and anti-Semitic, which was published in 1948 in response to Sartre's article "Le Portrait d'un antisémite" (1945).

But I like the way you wrote about that.

And in doing so, you used two words that really resonated with me and that you made me feel like expanding on: the words *withdrawal* and *contempt*. I'm not sure that they mean the same to me, but still . . .

To begin, I'd like to point out that my father was born poor, in Mascara, a modest village in western Algeria, all steep slopes and loose stones, stifling in summer, freezing in winter, whose only bit of life and bustle came from the Foreign Legion barracks.

His father, my grandfather, was a photographer, but he was a village photographer restricted by the prevailing anti-Semitism to photographing only the "natives," leaving to a "real Frenchman" the sole rights to the only worthwhile market, i.e., marriages and births among the "whites."

His house, which I came across much later, almost by chance when I was doing a report following the footsteps of Camus in his youth, was a one-story dwelling made of poorly assembled stones, without electricity or running water and with one of those floors of beaten earth that nowadays can be found only in Africa's shantytowns or the Brazilian *favelas*.

The little I know of my father's life there until the beginning of 1938, when, at the age of seventeen, he escaped to Spain, I learned through cross-checking, as he never confided in me. It confirms this picture of black poverty, unilluminated, unmitigated: a childhood in which before dawn the little boy, still half-asleep, had to walk to the end of the town to fill the water bottles for the day; an adolescence spent dreaming of a wooden shelf, just one shelf, on which to place the books by Romain Rolland or Anatole France he had pilfered from the school library; football to pass the time and later on revolution in order to abolish it; and finally the opium of a communist youth, with the double virtue of being both soporific and exciting that this type of opium has always had.

So, he was born into poverty, an absolute poverty, as monotonous as hell, where the milk had to be diluted, the soup was made with thistles and roots, where you got a thrashing if you were tempted to start the fresh bread before finishing the stale bread from the night before, a poverty I'm not sure that any French person today, even in the most deprived housing estate, can even begin to imagine.

And yet, after the war, at the age of not much over twenty, helped by his talent, his anger, and an unusual authority, and also perhaps the solidarity that came out of the early Gaullism and his affinities with the Communist Resistance, he changed his life radically and built up a thriving business, indeed one that very quickly became quite powerful.

The interesting thing (and the point I'm trying to get to) is that as far back as I can remember, I always understood that he loathed his native Algeria, which was for him synonymous with misery, but at the same time I could see that he mistrusted this "mainland" France where he had succeeded so brilliantly.

I always knew that he hated, for others no less than for himself, that atrocious, humiliating, killing poverty and yet at the same time that he equally—perhaps even more so— abhorred money, men with money, the customs, the insulting, arrogant behavior that went hand in hand with this money, which nevertheless had become his world.

He was bourgeois but despised the bourgeoisie.

He was a captain of industry who disdained captains of industry.

He had broken with the politics of the left he had sup-

ported in his youth but at table he would still describe someone as "right-wing" as if it were an insult or a flaw.

His profession was wood, international commerce and the
wood industry, like the left-wing Feltrinelli billionaire or
Wallace, the hero of *Gommes* by Robbe-Grillet (a detail that
did not escape the notice of my well-read mother: the same
background, the same poverty, except probably the good fortune to get a bookshelf). But with a single exception (the
young François P., who was his main rival, but in whom he
recognized someone else who was out of place, no less contemptuous of the "establishment," also inscrutable, having
come from afar, and remaining distant), it was a mistake to
mention any of his colleagues in the "Wood Federation" of
the CNPF employers' union* for whom he felt a collective,
definitive, and scathing contempt.

Neuilly was his city. Yes, we lived in Neuilly, as I suppose
he thought that nothing could be better than Achille
Peretti's† district, with its "bling" before the word was invented,
to banish from his children's minds the idea, the possibility,
the subconscious vibration of the utter destitution he had
endured as a child. But apart from two or three teachers
who were invited to dinner at the end of each year in a ritual
that, looking back, strikes me as even more outmoded, more
inconceivable than the presentation of prizes at Le Chézy cinema, I don't remember either him or my mother mixing with
anyone in this ghetto of the rich and, worse, the nouveaux

---

*CNPF: The Conseil National du Patronat Francais (National Council of
French Employers) was an employers' union formed in 1945 at the request of
the Provisional Government of the French Republic. It was transformed in
1998 into the Mouvement des Enterprises de France (Movement of French
Enterprises).

†Achille Peretti (1911–1983): French politician, lawyer, and member of
the French Resistance, who was mayor of Neuilly-sur-Seine from 1947 until
his death.

riches (in our family's criminal code, the supreme crime was bad taste), whose grotesque customs we mocked at every opportunity. The only thing I remember is his rage on the day when, at the age of fifteen, I came home from school and explained that I needed a dinner suit, as I wanted to become a member of one of the clubs the local young dandies were rushing to join, which were called "society parties."

He was as much of a stranger in his new milieu as his old one, as much of a stranger to his destiny as to his origin, to the man he had become as to the one he had left behind.

Among the people around him, he had sent packing any possible witnesses to what he no longer wished to be (burning, suffering, known for false starts). Yet he did not replace them, as those who become wealthy do, with contemporaries of this new era (he did have some of those, of course, but he kept them at a distance, obstinately refusing to allow any familiarity).

As a result, he had no friends.

He hardly saw anyone.

I suspect that in his youth he had a happy nature, was one of the small glories of Saint-Germain-des-Prés by night, a dandy, a gambler, a man surrounded by women. Yet now he took no interest in any company but that of a handful of gray men who in my eyes had no charm about them. They were consuls, proconsuls, satraps, microstrategists, and other counselors of this "Group," as he called it, of which he was so proud and which, when he spoke of it, sounded like that of an expanding empire.

He was a reclusive king.

As I said before, he played chess, but alone or with me, or, in the end, with a computer.

He was a radiant person, yet impervious to his own radiance and, strangely, he derived no benefit from it. Others basked in the warmth and light he exuded, while he remained in the shadows he sought, where he could give free rein to his new taste for austerity, solitude, and silence.

He was a real "self-made man," in fact the essential self-made man, that is, someone who wanted to make himself, abolish his history, to inherit nothing from anyone, to shorten his memory, as you would shorten a bridle. But he was a haughty self-made man, inflexible in his pride with an obsessive fear that was at least equal to his renunciation of, indeed his armed rallying against, the great and small pleasures which his new social status would have allowed him.

Dear Benny Lévy,* to whom I spoke one day about this odd relationship with oneself, replied with a shrug of the shoulders that such was the destiny of this type of Jew, whom he called "Jews of negation."†

Albert Cohen, in his portrait of Solal, the Jewish prince who acts the clown with Christians but thinks no less of himself, who keeps in reserve a spare authenticity, who in the cellar of his residence keeps a mangy pack, which he goes down to at night to talk to and mingle with in secret, puts forward another theory of the type of man my father was, what he calls the "neo-Marrano."‡

I myself sometimes see a crucial component of this abstract, unanchored man with his head in the sky, instead

---

*Political activist and Maoist in May 1968, forced underground because he was a stateless refugee. He was later naturalized and, coming under the influence of the philosopher Emmanuel Levinas, embraced Jewish Orthodoxy. With Bernard-Henri Lévy and Alain Finkielkraut, he cofounded the Institut d'Études Lévinassiennes in Jerusalem.

†*Juifs de negation*: a term first used by Jean-Claude Mimer in his book *Le Juif de savoir*, denotes assimilated Jews—the Western Jew who "barely touches the surface of his Judaism."

‡Refers to the Marranos, Sephardic Jews who were forced to adopt Christianity but who continued to practice Judaism secretly.

of his feet on the solid ground of one of the community
nations—for which I later provided a philosophical apologia
in my books, in particular *L'Idéologie française*—in his ascet-
icism, the way he snatched himself away from his past without taking root anywhere else, this decision to avoid at all
costs replacing one identity by another and substituting the
background he might have dreamed of for the one he had
known.

But today, at this moment, my first impulse is to say that
he was a perfect example of the "withdrawal" you spoke of, a
withdrawal so complete in his case, so perfected that it con-
fined him to the role of a hero and created around him a solid
halo of opacity and mystery. A soul like a pyramid, a soul like
a tomb . . . Because for a man like that, his soul is the tomb!
Not the body, as it is for philosophers, but the soul. Only
occasionally, rarely, did an event or meeting occur, when, as
I mentioned, a word would rain down on him like a blow
from a pickax, piercing the halo, sparking the fine dust of
unwanted memories.

It's quite simple.

I told you that my father and I were very close.

Indeed, I was one of the very few people he was close to
and in whom he could have imagined confiding, as he suffo-
cated in his tomb.

I realize now that this mystery was so unyielding, that
shadow into which he chose to retreat was so dense, the
remoteness from others and himself, to which he was condemned by not wanting to live either in the obscene satisfaction of his new success or in a conventional loyalty to the
child buried within him, was so well constructed that I don't
know what he thought about most of the important matters.

I don't know what role love played in his life.

I don't know what his idea of God was or even if he had one.

I don't know if he was afraid of death, if he was resigned or believed himself beyond its reach.

His sense of propriety, that is, his fear of words and the fire they contained, was so strong that on his very last evening, when part of him knew that this was the end, the last word he left me was a ridiculous business card on which he had scribbled for the nth time the financing plan for my film *Le Jour et la nuit*. He had been getting ready to produce it, the prospect of which gave him a naïve pleasure that wasn't like him.

His inclination toward secrecy was so strong—as was the faith he had in his son and his son's choices—that only in the glasnost of the Gorbachev years did I learn from loosened tongues the incredible story of that day on June 1977, right in the middle of the New Philosophers period, when I stood before the Soviet embassy in Paris at the head of a protest demonstration against Brezhnev's visit to France. Through one of those ironies that are the destiny of men whose life is like an iceberg, immersed except for its tip, my father happened to be inside, heading up the delegation that had come to negotiate the state contracts I was protesting against. To the astonishment of the colleagues who had accompanied him, and naturally without stating the real reasons for his U-turn, he set so many preliminary conditions, raised so many difficulties, in short complicated the process to such a degree that the share of those contracts that were due to be allocated to him, as they had been every year for the last twenty years, never came to fruition . . .

As for his military past, his commitment to Republican Spain, then the Free French Forces, he never spoke of that either. Several years after his death I found a ragged black folder with his decorations, the photographs from that time, letters sent from Barcelona to the fourteen-year-old girl he would lose sight of for eight years but who after the war became my mother, and the honorable mention from General Diego Brosset at Monte Cassino, which I spoke of in my last book and which brings tears to my eyes each time, like now, I copy it out: "an ever willing ambulance driver, day and night, whatever the mission; carried out evacuations through a hail of mortar with total indifference to danger, again and again going back to look for those wounded in the lines under intense enemy fire."

The other day I returned to the rue Saint-Ferdinand, where he had his offices, very near the building where Drieu la Rochelle* committed suicide.

I followed the route he took every day with his slow, sovereign step, as sovereign as his voice, never bowing to any urgency.

I heard once more his low voice, slow, muffled as the voices of those tending toward silence are, yet at the same time melodious, well tempered, a voice that commanded attention and for which I envied him.

I walked again in front of the tobacconist's where my first film was born about Bosnia at war.

Then, in front of the avenue des Ternes, where we went to speak of that other "work," his own, of which he was secretly proud and in which he tried to get me interested once in a while, with no hope of succeeding.

None of that exists anymore.

That Paris has disappeared and, even more so, those

*Pierre Eugène Drieu la Rochelle (1893–1945), French writer of fiction and political essays. Having collaborated with the Nazis, he went into hiding after the Liberation and committed suicide in 1945.

places. And in those places nothing remains of what he called his life's work, not even a sign, a plaque, a gray blind in the windows or the magnolia in a pot at the entrance to the building, behind the railings, which seemed to be there for all eternity. It reminds me of those defeated cities, on whose remains the conquerors spread salt in order to make sure that they remain forever bare.

So there you are, dear Michel. I'm glad that here, at this point, thanks to you and the words you held out to me, our exchange should contain this little, this tiny trace of someone who was a significant passerby.

Dear Bernard-Henri,

It's funny, I'd forgotten, but "À l'agité du bocal" is one of my favorite pieces by Céline.

In general, I think Céline is overrated. After *Voyage au bout de la nuit* [*Journey to the End of the Night*], it's all downhill, his style becomes increasingly flashy and ostentatious. There is a certain music, I admit, but music of a lower order, something between jazz (of the interminable *jam sessions* once the musicians set aside their scores! the joy they get out of it! the tedium for everyone else!) and the *goualante*—the *chanson* that epitomizes French popular music at the beginning of the twentieth century (impossible to listen to again—I checked recently). Nothing like Proust's delicate harmonics, their indeterminate vibrations (not what I prefer, to be honest, but to put Céline and Proust on the same level has always seemed to me an error of taste, or at least the mark of someone who does not quite know *what he's talking about*). Nor is it anything like the stripped-down instrument, the *rock and roll* urgency of Pascal in the *Pensées* (there's no immediate comparison with the music of his time, but I don't think Pascal was much interested in music). Still less (and, of all the routes that great literature has taken, this is the one that still inspires in me the same admiration) with the sublime symphonic constructions of a Chateaubriand or a Lautréamont—which, to me, give almost the same immediate palpable feeling of genius as Beethoven.

Deep down, the praise Céline heaps on music at the expense of *ideas*, which he loathes, serves a dual purpose: first, to give the impression that he himself was possessed of a superior form of music, when he merely used the popular music of his time, with all its limitations. Second, to hide the fact that, when it came to ideas, he had none—or only very stupid ones like anti-Semitism.

The fact remains that Céline, a good but not a great novelist, is at his best in his scurrilous tracts, a genre that best suits his malicious, vindictive soul, and that "L'Agité du bocal," like certain pages from his anti-Semitic tracts, is irresistible in its cruel wit and spiteful anger. I could never write anything as good; I can't get myself sufficiently worked up; I make a cutting remark and it's over; deep down I don't really care about my adversaries (what adversaries?). There is a real incompatibility, I am increasingly aware, between hatred and contempt.

Personally, I don't believe in Jews. Or, to be more precise, I don't want to believe. Or, to be precise, I don't know anything about the subject. I will therefore carefully avoid expressing an opinion about the interpretation of Benny Lévy, about *juifs de négation* and neo-Marranos. I immediately react, this time with a feeling of complete comprehension, to the simple sentence you wrote about your father: "He was as much of a stranger in his new milieu as his old one." This is something that is not particular to a Jew. It is something that may have happened to lots of people who were around twenty at the time of the Liberation.

My father was born, the third of four children, to an unreconstructed working-class family. They were not destitute (destitution comes when you don't know what tomorrow will bring, whether you will still have a roof over your head, still have enough to feed yourself and keep warm; when you are poor, you know; you know exactly). They lived the difficult, dignified existence of the working classes (in a period of full employment, there was a genuine *working-class dignity*— Orwell evokes it when he talks of *common decency*, Paul McCartney talks about it too, in discussing his childhood; it's not something invented by journalists). These people lived by their work, they never had to *hold out their hand.*

Their lives, therefore, were *dignified*, but they were also appallingly *limited*. Nothing illustrates it better than the photographs of "1936—the great turning point," where you see the people on their first paid holidays, on bicycles, on delivery tricycles, leaving their suburbs, and families seeing the sea for the first time.

Actually, my grandmother came from a family in Nord-Cotentin, part farmers, part fishermen, so the sea was hardly likely to impress her. On the other hand, what I think would bring tears to your eyes is a photograph of my grandmother at the age of fifty, taken by her son to see the Mer de Glace for the first time—the childlike look on her face.

My father always despised his own father (whom I never knew); he never spoke to me about him other than as an *ignorant old bastard*. The root of the rift between them was that his father had found him an apprenticeship when he was fourteen, after he received his diploma, even though his results pointed to a promising academic future. I don't know, these things I'm talking about are ancient history, they're almost like legend to me, but it might still be of interest to kids in the housing projects. My grandfather might have realized that education might be a passport to success and social advancement, but an apprenticeship with the SNCF offers job security, that's what he probably thought. All in all, he probably was, as his son diagnosed, an *ignorant old bastard*.

Apprenticeship falls through, France at war, he joins a variety of youth organizations (UCPA, the Club Alpin Français): a few years later, my father finds himself a member of the prestigious Compagnie des Guides de Chamonix. Quite a coup for a kid from Clamart.

A love of mountains, it's true, a genuine love of mountains. An unplanned, genetically unfounded love of mountains. A desire to lose himself in the snow, an admiration for colleagues who had had fingers amputated, an exacting love.

A few years later, my father left Chamonix for Val-d'Isère. He bought some land and had a big house built in the center of Val-d'Isère (which, at the time, was not an internationally famous ski resort; Val-d'Isère doesn't appear on the tourist map back then. Jean-Claude Killy* was still a pimply teenager).

Capitalizing on this initial investment by reinvesting at the right time, someone else might have built a real fortune out of this.

A few years later, I meet my father. (Let's not exaggerate; I had driven across France with him in a jeep, but we'd never really gotten along; every time we stopped I was afraid he was going to drive off and leave me by the side of the road.) He has not made a fortune. By now he is an *independent ski instructor*, which means he's not approved by the French ski school. The people who enlist his services (rich people, often

---

*Jean-Claude Killy (born 1943) is a former alpine ski racer who was a triple champion at the 1968 Winter Olympics.

very rich people) don't want to ski on marked ski slopes open to the public; what they want is to be set down by helicopter on the summit of a glacier and come down alone, surrounded by powdery snow, they want to do *real skiing*. But for that, they need a guide, a qualified *alpine guide*, otherwise it's illegal, it's too dangerous.

My father's most famous client was, I think, Valéry Giscard d'Estaing, but he only took him out once or twice. Another one was Antoine Riboud,* who was a good client; my father took him out at least a dozen times, and I even went out skiing with him. My one memory of this captain of industry was in a restaurant in the mountains where some people in the group were taking too long deciding what vegetables to have with their meal. I can still see his exasperated expression, the brusque, self-important way he turned to the waiter: "Salad for everyone!" And it was important, and necessary, otherwise there would be all kinds of things—French fries, steamed potatoes, rice . . . In my mind, an august captain of industry is someone who, when the time is right, knows how to say, *"Salad for everyone!"*

My father had other clients, less famous but just as rich, and there were no real social barriers, so I was invited to come along. This was how, when I was ten, I came to play games of Monopoly with children my age who lived in a *hôtel particulier* on the rue de la Faisanderie. Then, when the holidays were over, I'd go back to my grandmother's house, where there was no bathroom (we washed in the washbasin;

*Antoine Riboud (1918–2002) was a French businessman, the founder and president of Groupe Danone.

from time to time we'd heat a basin of water). None of this struck me as surprising. Children are strange creatures.

And then there came the worst. Sylvie. Now, here I don't know what happened, my father must have charmed the family, but whatever it was, she stayed at the chalet for ten days; I was there too. We must have been about twelve, thirteen at the most. One day she played some records and asked me to dance a slow dance with her, we were the only people in the apartment, and I said, "I don't know how to dance." She was pretty, with a mop of curly chestnut hair. She was probably as much of a virgin as I was, which means a complete virgin. She was delectable, a doe. I was probably delectable, a faun. It makes me sick just thinking about it.

I've seen some of her family on television from time to time. And people see me on television too from time to time.

But, while I was experiencing the first flushes of my natural disposition for social failure, what was my father doing—socially speaking, I mean? Well, not much either. As an independent ski instructor, he could hardly fraternize with *ordinary ski instructors*—they barely nodded to one another when they met by the cable cars. A qualified mountain guide and a mountaineer, he was, it goes without saying, *respected by his peers*. (They too were mountain guides, of course, but did not necessarily have the same achievements as mountaineers, while he had taken part in expeditions in the Andes and the Himalayas.) He was respected by them without ever really being liked, because in their minds he would always be a *Parisian*, not a true man of the mountains. (Actually, he was from Clamart, as I mentioned earlier; to him that made a great difference, but not to them.) He strove to keep in touch with the other members of his family, in spite of difficulties that grew greater as the years passed. It is not without a certain embarrassment that I remember the visits—about once a year—he made to his sisters. Both had married working-class men, men of their own kind; they had married within their own world and had each bought houses in Gagny (Seine-Saint-Denis). I can picture my father, clearly *a visitor,* in the dining room of the house that represented the culmination of their dreams. He would be talking about politics, about General de Gaulle, subjects like that, harmless in themselves; then he would leave, visibly relieved (although he loved his sisters in spite of everything and somehow managed to force himself to go on making these yearly visits).

Did he socialize with his rich clients? Not really. There were Sylvie's parents, whom I've mentioned. (To be honest, I only really remember Sylvie, but they must have had some sort of relationship, otherwise they would hardly have entrusted their daughter to his care.) Overall, there wasn't much, I think. I remember seeing my father with dubious characters, *local property developers* and the like, for meetings that never really went anywhere, but mostly I remember seeing him on his own.

Like me, he played chess.

He regularly beat me at chess, so regularly that it put me off the game.

And he made plans, and indeed carried them out, only to lose interest in them afterward. He must have had *bosses* early on in his life (although he managed to work on building sites and only for short periods). Later he had *employees* (not for long, just until he sold his share of the business). He was probably equally uncomfortable in both roles.

Here was a man who sacrificed everything in life, absolutely everything, to a single imperative: *not being dependent on anyone.* An absurd imperative, when you think about it, which leads one to reject the very principle of a social life. I can still see him cursing the monopoly of the French electricity board; the problems he had trying to get permission to have a generator installed on his own property. People like that may still have a place in Argentina or Montana, but not in western Europe. When I think about my father's political opinions, I think of something like *libertarian,** though the term didn't exist in French back then; something American-sounding.

What strikes me, over and above our fathers' differences and the similarities, is the curious nature of the times when they were young men; the France of the *Trentes Glorieuses*, say from 1946 or '47 (the point at which industrial production truly gets going again) and 1973 (the first oil crisis): more than twenty-five years of uninterrupted growth and optimism. It was also the France of the *baby boom*, which ends earlier, curiously, for no apparent reason, in 1964. Were I to try to come up with a reason, I would say something like: the passage from consumer capitalism to a more hedonistic phase—the passage from the washing machine to the transistor radio, if you like.

To get back to the heart of the mystery: the France of the 1950s, its optimism, its energy, its faith in the future and the slight stupidity that that entailed. It seems more distant to me now than the France of the 1890s or the 1930s. And yet this is when I was born, well, toward the end of the period; I too am a baby boomer.

---

*Liberterien, which denotes political as opposed to individual libertarianism, is a term that first entered French political discourse in the 1970s; it was coined by the economist Henri Lepage.

It is possible to be nostalgic for a time one never knew; all you need is a television. And when I see contemporary documentaries of young people (people just like my parents, wearing the same clothes they wore), dancing the twist, when I think about their energy, their joie de vivre, I realize that I'm not alone in being *depressionist*—our whole era is, even if it is beginning to refuse to acknowledge the fact.

A few weeks ago, I read in *Le Figaro* magazine (don't panic, I can give the classic excuse, I read it in a dentist's waiting room; I'm only joking, I know you're not like that, but I would like to point out that I don't buy the rag, I've never really got over the sort of police investigation they did about me when *The Possibility of an Island* was published)... what was I saying? Oh yes, I was reading a book review that praised the author for "avoiding the clichés of the corporate novel." There followed a list of the aforementioned clichés and as I read on I realized that *I* invented these clichés almost fifteen years ago in *Whatever*. It's things like this that remind you you're getting old.

That France (and not just France, all of Western Europe) slumped into depression after the *Trentes Glorieuses* seems to me completely normal. The optimism was too great, the belief in progress too explicit and naïve, the hopes too divisive. *Whatever* was, I think, a salutary book, and one that I think could not be published now. Because our societies have come to a terminal stage where they refuse to recognize their malaise, where they demand that fiction be happy-go-lucky, escapist; they simply don't have the courage to face their own reality. Because the malaise has not diminished, it's simply getting worse, you only have to look at the way young people nowadays drink: brutally, until they lapse into coma, to deaden themselves. Or they smoke a dozen joints one after the other until their panic finally subsides. Let's not even talk about crack.

. . .

A few months ago, I had the pleasure of finding myself in
Moscow with Frédéric Beigbeder (by accident; we were there
for different reasons and didn't plan to meet up). Twice we did
sets as DJs in nightclubs full of the sumptuous blondes popu-
larized by current affairs magazines. Twice Frédéric and I
noticed the same thing: young Russians adore the Beatles, they
react to their music immediately, they like it (whereas I'm
sure they didn't know the music before, they only discovered
western music in the 1980s through groups like U2 and *a*-h*a*).
And not only do they like the Beatles, they like early Beatles,
songs like "Ticket to Ride" and "Love Me Do." The music, made
eternal by their genius, their enthusiasm, their joie de vivre;
the music of youth, of heading off on holiday (the music of economic growth, of full employment).

Back in France, the magazines ran headlines about a new
idea: economic decline. A very different atmosphere, obviously.

The worst thing is, the ecologists are right. Of course, none
of the problems facing humanity can be tackled without stabilizing the world population, without stabilizing energy consumption, without intelligently managing nonrenewable
resources, without tackling climate change.

And yet coming back to Western Europe I felt like I was
coming back to the dead. Of course, life is hard, very hard in
Russia, it is a violent life, but they *live*, they are filled with a
desire to live that we have lost. And I wished I were young
and Russian and, ecologically speaking, irresponsible.

I also felt I needed idealism (a rarer commodity, I admit,
in contemporary Russia). I wished I were part of a time when
our heroes were Yuri Gagarin and the Beatles; when Louis de

Funès made everyone in France laugh; when Jean Ferrat was adapting Aragon.

And, once again, I thought about my parents' youth.

I'm sorry to take all of my examples from popular music (but you know how much it mattered to people my age). An overview of the literary situation would, I think, lead quickly to radical conclusions. When a country is strong, self-confident, it is prepared to accept any amount of pessimism from its writers without turning a hair. The France of the 1950s accepted people like Camus, Sartre, Ionesco, Beckett. The France of the 2000s has trouble putting up with people like me.

So, well . . . I'm getting old now, I'm getting weaker, I would like to be happy before I die. So I think I'll go back to Russia.

Dear Michel, you're the *depressionist* but I'm about to be the obligatory killjoy.

Unlike you, I have absolutely no desire to be Russian or to return to Russia.

I used to love a certain idea of Russia.

I loved and defended this idea of Russian culture, which in the 1970s and '80s conjured up a whole hodgepodge, Solzhenitsyn and Sakharov, the Slavophiles and Europhiles, the disciples of Pushkin and those of Dostoyevsky, the dissidents on the right and the left and those who, in the words of the mathematician Leonid Plyushch,* belonged to neither of these camps but to the concentration camp and whose defense I was taking up while my father, in the episode I told you about, was signing (or rather, was not signing, *deciding* not to sign) his contracts with Gosplan's† wood branch.

Then there's what Russia has become, what appeared

---

*Leonid Plyushch: Russian mathematician held by Soviet authorities in a psychiatric hospital. He was released in 1976 as a result of an international petition initiated by the French mathematician Henri Cartan.

†Gosplan: Soviet State Planning Committee, the central board that supervised various aspects of the Soviet Union's planned economy.

when the breakdown of communism, its debacle—what a mountaineer like your father would call its "thaw" or "collapsing ice" (the real meaning of debacle)—revealed to it and the world the Russia of Putin, of the war in Chechnya, the Russia that assassinated Anna Politkovskaya* on the stairway in her building and that the same Anna Politkovskaya described in her wonderful book *A Russian Diary,* just before she was assassinated. It's the Russia of the racist packs who, right in the center of Moscow, track down "nonethnic" Russians, the Russia that chased out the Chinese at Irkutsk, the Dagestanis at Rostov, the same Russia that persecutes those it called the *Chernye,* meaning the "swarthy" ones, the Russia that has the nerve to explain to the world that it has nothing to do with democracy and human rights since it has its own democracy, a special, local democracy that is quite unrelated to Western canons and rights. It's the country of such specialties as its party, the Nashi, meaning "our own," which, to call a spade a spade, is a Stalin-Hitler combo, the Russia that, incidentally, is giving new life to the anti-Semitic European pamphlets of the nineteenth and twentieth centuries, the same Russia that made a best seller out of a stupid *List of Masked Jews,* which lumps together Sakharov, Trotsky, de Gaulle, Sarkozy, and Yulia Tymoshenko, the mastermind behind the Orange Revolution in the Ukraine. It's the Russia that—since you mentioned music—put on the cover of one of its popular magazines the singer Irina Allegrova dressed up as an SS camp guard, holding a ferocious hound on a lead. This Russia, which, apart from this kind of idiocy, believes in nothing at all, absolutely nothing, just the religion of the marketplace, consumption and brands. This Russia,

*Russian journalist and human rights activist who was assassinated in 2006 after writing *Putin's Russia* and opposing the Chechen conflict.

which, the last time I went there, struck me as having had its culture erased and its brain washed, this Russia, whose most discouraging side, according to Anna Politkovskaya, to mention her yet again, was its amorphousness and passivity, the way it accepts, for example, that it hardly has any employment legislation left and that its workers are treated like dogs, the same Russia that leaves the nightclubs where you went to have a laugh and dance with Frédéric [Beigbeder] to rot in a terrifying poverty. In this Russia, no less than under communism, people are ready to betray their parents to steal a broom, a bowl, a badly screwed tap, or—as in Brecht's *Messingkauf Dialogues*—bits of scrap iron at night from deserted building sites abandoned by oligarchs on the run or in prison . . . Not only does this Russia inspire no desire in me, it fills me with horror. I'd go so far as to say that it frightens me because I see in it a possible destiny for the late-capitalist societies. Once upon a time, during your postwar "glory days," the middle class was terrorized by being told that Brezhnev's communism was not an archaism restricted to distant societies but rather a picture of our own future. We were wrong: it was not communism but postcommunism, Putinism, that may be the testing ground for our future.

But you already know all that.

You know it at least as well as I do.

Just as you know what you're saying when you say that Céline, that "overrated novelist," only wrote well in his pamphlets.

So I will spare you any more of this lecture by a moralist, redresser of ideological wrongs, and staunch defender of high-minded principles, who, when you mention the Beatles, replies—shock, horror—that Russia is not what it used to be, and how is it possible to laugh and sing in terror, among the corpses?

No, the real question here is our different attitudes to this reality, with which we are both familiar. How is it that, knowing what we know, one of us could act as if nothing was more important than to go on listening to "Ticket to Ride" in the company of gorgeous blondes, while the other gets up on his high horse muttering that we don't have the right, that we can't simply wash our hands of this rotten Russia? The real question (at least the one you make me feel like raising, and too bad if that seems pompous) is what's going on in someone's mind when they decide or pretend to decide that they don't care about the destiny of the human race and, on the other hand, what goes on in the mind of someone who, in the face of Africa's forgotten wars, the massacres in Sarajevo, the Pakistani madrassas where jihad is taught, Algeria in the grip of mass terrorism, Russia today and Chechnya laid waste, chooses to act as if the misfortune of others concerned him, as if he were accountable and even a little responsible and as if it were not possible to be really a "man" without feeling responsible for others—at least some of them—and in some sense their hostage.

You are right when you say that our improbable exchange will have at least the (minor) virtue of exploring a little this "literature of confession," which I feel I must point out you were not that much closer to than I was. (I can make out from here the faces of the biographers, webmasters, chasers of literary prizes, police and customs officers of the imagination that you also have at your heels and who rave about your date of birth, your way of life, your Ireland, your dog, your relations with women, and your body—I can see them from here and I must say that the thought of them reading what you threw at them about your father's whimsicality, his eccentricity, his remoteness, and his skiing clients makes me laugh out loud.)

But if it—I'm still talking about our exchange—also succeeds in forcing us to reveal ourselves through questions such as "concern or not about the human race," if in my case at least it allows me to return to the roots—no bluff, no pretending—of this need I have to feel that I am the one "under an obligation," the "guardian," what Levinas* called the "substitute" for my neighbor, if it could help me to understand and say why a man like myself, who could stay quietly at home enjoying life and writing novels, should spend so much of his life running around the world, denouncing its injustices and disorder, and why, although nobody asked him to do so, he keeps giving his learned opinion week after week on how to fix things—if our exchange could do that, I must admit that I would be pleased.

The problem, I insist, is not only that nobody called on me to do this . . .

It's not only that, unlike those whose profession it is, in particular journalists, I could easily live without bothering with this.

The strange thing is that when I think about it, I am at least as inclined as you toward skepticism, doubt, and a sense of futility.

I'm a pessimist.

In philosophical terms I'm not at all what is usually called a progressive.

*Emmanuel Levinas: a Lithuanian-born philosopher and Talmudic scholar who became a leading French thinker in the 1950s and developed "the ethics of the Other."

Actually, I believe that people who want to get too mixed up in the lives of their fellow men, to redesign or regenerate humanity excessively, are either dangerous lunatics or crooks, or both.

Indeed, for the record, it's that conviction that cost me the Prix Goncourt the only time in my life that I had a real chance of winning it. It was the year of my *Last Days of Charles Baudelaire,* and there was a passage in the novel in which I had the author of *Les Fleurs du mal* say that it was no coincidence that horrible Marat had called his newspaper *L'Ami du peuple* or that the abominable Robespierre believed he was a friend to humankind. On the jury was the late André Stil, who had two religions, or rather three—the Party (he was the only Frenchman to receive successively the Stalin Prize and the Prix Populiste Littéraire), Grasset* (he was the only juror in the history of the prize to have made a point of honor of never letting his emotions get in the way, and, over the fifteen to twenty years of his reign, always voting for his publishing house), and Robespierre (he harbored a puerile but intense devotion for "The Incorruptible," following the line of a party that only ever saw the Bolsheviks as the reincarnation of the Committee of Public Safety and its blazing intransigence). You can guess the rest. There was unease in the civilization of Robespierre and Stalin. *Between my Party and my publishing house, I must choose my Party.* And by one vote, his, a Goncourt that had been in the cards slipped away and went to an undeniable lover of the human race, my comrade Érik Orsenna.

I wanted to tell you that I know how it goes.

I want it to be clear that I am aware of what, metaphysically speaking, may militate against the need for "commitment."

---

*Éditions Grasset, a major French publishing house.

Nevertheless, in spite of that, in spite of all that, despite all I know about dangerous pity and its snares, despite the murky, suspect, even vaguely ridiculous aspects of this pose of the great intellectual hoisting the Enlightenment flag in all the dark rooms of the conscience and of the world (isn't it Norpois who in [*À*] *la Recherche* [*du temps perdu*] exhorts the BHLs and Houellebecqs of his time to lay claim to the "great causes" and warns them that if they fail to do so they will be nothing more than "flute players"?), that is what I've spent my life doing. Instead of writing my novels and real philosophical tracts, I've traveled the length and breadth of this vast world looking for wrongs to be righted and causes to be defended.

Why is that?

I won't mention the official, noble, blameless reasons, although they do count for something.

Even if, in my case, these words are not merely hot air, I won't mention anger, indignation, the unbearable sight of the world's poverty, the immediate, mandatory, instinctive sympathy for history's victims, those it has ignored, its damned.

I will attempt to name the other reasons, the petty ones, the ones that are less easy to admit, but that count almost as much, if I try to be honest with myself and thus take seriously our decision to travel this part of our path together, following the route of confessional writing. There are three points to be added.

Certainly, there's a taste for adventure. That may seem lame or frivolous. But it's true that I'm attracted to adventure and that this has contributed to the habit I've formed since the war in Bangladesh of traveling to the ends of the earth looking for reasons to fight and write. I like traveling, moving, sending my body and soul into unfamiliar surroundings, operating within reference systems whose parameters are different from those that underpin my ordinary life. I like to harness my energy according to some other system, to experience sensations, emotions, a form of relationship with others and myself, a relationship with death and therefore with life, with the fear and therefore with the feeling of existing that are unlike anything you'll experience in fortunate places among the well-to-do. I was happy in Sarajevo. I have pleasant memories of my time in Huambo or Luanda, in Angola. In Tenga, in the suburbs of Bujumbura, I was caught up in a shoot-out, which I have described in one of my books. Obviously, that's not a good memory, but it taught me more about myself, my reflexes, my most obscure desires than hours and pages of patient introspection. My report from this year in Darfur came from that desolate savannah where the people live in fear of seeing a Janjaweed soldier appear at any moment in that desert that has been so methodically desertified that you can travel for days without coming across any trace of another human being or even a ruin, nothing but the odd, vague animal looking at you with the eyes of a child. I lived through moments there that were very strange, not at all unpleasant, that made me reflect on time, forgetting, memory, debris and the end of debris, the body's mute words, its freedom. I know that this isn't a good thing to say, that it makes me a tourist of disaster. But it's true.

Then, there's a taste for performance, which I've always had. I've always been tempted (this is even more indecent, obscene, attention-seeking, inappropriate, but I'm telling you the truth) to do what other people don't do, or if they do, to do it in some way that belongs to me alone. I liked going off to take part in the revolution in Bangladesh, while in 1971 my comrades believed that Paris was where the revolution was taking place, and thirty years later I enjoyed writing a preface for Cesare Battisti,* when all of the press in France and Italy were calling him shallow, scabby, a brute, a bastard, a born criminal. I liked setting off on the tracks of Daniel Pearl when everybody else seemed to have forgotten him, helping to turn the case of Hirsi Ali, whose name was unknown, into a French national cause, going to Sarajevo before everyone else, when the city was still being blockaded . . . In my Darfur struggles, I liked not going through the official channels used for most of the testimony you can read anywhere. And, on my way back, I loved being able to suggest, insidiously, with an appearance of false modesty but in reality terribly pleased with myself, that I wasn't one of those naïve American actors who believe that they have "been there" just because some Sudanese walked them around a couple of refugee camps. This morning I enjoyed being able to point out in my "Bloc-Notes" that I am one of the only French people to have spent a day—during my "forgotten wars" period—with Iván Rios, that FARC [Revolutionary Armed Forces of Colombia] commander who was killed by his bodyguard and whose severed hand was brought back to the commander of the San Mateo barracks. I also liked, in the same series of reports, having been one of the very, very few to have succeeded in traveling through the bush on board an improbable sort of rickshaw into the heart of the Nuba Mountains among people who

*Italian member of a violent left-wing group during the so-called Years of Lead in Italy, which lasted from the late 1960s to the early 1980s, characterized by widespread social conflict and acts of terrorism by both right-wing and left-wing paramilitary groups. Battisti fled to France to avoid a life sentence, and later to Brazil when a change in French law would have led to his extradition to Italy. He remains in Brazil, where he has been granted political refugee status.

hadn't seen a white person since Leni Riefenstahl. Once again, I'm embarrassed to tell you this. In doing so, I'm quite aware that I'm making myself look less deserving against the horizon of a humanist and "committed" eternity. But that's how it is. Jean-Marie Colombani and Edwy Plenel will remember. They are the ones who approached me with the suggestion that I should report for *Le Monde*. I named only one condition (presented, naturally, as a choice dictated by cold military efficacy and not at all by this desire I'm sharing with you, of being the best and first at everything): that I could take the collection of papers over, let's say, the last fifteen years and go to those places that their reporters had not or had hardly visited . . .

There's one more thing, and this time I don't know how to say this without sounding completely ridiculous. It's wanting to exceed my limits, to live beyond myself, literally to live beyond my means. The idea, if you prefer, that there is life and there is a greater life and that although the first may seem futile, although at the end nothing of you or your projects will remain, the second and only the second, that greater life, means that a person's life was worth living. The greater life . . . The expression comes from Malraux. But it's also used by Malebranche* when he explains in one of his *Letters to Dortous from Mairan* that man is only great "through his relations with great things." I like that expression, the idea that for each person there's the possibility of a

*Nicolas Malebranche (1638–1715): French philosopher and physicist. A Cartesian and opponent of the British empiricists, he was also a devout Christian who sought to synthesize the thought of Descartes and St. Augustine in order to demonstrate that God was active in every aspect of the world. This led to his doctrine of occasionalism, according to which God is the only causal agent and "creatures" merely provide an "occasion" for divine action.

greater or lesser life. I like—and don't care whether this seems antiquated, useless, incomprehensible to certain people— this possibility of being a little greater than yourself. (The image is still from Malraux, in the second-last section of the *Antimémoires*, where he has Clappique meet an older Méry, who only has a few weeks to live but who is nevertheless "too tall for his height.") I like the thought that you can raise your-self above yourself, above your height and the destiny you were given. And I don't mind this being done, if necessary, by perching on top of major events or, when needed, on minus-cule events such as those wars without names, archives, or a history that have so often spurred me to action. We're all more or less guided by a star, aren't we? Well, there are bad stars—which the Romans called *sidera*, whose property is to attract you toward the depths, the chasm, the abyss, and first and foremost the abyss in yourself: the vertigo of introspection—rather than being star-struck, being struck down by the intimacy my father was so afraid of, and the mistrust of which I inherited. There are the good stars, the *astra*, which, on the other hand, make you raise your head, look to the sky, especially the sky of ideas: there's the star of the sailors of the Île de Sein and the humble fishermen of Brest and Saint-Malo immediately joining the Free French; the idée fixe that, despite the shooting and the slaughter, made the inspired soldiers of Monte Cassino rise to the assault, the light guiding the first French pilots in the Battle of Britain through the night as they resisted the fascination—again, starstruck—of what de Gaulle called "the frightening void of general renunciation." I'm nostalgic for that. Like all my generation, I miss those stars whose heat reaches us now only from very far away, almost abstractly, and yet were the best thing about the (last) century. And ultimately it's this too, this unparalleled heroism, these true legends, myths of flesh and thought, these living examples, all the more alive for appearing unreal, that have me running around.

So you see that we don't always break with the law or with our mimicry of the father . . .

Well, I'm glad you brought up the subject yourself, because I don't think I would have dared to ask you straight out: Deep down, dear Bernard-Henri, why are you a "politically committed intellectual"?

For many years, twenty or thirty years maybe, people have come up to me and, without me even asking, told me things they have probably never told anyone, things they'd possibly never *thought*—consciously thought through—before they told me. This is precisely why I became a novelist. (Actually, let's be precise: this is the reason I wrote a number of novels.) Nothing otherwise predisposed me to it: I've always preferred poetry, I've always hated telling stories. But from the beginning I felt (and I still feel) a sort of *duty* (the word seems strange, but right now I can't think of another one): I was required to save these phenomena, to furnish as best I could a retranscription of the human phenomena that so spontaneously appeared before me.

The context here is different: you're not some aging sales rep in a hooker bar in Pattaya, or a wife-swapping social worker trying to breathe new life into her relationship. You're more than capable of retranscribing the human phenomenon you represent without the need of a scribe; nonetheless, I'd like to think that, like others, you sensed in me those characteristics that led me to become and gradually to identify myself with the role of the *recorder*.

The lack of a sense of the ridiculous, for a start. A politically committed intellectual is not, to my mind, as you may have gathered, someone *ridiculous*. I can picture it, I can imagine the half-smiles, whatever you like, but deep down I don't feel that a politically committed intellectual is ridiculous; because deep down I feel that very few things are ridiculous. I've probably withdrawn too much from any concrete sense of social belonging—and by the same token, withdrawn a little from humanity (but let's not get ahead of ourselves)—to truly have a sense of the ridiculous.

You will have gathered, too, that you can tell me you're a disaster tourist without provoking any real disapproval (besides, coming from so far and having no real power, how could you not be something of a tourist?). Disapproval is a mental category I use rarely. And yet I do have a sense of good and a sense of evil, indeed they can appear with surprising violence when called on (I never seek to excuse a criminal; I never relativize an act of charity). But I call on them very rarely, *a minima*. And I am happy to live in a peaceable world in which the moral fiber of a man is rarely truly tested, where most actions are morally neutral.

Don't worry, I am going to get around to talking about myself. Following your example—first the honorable reasons, then the more questionable ones, and so on to the worst—I'll explain why I *am not* a politically committed intellectual.

(Leaving aside the fact that, in any case, I'm not an "intellectual"; otherwise I'd need to explain why I studied at an

institute for agronomics rather than *khâgne** or Sciences Po,
but that's another matter.)

To talk about political commitment, I have to go back to
Russia, where I've been twice, in 2000 and 2007. The first
time was impressive. In the deserted avenues of Moscow,
4×4s with tinted glass windows thundered past. The restau-
rants and the cafés were empty—except for Westerners; in
the streets and the doorways, young people shared bottles of
beer and vodka (drinking in the bars was much too expensive
for them). A few young women were dressed like prostitutes;
the others were barely modernized babushkas.

Nowadays, it's almost impossible to drive through Moscow;
the cars now are Nissan Micras, Volkswagen Golfs. The res-
taurants and the cafés are full of Russians who drink according to their budget; young women wear the current fashions.
In other words, a middle class has formed, and the first thing
one notices is that the pockets of "terrifying poverty" have
vanished; the mysterious, almost mystic formation of a *West-
ernized middle class* (or that, at least, is how it is usually
referred to).

These middle classes voted en masse for Putin, voted en
masse for Medvedev; they believe they have no credible alternative; like their government they consider the rebukes of the
West (over Chechnya et al.) to be *unacceptable meddling*. It
must be admitted that, in this, the Russian government is on
the same wavelength as the populace.

Nor has Russia, and here I have to contradict you, become
a cultural desert. In the numerous bookshops, literature from
around the world is freely available with no restrictions. The
books are exceptionally well made and well printed and, most

---

*Khâgne is the preparatory course for the arts section of the prestigious
École Normale Supérieure.

important, they are very cheap, even on a Russian budget. In short, in Russia, many people still regularly buy books—more so than in, say, Brazil or even Italy or Spain.

It's true that Solzhenitsyn is considered to be an orthodox old pain in the neck; he, I admit, has every reason to feel disappointed in the recent evolution of Russia, to feel that it has "betrayed its soul"; and I'm not sure that Dostoyevsky would have *adored* the nightclubs ... Then again, I'm not sure whether I *adore* the nightclubs, but I was glad to see Frédéric again and the *sumptuous blondes*, well, you know the terms of the equation, I've written enough books on the subject.

On my second trip to Moscow, I had a very interesting conversation with a civil servant in the Ministry of Foreign Affairs. (These people lead a strange life; they spend a few years in a job, develop a temporary sense of belonging, only to be uprooted; their conversation is often fascinating.) I was telling him that in France after the war, it was said that the country was ungovernable, the Fourth Republic, the frequent changes of government, etc.; none of which prevented France from fast-track development, so much so that this period of government irresponsibility remains, from an economic standpoint, the most flourishing period in our history. He replied that though Putin's Russia could be accused of all the evils in the world, though not of "governmental instability," the same phenomena were evident (the rise of the middle classes, consumer capitalism).

There was silence for a few seconds, then he said something like: "All in all, maybe it's for the best; it proves that society has its own momentum and the system of government superimposed on it with its regulations, its government officials, is simply a form of parasite."

Then he stopped, remembering that he too was a government official, a civil servant at the Ministry of Foreign Affairs, to be precise; there was an awkward silence, which I easily managed to dispel, since I'm quick to play the fool by asking for more vodka. Another example of the tendency of people to *tell me things* that they themselves hadn't expected; even so, we changed the subject pretty quickly.

There you are, dear Bernard-Henri, the first root (the one I consider to be honorable) of my lack of political commitment: an ideological diffidence verging on atheism. Russians certainly do not feel that they are *living in a democracy;* I think for the most part they don't give a damn and who am I to disagree with them? For many years, I lived in a country (France) where I had the right to vote, a right I barely exercised. From a political point of view, many measures were implemented, concerning public health especially, of which I completely disapproved. Off the top of my head, I would mention the banning of products considered to be "drugs," the constant hectoring campaigns against alcoholism, in favor of using condoms, against cocaine, sugary foods, and who knows what-all, the absurd inability to buy most common medicines without prescription, and more than anything, the thing that in itself is symbolic of all the others: the slow, pitiless pincer movement that in a few short years closed in on *smokers*. All these things contributed to my cutting myself off from the world, of becoming someone who absolutely does not consider himself to be a *citizen*. Sadly, I'm not exaggerating; I have gradually grown to see public spaces as a hostile territory bristling with absurd and humiliating bans, which I negotiate as quickly as possible to get from one *private* residence to another *private* residence; a territory in which I am deeply unwelcome, in which I have no place, in which nothing interesting or pleasant can happen to me.

Having done a little research over several elections, I quickly discovered that all the parties courting my vote held almost identical positions on these public health issues; that there *existed a broad consensus of opinion on the subject*. So what did I do when I came to the ballot box? With a goodwill that in retrospect seems to me absurd, I hesitated endlessly, painfully, sometimes for hours between different candidates, different electoral platforms; I hesitated for a long time before eventually, on almost every occasion, abstaining. You see, I have never had the sense of *living in a democracy;* I've always had the sense of living in a sort of technocracy, though without necessarily feeling that this was a bad thing; maybe the technocrats are wise and just; maybe I should give up alcohol; maybe I should even *give up smoking*.

And I would be wrong to accuse these decent technocrats who doubtless have all the relevant qualifications necessary to carry out the difficult task of formulating laws; these public health measures would no doubt be approved by our fellow citizens in a *crushing* majority. Thereby literally *crushed,* all I can do is shut up and accept that I live in a world where the general will "exercises too great a pressure on the will of the individual." In practice, I can try to find a corner where I can go and die, some isolated spot where, all alone, I can give myself over to my modest vices.

It must be said that in the years since I have been living in Ireland, things have been better. Not that the public health policies are any different, they are European, and Ireland has enforced them more swiftly than other countries; but my situation here is profoundly different. The Irish government has never proposed that I *participate in the democratic process,* nor given me the impression that I had to take part in any way, shape, or form in the political decisions taken by the country. The level of taxation, which is extremely low for earnings relating to artistic work, is quite low in general; almost no one in the country pays much tax; it is a different concept of State. With this level of taxation, you can feel you are dealing with essential, incontestable expenditure—law and order, refuse collection, road maintenance; you never think that the government has committed itself to some bold policy on which you would be called on to have an opinion, for which they would ask for your support. All this is calming; you don't really have the impression of participating, or at least you don't have to ask yourself any questions; all this, in a word, *depoliticizes*. I suppose there is a *psychological threshold,* which it is dangerous for a government to go beyond. On that subject, it is interesting to note that different churches, regardless of the geographic or historic conditions that shaped them, are more or less agreed on the extent of the financial contribution they can expect from their faithful: 10 percent of their income, no more.

A few years ago, I remember talking with Sylvain Bour-meau. This, incidentally, is a second honorable reason for my *lack of political commitment:* never has my friendship or my respect for people, little though it might be, been marred by their political opinions. I know that Sylvain Bourmeau is a fine representative of *la gauche morale*—the moral left—and indeed he is passionate on the subject, which, to be honest, bores me, but it's his pet subject. I nonetheless consider him to be an honest and thoughtful literary critic, one of the few in France whose opinion of my own work might affect or sway me. I also—more important—consider him a good guy.

Anyway, chatting with Sylvain, I told him that although I was in favor of immigrants in France being allowed to vote, in all elections, obviously, I was against the French abroad being allowed to vote. I couldn't see why, having consciously decided to live outside France, I should have any right to pronounce on the politics of the country. He replied, or rather he was thinking aloud: "Yes . . . reserve the right to vote for *users*."

Thinking about it some months later, I realized that this ugly little word *user* (and I realize this is going to plunge Régis Debray* into despair) precisely describes my relationship with the government of my country, of any country. As regards France (or any other country where I might decide to live), I do not feel (deep down I never truly felt and would come less and less to feel) like a *citizen*, but, in banal terms, like a *user*. There, I've said it. It's a little sad; it's a sense of belonging that is failing, deteriorating. But we have reached the point where we can tell each other the truth more or less, haven't we?

As we come to the dishonorable reasons for my lack of political commitment, you have the right to shudder. Don't worry, I'll be quick. I completely understand that the trips to Darfur, the danger they entailed, may have speeded up the process of giving you a sense of yourself; but, sadly, no one or almost no one can go through life without encountering precise situations in which he can get a pretty clear idea of his moral worth. So don't worry: I am not speaking on the strength of self-examination but from experiences that enabled me, concretely, to appreciate my own worth.

Almost incapable of physical violence, I have, in addition, never taken any pleasure in it, even in those—rare—cases where I had the advantage. In fact, giving up physical violence as the principal means of settling disputes seemed to me one of the only advantages of becoming an adult. I have

---

*Jules Régis Debray (born 1941) is a French intellectual and journalist most noted for introducing the discipline of "mediology" in his book *Transmitting Culture*.

never been fascinated by weapons, nor really by games of strategy.

I am, besides, organically, viscerally incapable of *obeying*. When I sense that I am being given an order, something inside me freezes, transforms itself into a sort of painful, impassable mental nodule. Since more often than not I am too much of a coward for confrontation, I am evasive; I give the impression that I will obey when the time comes. And then, at the last minute, without thinking ahead, in an impulse so irresistible it seems like a reflex, I disobey.

Incapable of taking orders, I take no pleasure in giving orders. It is something I do reluctantly, only for brief periods and only when it is absolutely necessary.

Given all of this, it is not difficult to imagine what kind of soldier I would make. I have no doubts, dear Bernard-Henri, that in the event of war (and I think this is what one must envisage as the last resort when discussing commitment), I would fight little and badly. I would throw a few punches or fire a few shots depending on the context (ideally, the whole thing would be played out on a computer screen); and pretty quickly I would start wondering what I was doing there; the vague thrill of combat (I am, I suppose, capable of secreting a little adrenaline) would wear off. And, at the first opportunity, I would quite simply *do a runner*. I would join the vast throng of those who fought little and badly; of those who waited, without quite daring to say as much, for everyone else to *stop their fucking nonsense*. Of those who do not care about the fate of democracy, of Free France, of Chechnya or the Basque country; about those who succumb, as de Gaulle rightly said, to the spell of the "terrifying emptiness of general renouncement." I am one of those. Of those whom nothing general and universal (nor specific and domestic) can really move. Of the vast troop of people who endure history, interesting themselves only in that which directly concerns them and those close to them.

I find it extremely unpleasant that choosing to take the standpoint of selfishness and cowardice may, in the eyes of my contemporaries, make me *more likeable* than you who advocate heroism; but I know my peers and that is precisely what will happen.

I'd like to speak on behalf of a superior heroism, that of the Dalai Lama, say. In the writings of a Tibetan monk I was struck by the thought experiment he describes, where he imagines lying down on a railway line just before a train comes. The monk, he says, understands the phenomenon of his body being cut to pieces, and envisages it calmly as a representation of his spirit. This guy wasn't joking; this was how far he'd got.

I haven't got that far and in practice I speak on behalf of nothing very much. Of some vague concept of progress, maybe, which to my mind is scientific or technical. A vestige of the seriousness I had in childhood, continued through my studies, that means that I consider war (civil or religious, of independence or of conquest) as so much *waste of time*. The important thing, surely, is to invent the steam engine, develop industrialized production, control the weather. It is more than a vestige, in fact; this is how I was brought up, I can't help it.

So, there are the good students who go home after class and do their math homework for the next day; and the bad, the morons, who hang around the streets looking to play some mean trick, to start a fight.

Later, there will be honest engineers who build railway viaducts and office buildings; and bloodthirsty clowns who seize on any pretext, ideological or religious, in order to destroy them.

Is this, then, the core of my beliefs? Is it as simplistic as this? Sadly, I fear it is. I have always felt the deepest mistrust for those who *take up arms* in the name of whatever cause. I have always felt there was something deeply unwholesome about warmongers, troublemakers, rabble-rousers. What is a war or a revolution, in the end, but a hobby fueled by spite, a bloody, cruel sport?

I have infinitely sympathized with, felt, and finally embraced the maxim by old Goethe: "Better an injustice than disorder."

Above all, I have been fascinated by the phrase, so mysterious in its generality, from Auguste Comte, "Progress is nothing other than the development of order."

Are we going to have to resort to philosophy for the rest of our exchanges? It bothers me that I still don't have access to my books. Go on, let's let the old mother sleep a little longer. And since you conclude your letter with another story about your father, I will tell you a story about mine, though I admit mine is a little more ambiguous.

Let's be clear: my father was too young to be part of the "French Resistance." There were of course exceptional cases; I think there may even have been fifteen-year-olds who were executed; let's say that he could just about have been involved, but he did nothing about it. To tell the truth, even if he had, he wouldn't have boasted about it; but I would certainly have known about it from his sisters, so proud of him, so quick to cut an article out of a newspaper if there was some mention of one of his Himalayan expeditions. If there were any heroic feats, I would have heard about them, but as far as heroic feats go, there were none.

Nor on the other hand did he collaborate with or get involved in the acts of violence perpetrated by the Milice; I don't think he was even involved in the Chantiers de Jeunesse,* or at least he never talked about it. Actually, I believe (and it's disturbing when you think about it) I never heard my father mention General de Gaulle or Marshal Pétain. From which I am forced to conclude that he spent the war years pursuing purely personal projects (of the sort, I imagine, that every teenager does).

Once, only once, he told me a story that reminded me that he had lived through the war. It was about two young French Resistance fighters who had killed a German officer in the metro. (Had my father had some sort of contact, whether close or distant, with these young men? I have no idea, but thinking back on the way he told the story, that's what I believe.) And what did he, personally, think about this act of resistance? He had concluded that it was "not very interesting."

I can still picture him as he said those words and I regret the fact that I did not question him further. That "not very interesting" is as frustrating in its laconism as a Zen koan. Did he mean to show his contempt for an act of resistance that would immediately have triggered the execution of a dozen French hostages in reprisal? Was he trying to tell me that the idea of *Free France* was not, in itself, a subject likely to fascinate him? Or was he, more profoundly, trying to let me know that it seemed to him "not very interesting" to assassinate someone in the metro regardless of the motive? I don't know, I still don't know; but doubtless, in my case too, the mark of my father still carries weight.

*Les Chantiers de la Jeunesse Française was a French paramilitary organization during World War II known by the occupying German forces as Französische Arbeitsdienst.

March 21, 2008

I don't know which of us will get first prize as the better "recorder."

But I have to say, dear Michel, that you are surpassing yourself when it comes to enormous, provocative confessions that will give the blabbermouths something to talk about.

Let's go over all this slowly, calmly, without being contentious and particularly without getting annoyed. (It's quite possible that in our little exchange you've already won over the mockers, the sniggerers, those with a sense of humor, whereas I'm known not to have one, so I'm not going to add to that . . .)

The problem with your last letter is, of course, not your civic abstention, your nonallegiance, your attitude of "just pretend I'm not there, actually I'm not there anymore, I go from bubble to bubble, from one private home to another, I don't identify with any community, I feel less and less of a citizen, more and more depoliticized and free, a literary Bartleby with his *I'd prefer not to,*' throwing open the door to the 'possibility of an island.'" Why not? After all, that may be an acceptable definition of a writer.

Nor does it have anything to do with your living in Ireland

and your fiscal expatriation. It's true that in my case I could technically do this too, since between my American adventures, my trips, and the way I live, according to my lawyer's expert calculations I end up spending far less than the famous "six months a year" that qualify you as a tax resident in Paris. The fact is, I don't take advantage of this and continue to pay those confounded taxes like a good boy, a good citizen. But why, fundamentally? Is it really out of virtue? Purely out of my civic duty? Or is it also—let's be frank— because I don't dare, I haven't got your nerve, and it would make a mockery of the big fuss I make with my concern for mankind. ("What, he makes us feel guilty, he makes us look like swine who put their interest before honor, happiness before justice! He spares us none of his indignation! He denounces so-and-so! He calls on you to vote for some other one. And now we find out that he's stashed all his money away in Ireland or Malta, yuck . . .") So it's nothing to show off about. Nor is it a good idea to try to be too crafty.

What troubles me, what I find staggering, is not even what you say about war, that it makes you feel sick, the lack of courage you attribute to yourself, your "good soldier Schweik"* side, hesitating as in Hašek between disobedience and lack of respect, passive resistance and militant anarchism, affability as a strategy, internal desertion, shirking, the silent revolt. That's how everyone functions. No one, apart from fools, deliberately exposes themselves to danger. It's only in books and particu-

---

*Reference to *The Good Soldier Švejk*, a novel by the Czech author and humorist Jaroslav Hašek, acclaimed as one of the great satires of world literature. Set during the First World War, the novel relates a series of adventures in which Švejk manages to outwit various bureaucrats and military superiors despite being a feebleminded drunkard.

larly in the weak novels of Drieu, Jünger,* or Montherlant†
that combatants are courageous in the sense that you seem to
give the word. I'll even let you in on a secret: I'm not sure that
I'm any braver than you are. It's possible that violence, the real
violence I saw in Sarajevo, Africa, Southern Asia, Afghanistan,
frightens me just as much as you, precisely because I know it,
because I can smell its usual packaging from miles away. You
can't imagine my state of panic in 1998, for example, when I
was reporting for *Le Monde* in Panjshir and had to stay close to
Massoud, who didn't bat an eyelid as shells from 155s fell a few
feet away from us, whereas I . . . As for these men of war, like
Massoud for example, whom I have spoken of so highly, as for
the ones I ended up becoming an adviser and friend to, like the
Bosnian Izetbegović,‡ I would like to point out that it wasn't so
much their heroism that fascinated me but their way, as Malraux said, of *making war without loving it.* There too, we are
more or less in agreement. And it's my turn to reassure (or dis-
appoint?) you, by telling you that you are not less "ridiculous"
but less of a coward than you think.

But there are two other things in your letter that are unacceptable or that I, in any case, cannot accept. The anecdote
about your father and that ugly line of Goethe's about injustice and disorder.

First, the anecdote.

*Ernst Jünger: German writer who is best known for his account of the
First World War, *In Stahlgewittern* (*Storm of Steel*).

†Henry de Montherlant: French essayist, novelist, and playwright.

‡Alija Izetbegović: first president of Bosnia and Herzegovina (elected in
1990), in office during the war between the Bosnians and the Serbs, and
author of the books *Islam Between East and West* and *The Islamic
Declaration.*

It's certainly a pity that you did not have the time or inclination to ask him more about it.

Of course, that's often the way.

You don't think about it when your parents are there.

When you do think about it, it's because they're no longer
entirely there and you don't dare.

And when, like myself two weeks ago—perhaps because of
our correspondence, who knows!—you summon up the
courage to phone a ninety-four-year-old aunt, your mother's
elder sister, the last witness to so many things (and also the
first witness, incidentally, to my existence, since she was the
midwife in Béni Saf, the Algerian village to which my mother
returned to give birth to me), when you cross the line and
think, "It's too silly to leave all these unanswered questions,
these shadows that remain, this suspended family saga, I've
made up my mind, I'm going to phone," then the devil gets in
the way . . . She died, just a few days before we were to meet,
on March 9 at Melun. So sad . . .

But in your case it's almost worse.

I imagine you realize that this story of the German officer
taken out by two members of the Resistance, this image of
your father, and the fact that, after hearing this story, you
never thought of digging deeper than his laconic comment
you say you remember of "not interesting" to really go to
the heart of the matter and what they say about it is rather
odious.

Your story states your refusal ultimately to take the side
either of those young people or of the officer.

It puts on the same "uninteresting" level the Nazi idea of
the one and the Free France to which the others aspired.

It excludes the idea that some wars are more just than
others or that, when faced with extreme filth, when it's the
very idea of being human that is at stake and there is no other

way of saving it, violence must be espoused, with a heavy heart if you choose, dragging your heels if you say so, but all the same it must be taken up and it must triumph.

In other words, your story puts on an equal footing the absolute evil that is Nazism and the violence of reaction, that last-ditch resistance, which is not its own end but is just trying to stave off the worst. In passing, it should also be noted that it confuses, by gathering under the same dubious banner (I'm quoting you) the warmongers, those who "take up arms for any cause whatsoever," the Basque separatists (who are, as I'm sure you're aware, unscrupulous terrorists, killers of civilians, wreckers of a real democracy), and the Chechnyans (and I'm sure you're also aware that they have only rarely succumbed to the temptation of terrorism, while they are the target of a total war, up to extermination, instigated by a KGB president who has sworn—Putin, this time in his own words—to "finish them off" right down to the last one, if necessary hunting them down "even in toilets").

Dear Michel, I'm not going to give you a lecture.

Once again, you know all this so I'm not going to preach.

But I'm sure you understand that we're no longer back in the Hašek days.

Or those of the mutineers of 1917* and other "men against" in Francesco Rosi's film.†

---

*The French army mutinies of 1917 took place after the disastrous failure of the Nivelle Offensive in April of that year and involved primarily infantry soldiers who had had enough of trench warfare. The mutinies led to mass arrests, mass trials, and a number of executions. For a long time this was something of a taboo subject in France (so much so that Stanley Kubrick's film *Paths of Glory*, released in 1957, was not shown in France until 1975). In a controversial move, those court-martialed were pardoned by French premier Lionel Jospin in 1998.

†Francesco Rosi's pacifist film *Uomini contro* (released in 1970), which portrays the follies of war, also set during the First World War (in Italy).

Or even in the lyrical and ultimately rather grotesque merry-go-round in *La Comédie de Charleroi,** Drieu-style.

We're with Giono,† inches away from his "integral pacifism." And I'm sure there's no need to show the inevitable sequence that led this otherwise admirable author of *Roi sans divertissement* and *Jean le Bleu* to become a supporter of Pétain.

I hope you understand that I'm not accusing your father.

I haven't overlooked or ruled out the thousand possible explanations you might have uncovered for his strange attitude: modesty, prudence, protecting a third party, even— who knows—the double dealing of a hidden member of the Resistance, as in René Clément's *Le Père tranquille.*

No.

What interests me in this story is you.

What I find worrying is how you use the anecdote and your way of being apparently satisfied with the most pessimistic, the most distressing explanation, as if this indifference suited you today.

You can be a pure writer, dear Michel, and still feel summoned to a rendezvous with history—see Rimbaud and the Commune.

You can be concerned only with the absolute, the supreme book, etc., and still keep an ear open for human sobbing—see the little-known *Conflit et confrontation,* in which Mallarmé claims to offer "points of clarity" to the "blind flock" of "navvies." He doesn't give an inch when it comes to his

*A collection of short stories by Pierre Drieu la Rochelle (published 1934). The title refers to the Battle of Charleroi, which took place on August 21, 1914.

†Jean Giono: French author whose fiction is infused with pacifism and the themes and values of the Provence countryside.

poetry; on the contrary, he sees conflict and confrontation as the spiritual brothers of poetry.

Or you can be like Proust in Norpois's words, a "flute player." You can see the public space as a hostile place that makes you literally ill and whose only virtue is to allow you to pass from "one private home to another." And yet you can still have an infallible radar for detecting an opponent of Dreyfus.

But a word to the wise is enough; sorry to go on.

Now to Goethe's saying.

First of all, I'd like to point out that Goethe's exact words ("I prefer to commit an injustice than to tolerate disorder") were said during the French Revolution in front of the city of Mainz, which had been recovered by the Prussians. He said it only minutes after personally intervening to prevent the lynching of a French soldier who had been evacuated by the troops of the duke of Weimar. In the context, the "injustice" consists of sparing an enemy soldier who may be a great criminal. The "disorder" is that of the unleashed, bloodthirsty rabble, ready to tear a man to shreds. Thus, in his mouth the phrase really means the opposite, exactly the opposite of what you say he meant. Indeed, since Barrès,* he has always been misrepresented.

So there you are. I hate that line as everyone quotes it and as you in turn apply it.

I hate it because of Barrès, who, since he was the first to distort it in this way, was also a sort of second author.

I hate it because of Dreyfus, the innocent Dreyfus, who was the real target both of Barrès himself and of the dirty "intellectuals" claiming to rehabilitate Barrès.

I hate it because of all the innocents it has allowed, since

---

*Maurice Barrès, French writer, nationalist, and, alongside Charles Maurras, leader of the anti-Dreyfusards during the Dreyfus affair.

Dreyfus and like Dreyfus, with the same clear conscience and in the name of the same reasons of state, to be unscrupulously condemned.

I hate it because of those judges who at least once in their career come into possession of "new evidence" indicating that someone who has been convicted may be innocent but close the file with a sigh because, *well, that's how it is, you're not going to start up everything from scratch, set the whole machine in motion again, discredit it, weaken it, instill doubt . . . better to drop it, calmly put on your slippers and have your dinner . . . better an injustice than disorder . . .*

By chance I had dinner the other evening with a great judge, Philippe Courroye. You would need to know the history of my relations with him to understand. I would need to tell you about that morning five years ago when he interrogated me for hours about a financial misdemeanor. Thank heavens I hadn't committed it, but only a literary argument, a purely literary argument, managed to convince him that I was telling the truth. Next time, maybe. In a future letter, if it comes up and especially if I'm allowed to (I'm not sure about that, to tell the truth). But what I want to tell you here is that he spoke to me the other night about a recent case, very recent, which he came across in his role of public prosecutor in Nanterre. A man had received a heavy sentence. The matter appeared to be classified as ultrasensitive. The formidable Courroye, on examining the file, finds that it's not that clear, that this man was a simple soul, a Pierre Rivière* without the

*A Norman peasant who killed his mother, sister, and brother and wrote a memoir (1835) while in jail that became the subject of a book by Michel Foucault, *Moi, Pierre Rivière, ayant égorgé ma mère, ma sœur et mon frère . . . Un cas de parricide au XIXe siècle* (*I, Pierre Rivière, Having Slaughtered My Mother, My Sister and My Brother . . . A Case of Parricide in the Nineteenth Century*).

madness, and that he might have confessed to a crime he hadn't committed. And the reactions of the colleagues Courroye asked to check, reinvestigate, possibly rejudge were inertia, apathy, the unwillingness of a machine that does not at any cost want to be challenged. Over a century later this is the same tune, the same story, the same distant but distinct echo of the mechanism of the Dreyfus affair, still this same "better an injustice than disorder."

Courroye is certainly not a representative of the moralizing left you mention.

We certainly do not belong to the same part of the ideological and political spectrum.

But in this case, he was the one who was right.

When I left him, I said to myself—and I repeated it when I read your letter—that fortunately there are people within the institution who take the view that there can be no order worthy of the name if it is nourished by injustice.

In short, that line is detestable.

Even outside the courts, it's a line that gets around, and everywhere it goes, it injects its poison.

It's the line that springs to mind when you don't want to bother with the destiny of a small people whose martyrdom doesn't have even a butterfly effect on the workings of the planet.

It's the phrase muttered to themselves by those bastards when you ask them to take sides with a handful of Tibetan monks—oh yes, those Tibetans! Not always such pure spirits as the Dalai Lama, ready for the mystical experience of having their body sliced through by a train—who are in the middle of screwing up their little diplomatic games.

It's the typical line of someone who knows, on the one hand, that there's injustice in Tibet and, on the other, that there will be a great disorder if we annoy the Chinese and they decide to punish us by selling their dollar reserves and not flying to the aid of Goldman Sachs or Lehman Brothers.

It's the phrase that would have occurred to the neighbors across the way from Family X, arrested one morning in July 1942 by the national police, by order of the Gestapo. What does one Jewish family matter? Isn't France already in enough trouble as it is? Aren't the French police, led by the valiant Bousquet and Papon,* going through hell to save anyone they can and give blankets to children? And frankly, is it really the moment to cause an almighty scandal, such disorder, because of some local injustice?

It's a line that kills, it's the most odious line of all time.

I don't wish to offend you. I'm just saying what I feel. It's a line that makes my blood run cold, and it distresses me to think that you seem to have made it your own, without giving it a second thought and moreover assuming—I wonder why exactly—that our contemporaries are likely to take your side . . .

I'll go further.

Or perhaps not so far—I don't know.

You may think that I'm overreacting, that I'm making this too personal and that this weakens my argument. But too bad, after what you threw out at me, I must be allowed to cross the line.

This sentence in itself turns my blood cold.

But it also turns my blood cold on a more personal level.

And I'll even say that if it turns my blood cold, if I find it physically unbearable to read it in general and particularly

---

*René Bousquet and Maurice Papon, high-ranking officials in the Vichy regime, both charged with crimes against humanity in the 1990s.

when written by you, that's because it resonates in me with obscure fears, irrational terrors, threats that are difficult to formulate and probably childish, ghosts. It's because—I'm going to say it straight out—part of me has always believed that one day that phrase could apply to me.

There are things like that, that you just know.

For example, I have the impression that I more or less know what the last book I'll write will be and even the last one I'll read.

I have a vague idea—I've always had one—about some of the appointments I still have to honor.

And this is the same. This may seem very silly but I've always felt that the day might come, I don't know when or where, how, in what context, whether literary, judicial, political, revolutionary, where I might hear, "An injustice for Lévy? A serious injustice? Very serious? Well, he went looking for it. He shouldn't have been such a show-off. In any case, better that injustice—a thousand times better—than disorder in the world!" And I know that the phrase will sound so fair, so obvious and reasonable, that there will be no one to protest, to contest it, to petition or rebel against it.

It's the story (which has haunted me since I first read the book in the summer of 1968 at Antibes) of Solal in Chapter 5 of Albert Cohen's *Belle du Seigneur*, alone in his cave in Berlin with the dwarf Rachel, exiled by the League of Nations, stripped of his honors, abandoned by everyone, condemned.

It's the last words of Emmanuel Levinas's *Proper Names* (I don't have my books with me either, as I'm writing this time from Salvador da Bahia in Brazil, and I don't even have the Internet)—it's that last, lugubrious page, in which Levinas evokes the naïveté of one of those who used to be called French Jews: sure of himself and his place in this world, cosseted, rich in talents and titles, surrounded by friends, possibly powerful. But then overnight, without warning, an icy wind blows through the rooms in his house, the tapestries and drapes are torn from the walls, all the poor glories of his life are swept away like rags, and in the distance he hears the screeching of a pitiless crowd.

In fact, it's the story of Alfred III, the grocer in Friedrich Dürrenmatt's *The Visit*. I suppose you know Dürrenmatt? If you don't, get to know him at once. He's not much worse than Goethe. He wrote that brilliant text, which has also haunted me for twenty years and tells the story of an "old lady" who as a child lived in Güllen, a small town that used to be wealthy and is now ruined and that Goethe, no less, is supposed to have visited once. She left Güllen and made her fortune elsewhere. She returns as a total show-off, broadcasting her success as the town's prodigal daughter. After a few days of psychological preparation, as shifty as it is intense, she announces to her former fellow citizens, "You remember Clara, the mason's daughter, who was in love with Alfred but was abandoned by him when she became pregnant? She went through hell, that little Clara. She snuck off like a thief, fleeing the insults of those who mocked her red braids and her advanced pregnancy. Well, I'm Clara. I've come back to avenge myself and at the same time to save my town, as you're about to go under, aren't you? Your factories have closed. Your young people are unemployed. Don't worry, citizens and friends. I'm offering fifty billion plus another fifty billion to share among yourselves. All I ask in return is one thing, the head of the man who dumped me and whom you must kill." Naturally, the village cries out, "That's blackmail, outrageous. Have you ever heard of honest citizens, respectful of the spirit of justice, agreeing to such a transaction?" The old lady smiles in a corner and replies, "That's all it will take. I'll wait.

When you change your mind, I'll be there with my valets, my eighth husband, my chambermaids, my trunks, and my billions, at the Inn of the Golden Apostle, near the railway station." And indeed it doesn't take her long to get her result. It begins with an epidemic of new yellow shoes that invade the town, then dresses for the young girls, colorful shirts for the boys. To his surprise, Alfred notices that the police officer he turns to when he notices the grim way people are staring at him is sporting a magnificent gold tooth. The curate who gives him refuge has received a new bell for his church. Everyone gets televisions and washing machines. Unlimited supplies of pilsner. Prosperity at all levels. You get the point. As the old lady predicted, the entire village has begun, just begun, to let itself be bought. "That Alfred, after all . . . Isn't the old woman somewhat right? Didn't he behave like a swine at the time? And even today. Look at him even today. First off, he's an ugly bastard, we never realized what an ugly, two-faced look he had . . . And then, doesn't he understand the awful situation the town is in? He was there the other day when she made her proposal. He understood just as we did that all that was needed was a word from him, a gesture, for our prosperity to return and Forge X and Mill Y to be saved. Of course we acted indignant; it was a question of principle. But what about him? Why didn't he make the gesture? Why does he not sacrifice himself for this city, which he says he loves? He says it's unjust, that it would be an injustice to give in to that old lunatic's caprice. But where does the injustice lie, I wonder. Can you really talk about injustice when a whole community can be saved? What an egotist. What a bad lot. And what fools we are to be so kind." I'm not so sure of the details. But that's how it goes, in general. And there's poor Alfred in the last scene, assassinated in a corner of his grocery store, shabbily strangled, while, as the price for this small injustice, happy order returns to Güllen.

I know writers who identify with Céline, Proust, Paul Morand, Drieu, Montherlant, Romain Gary.

I even have a friend, not a bad writer, who, when he's not feeling well, declaims in front of his mirror the "Ode à Jean Moulin" by André Malraux.

But on my good days it's Solal I think of, in his cave, abandoned by everyone except his dwarf.

On the bad ones I'm haunted by the destiny of Dürrenmatt's grocer, not a real bastard, not entirely innocent, assassinated by a crowd of his fellow men.

At times I also think of the story (a true one in this case, and it has pursued me since it was revealed a dozen years ago by a Swiss historian) of Marc Bloch, whose "great friend" Lucien Febvre implored him to give in to the Germans, who were asking for just one thing, one small thing, to authorize the republication of the journal *Annales*,* and to consent to having his name removed from the journal's list of contributors. What? Febvre grew impatient. Bloch was hesitating, complaining? Weighing the pros and cons, moralizing, flaunting his high principles, quibbling? What selfishness! What an inflated ego! What a lack of any sense of or concern for the common good! Naturally, Bloch eventually gave in. But what prevarication, what complications before finally going over to the only worthwhile view. What a prick.

I repeat that all this makes no sense.

It's almost unseemly to identify with Marc Bloch, who was ultimately executed by the Nazis.

Annales: the journal *Annales d'histoire économique et sociale.*

And I authorize you to object that there is something about these ghosts that tends to undermine what I told you the last time about my inability to experience and see myself as a victim.

But that's how it is. I suppose we're all entitled to our little contradictions. Moreover, in my defense I'd say that there is my daytime thinking, my conscious, everyday life, where being a victim has no place, and then there's my other, nocturnal life, not usually acknowledged, where I'm less proud and endlessly vulnerable.

In any case, that's the truth.

This is my primal and secret scene, my obsession, my nightmare.

And that was my fifteen minutes of being pathetic or paranoid, as you will.

I'm afraid no, dear Bernard-Henri, the problem is that it is not a piece of provocation and I believe I understand Goethe's maxim exactly as he intended it.

Injustice can, in effect, mean sparing a French (or German) soldier who may be (or may not be; let's say who probably is) a major criminal.

There is disorder in any case that involves killing someone at random. Because that, may I remind you, was precisely the aim of acts of the Resistance: to spread terror through the occupying army; to ensure that not a single German soldier felt safe in the metro.

Greater disorder in a case where that same soldier (whether German or French) is lynched by a mob—greater disorder, I must point out, simply because in the second case, the death will be that much more disgusting. Although perhaps that is to exaggerate a little; there are always a few clumsy oafs in a crowd, the death blow must come pretty quickly. Well, I say that mostly to reassure myself; the moments preceding the death blow must nevertheless be utterly appalling.

Disorder, too, in the planting of a bomb in a crowded place. Anarchists, Al Qaeda . . . there are few people, to be honest, in history, few people to *justify* the act (but many, almost as many as you could want, to carry it out).

No, obviously I don't like disorder: I am one of those who believe that disorder results in the greatest injustices.

Goethe's maxim, deep down, is that of all those who believe that the authorities in charge of a situation should make a decision, *any decision,* be it vague or unjust, rather than leave the last word to the "crowd," or to the "street"—to the big nasty impulsive animal always ready to pillage and massacre. That of all those haunted by the idea that we are never far from primal savagery, that civilization is merely a veneer. To believe that, one doesn't even need to be caught up in a civil war; it is enough, as we talked about earlier, to witness what a pack of children or of teenagers is capable of when they've chosen a victim. It's enough to have been in a crowd when access to the emergency exits is blocked. The ease with which they lash out and trample. Maybe we would be better off talking about cheerful subjects.

I have absolutely no idea in what sense Barrès understood it, and I confess that I don't really understand. (In what sense can reopening a case that was badly conducted constitute a cause of disorder? Isn't this how the judicial process normally works?) I don't really know anything about Barrès; I remember starting La Colline inspirée,* slogging through and finally giving up without finishing the book. In a nutshell, I can't say he is an author that particularly impressed me.

I later heard he was some sort of *nationalist.* In short, someone not very interesting. Developing an overweening national pride is always a sign, to my mind, that you have nothing much else to be proud of.

The Sacred Hill by Maurice Barrès, translated by Malcolm Cowley (New York: Macaulay Company, 1929).

Okay, I know what you're going to say: Barrès is an important author, I read the wrong book. In that case, tell me which book I should read, because so far, in my opinion, quite frankly, Barrès is a nonentity.

Let's wait until I've read Barrès; but where does the German soldier fit into all this? No, of course I wouldn't have done it. I think I would have trouble killing a pig, And you're right, it's not (or not principally) about cowardice. The expression I find odious, almost unbearable, is a simple, anodyne phrase (one that you didn't use, but if I had to be disagreeable, let's say I think it was implicit in "with a heavy heart" and "dragging your feet"; thankfully, in the end, you didn't say it). This simple phrase which, to my mind, carries within it every crime is "The end justifies the means."

With the appropriate judicial proprieties, yes, maybe, I think I could kill. I could manage to be part of a firing squad. (Though I am happy never to have had to do so; I know that, in any case, the condemned man is blindfolded, and I wouldn't want to have to look him in the eye, but I would fire, yes, I would fire, if I believed that the man had been fairly tried.)

I am not really convinced, to finish with those points on which we disagree, by the distinction you make between the Basques and the Chechens. The Basques (*some* Basques) believe it is important to have an independent Basque state; they fought for it under Franco, they went on fighting under various successive Spanish governments; in what sense has the nature of their cause changed, simply because they are now fighting a democracy? As for the Chechens, I don't know much about them; I don't think that an independent Chechnya has existed in past centuries. From time to time there has been a movement in favor of independence (isn't there some mention of it as early as Tolstoy?); it's quashed, usually by military force, by the Russian government of the day. So yes, from all I know, I do still consider it an *internal matter for Russia*.

What precisely confers legitimacy on a nation? The length it has existed? A *common will*? I wonder. If it is a common will, I don't understand why people don't use the simple means of a referendum on self-determination. In the case of Corsica, the outcome would be a foregone conclusion (I say this because I know the area quite well). In the case of the Basque country, of Chechnya, of Flanders? I confess, I don't have a clue.

The case of Tibet is very different. Tibet has an age-old, a millennial existence; it was a sort of theocracy that developed a very interesting variant of Buddhism. And then brutally, fifty years ago, it was invaded by Communist China. At that point the resistance began, under the leadership of their spiritual leader, who was forced into exile. Since then, the resistance has never ceased.

I do not personally consider the Dalai Lama to be a "pure spirit," I consider him rather to be a tactician and a subtle one. And if, at the present time, he refuses to call for a boycott on the Beijing Olympic Games, I suspect he has his reasons. He can, of course, like any of us, be mistaken; but I am more or less sure that in terms of the *media coverage*, he has made his calculations.

Let's go further and say that the adoption of an attitude of nonviolent resistance, or a morally admirable form of resistance, perhaps, may also be a form of calculated self-interest; nor is it necessarily a losing strategy.

Stalin's famous phrase—"The pope! How many divisions has he got?"—is somewhat laughable given the not insignificant role that Pope John Paul II would play decades later in the final collapse of communism. Stalin, in short, was a stupid arsehole. Or, to be more polite, his view of human nature was rather limited.

Let's state the obvious: man is not, in general, a morally admirable creature. To delicately state something less obvious: man, in general, has enough in him to admire that which, morally, is beyond him and to behave accordingly. Tibetan resistance, from the outset, *commands respect*. And, in the long term, to command respect is not necessarily a losing strategy. I don't know who the idiot was who coined the phrase—like the title of a dissertation: "Kantian philosophy has kept its hands clean; but it has no hands,"* but I do know that he would have been better off saying nothing that day. Moral law does have hands, and powerful hands at that.

Because what is at stake in Tibet is not the vague, historically variable entity the nation-state; what is at stake in Tibet, in the eyes of the whole of the civilized world, is moral law; yes, itself, personified, as is manifest by the impeccable behavior of the victims. And what motivates the Tibetan people is not the fickle phantom, that mixture of frustrated resentment and silly pride we call national feeling; it is a principle of a spiritual nature, the most difficult thing in the world to defeat (something that is perhaps, strictly speaking, invincible).

I certainly have no wish to put the "spiritual" on a pedestal; it is also a *principle of a spiritual nature* that motivates the Islamic revolution throughout the modern world; in fact it is this that makes it so terribly dangerous.

---

*A reference to Charles Péguy's statement "Kant a les mains propres mais il n'a pas de mains" (Kant has clean hands but he has no hands).

Moral law was also at stake, to the greatest possible extent, in Nazism. There, too, there was a *principle of a spiritual nature* (one that you obviously know much more about than I do). There was only one (one can hardly define as "spirituality" a mishmash of Nordic mythology, a tedious *remix;* Chesterton noted that even a committed freethinker would give himself a serious headache if, in the space of an afternoon, he had to come up with a blasphemy intended to offend the great god Thor).*

And it was a spiritual principle that triumphed; or at least in retrospect one can read history that way.

Problems, real problems, begin when two spiritual principles come face-to-face; this is why I am not terribly optimistic on the subject of the conflict between Israel and Palestine.

I have made my choice, it is the same as that of Maurice Dantec[†] (though we express ourselves differently and do so for different reasons). Maurice converted, good for him; but for my part the choice continues to be one of uniquely moral considerations. I am gathering together the conditions for perfect objectivity on the subject: I have, as far as I am aware, no Arabic or Jewish forebears; the religions they practice seem to me almost equally absurd. But there is, to my mind, an essential, crucial difference between a *blind attack* and a *targeted strike.* You see the importance I attach to the *means*! They go so far as to influence my judgment of the *end*.

---

*"Blasphemy depends on belief, and is fading with it. If anyone doubts this, let him sit down seriously and try to think blasphemous thoughts about Thor." From *Heretics* by G. K. Chesterton.

†Maurice G. Dantec (born 1959) is a French-born science fiction writer and polemicist resident in Canada. In addition to his science fiction novels, he has written a number of polemical essays on radical Islamism. Dantec is an avowed Zionist and convert to his own Christian-Futurism, which informs his post-9/11 trilogy; the trilogy interconnects metaphysical research (Esotericism), technology, and the post-human.

. . .

Well, well, well. I believe I have just proved that I too could easily have been a pontificating/grandiloquent/sincere individual. Let's go back to the admittedly more trivial question of the *nation*. Here too I think I need to go back a little. Some years ago, I was included (together with Maurice Dantec, Philippe Muray,* and a number of others) as one of the leading figures in a small, easily readable book that described us as the *new reactionaries*. My first reaction was one of amusement; then, some weeks later, I began to feel annoyed. Not because of the whiff of shame attached to the term *reactionary,* that seemed rather funny; but because it's important to agree on the meaning of words. A reactionary is someone who favors some previously existing social configuration— something it is possible to return to—and someone who militates in favor of such a return.

Whereas, if there is an idea, a single idea that runs through all of my novels, which goes so far as to haunt them, it is the *absolute irreversibility of all processes of decay* once they have begun. Whether this decline concerns a friendship, a family, a larger social group, or a whole society; in my novels there is no forgiveness, no way back, no second chance: everything that is lost is lost absolutely and for all time. It is more than organic, it is like a universal law that applies also to inert objects; it is literally *entropic*. To an individual convinced of the ineluctable nature of all decay, of all loss, the idea of reaction would never occur. If such an individual could never be *reactionary,* he would on the other hand, obviously, be *conservative*. He would always consider it best to conserve what exists, what works more or less, rather than

*Philippe Muray (1945–2006) was a French essayist, critic, and novelist.

rush headlong into some new experiment. More attuned to danger than to hope, he would be a pessimist, melancholy by disposition, and generally easy to get along with.

In short, I was angry with Daniel Lindenberg, who, in calling me a reactionary, demonstrated such a complete lack of understanding of my books that it occurred to me that maybe I was a bad writer; then I thought maybe he was a bad reader (or that he hadn't read me, that he was working from index cards). Eventually I reread the magnificent article Philippe Muray devoted to *The Elementary Particles*, entitled "And, in Everything, Foresee the End," and I felt serene.

All things, therefore, die, including mental constructs, and as for the French nation, French patriotism, they are already dead. They have been dead for a long time; specifically, they have been dead since 1917 at about the time the first mutinies took place because, to be frank, it was all getting to be a bit too much.

Here too we need to step back a little. Here is a verse from a song that, at the time, everyone in France would have known:

The Republic calls us
Let us prevail or let us perish
A Frenchman must live for her
*For her, a Frenchman must die.**

Okay. It must be admitted that the Third Republic, with its famous *Black Hussars*, had clearly succeeded in something for an entire generation to go off to be massacred in 1914 with the feeling that they were only doing their duty and, in some cases, go off *enthusiastically*.

A few days ago, the last French combatant in the First

---

*"Chant du départ" (1794), music by Étienne Nicolas Méhul, words by Marie-Joseph Chénier.

World War died and, to mark the occasion, we heard again the testimony of his comrades, the former *poilus*. People have always been killed in wars, that's what wars are for. But back then men lay howling and dying for days at a time, a few feet from their comrades, and then rotting and decomposing, still only a few feet from them. These men who had to share their trenches with rats, their rations with worms, who were riddled with lice, who had to relieve themselves in the trenches wherever they could; and all this went on for months, for years, for a war that was utterly absurd, the reason for which no one can quite remember.

A government can ask much of its citizens, of its subjects; but there comes a moment when it asks *too much;* and then it's over. In going beyond the acceptable in that appalling, unjustified war, France lost all right to the love and the respect of its citizens; it brought discredit on itself. And such discredit is, I repeat, permanent.

This, it seems to me, explains a lot of things.

The nihilist rage of Surrealism and Dadaism, the surge of fury André Breton sometimes felt at the sight of a uniform or a flag.

The ease with which a generation of working-class people (whose parents and grandparents were probably irreproachable patriots) was convinced that the *country of the workers* was the Soviet Union and there could be no other.

Finally, the lack of enthusiasm with which the French fought in 1940. When people condemn the *spirit of Munich,* I always feel a certain unease, because Munich after all was in 1938—twenty years after 1918. Twenty years isn't much. And I think one has to beware of reading it as ideological. Because the first thought that occurred to most French people in 1940 was not, I think, "The struggle against Nazism has started," but something more like "Here we go again with the Huns."

If I don't know quite what my parents did during the Second World War, I know even less about what my grandparents did during the previous war. There is, however, a number I remember because it struck me at the time. My grandmother was part of a family that in 1914 comprised fourteen brothers and sisters. By 1918, there were only three left. This is what they call "taking a heavy toll."

For my part, I have little with which to reproach France; I didn't even do my *service militaire*—I was exempted category P2 or P3,* I don't remember now. (Nowadays things are okay, we have a professional army; under such circumstances it's easier to love one's country, since the love is risk free.) But it's like being in a relationship; you can't quite remember what irritated you about your partner, you can even find some good things to say about them, but there's nothing to be done, when it's over, it's over, and I won't fight for France or for the Republic or for anything like it (always supposing I'm prepared to fight for anything).

In short, our different families have given us different visions of France, something confirmed rather amusingly by the way you write about taxes. When you say you "haven't got the nerve" to be a tax exile it's obvious that you think of it as morally reprehensible, whereas I can honestly say that I don't.

---

*P1 through P5 were clinical reasons for which one might be exempted from compulsory military service; P2 related to depression or drug problems, P3 to anxiety or instability.

I can assure you, dear Bernard-Henri, that I have absolutely no feelings of guilt. I have never felt any duty or responsibility toward France and choosing which country I live in has about as much emotional resonance for me as choosing which hotel I stay in. We are only passing through here on earth, I understand that perfectly now; we have no roots, we bear no fruit. In short, our mode of existence is different from that of trees. That said, I'm very fond of trees, in fact I've come to love them more and more; but I am not a tree. We are more like stones, cast into the void, as free as they are; or if you absolutely insist in seeing the glass half full, we are a little like comets.

I find what I've just written a little sad, suddenly; but it's true, unfortunately, that in my life I feel as though I'm in a hotel; and I know that sooner or later I'll have to *check out*. I can't cope with this; I'm going to try to tackle some lighter subjects.

It's possible that one day I will come back to France, and it would be for a very simple reason: I will have had enough of speaking and reading English every day. It annoys me that I feel so attached to my language, I feel it smacks of *literary posturing*, but it's the truth. Besides, why should it be reserved for writers? The language we speak, that we use to express ourselves, is an important thing in a man's life—at least as important as the food he eats.

And the French language is truly one of the successes of this country, harmonious, a little muted with limited tonalities. When traveling, I have sometimes felt the violent, irresistible urge to read even just a few lines in French; in this state of withdrawal I have sometimes gone so far as to buy *L'Express*.

(There are places in Asia where you can't buy a newspaper

or a paperback book in French, but you can still find the international edition of *L'Express*.)

(I have to say it is an incredibly bloody boring magazine.)

(But it's got great distribution.)

There is also what one might call *the France of Denis Tillinac**—all local color and duck confit. I had barely experienced it until two or three years ago when, for a variety of reasons, I had to crisscross the country. And I have to admit, Denis Tillinac is right: it is a very beautiful country. The rural areas with their subtle patchwork of tilled fields, open meadows, and woodlands. The villages, here and there, stone houses, the architecture of the churches. Fifty kilometers farther along all this can change completely and you find a different arrangement, just as harmonious. It is incredibly beautiful what generations of anonymous peasants through the centuries have managed to create.

Ooh-la-la, I feel like I might be *losing it*; admire a rural landscape these days and you can find yourself being accused of *neo-Pétainism*. I like Prague too, you know, and even New York at a push (though the weather there is a little harsh).

Be that as it may, Denis Tillinac is right; he is absolutely right to live in this France (it's true that la Corrèze is among the most beautiful areas of France) but he is wrong to believe that it will disappear and to feel nostalgic about it. Worldwide, tourism is now the largest economic sector and selling points like that don't just disappear: they're worth a lot of money. This is what young British people have come to look for

---

*Denis Tillinac (born 1947) is a French writer and editor of *La Table Ronde*, who writes "gentle, tender" novels, essays, and biographies that are quintessentially French.

when they retire after their careers in the *City* (and now that they've grossly inflated prices in the Dordogne, they've started buying up the Massif Central). This is what, with all their feverish, financial hearts, the Japanese and Russian *nouveaux riches* hoped to find; and we gave it to them. They have their raw-milk cheese, the Romanesque churches, they have their duck confit. We will give the same warm welcome to the *nouveaux riches* from China and India.

As an economic activity for France in the future, that will be more than enough. Does anyone really believe we are going to become world leaders in software development or microprocessors? That we are going to maintain a *major export industry*? Come on . . . We will still have some manufacturing, that's true, mostly in the same sector (haute couture, perfumes, Joël Robuchon packaged dinners). Trains will be another exception; the French love trains.

Does this mean that I *meekly accept* the new international division of labor? Well, yes, nor do I see how I could do otherwise. The "emerging countries" want to earn money, much good it may do them; we have lots of things for them to spend it on. To put it more crudely, do I really want to turn France into a dead, mummified country, a sort of *tourist brothel*? To do to France what Bertrand Delanoë,* that wonderful trailblazer, is in the process of doing to Paris? Without a second thought, I say YES.

You wouldn't think it, but I have, in a few sentences, just saved the French economy; which just goes to show that our letters are not a waste of time.

---

*Bertrand Delanoë (born 1950) is a French politician, and has been the mayor of Paris since 2001.

I was happy to see you the other morning, Michel, although obviously disappointed by the power cut that prevented me from seeing your film.

But apart from the fact that it's only been postponed and that we'll see each other very soon, I must confess that I enjoyed our playacting in front of all those people waiting with us and who, I believe, we managed to fool into thinking that we hardly knew each other, that we were glaring at each other and had nothing to say.

I've always thought I'd have made a good secret agent.

Clearly, you wouldn't have been bad in the role either.

And, as an aside, I think that a greater interest should be taken in writers who in their real life were real secret agents.

They're always going on about writers who were diplomats, this unnatural alliance, this oxymoron. (Luckily, Claudel* forgot that he was an ambassador when he wrote *Connaissance de l'est* [*Knowing the East*]! And I can still hear Arielle's†

---

*Paul Claudel, French poet, dramatist, and diplomat who was the French consul in China from 1895 to 1909 and in Japan from 1922 to 1928.

†Arielle Dombasle, Lévy's wife.

grandmother, the wife of Ambassador Garreau-Dombasle,* who was also a good poet, celebrated as such by a handful of Surrealists and indeed also by Paul Claudel, sighing that the dinners, the letters from the castle, the *performance* had cost her her work . . .)

But the case of writers who were spies is so much more exciting! And there's much more of a link with literary activity, the literary profession. Read any biography of Koestler, Orwell, or even le Carré. Take the case of Kojève,[†] who we now know worked for the KGB. Look at Voltaire, the honorable correspondent of Louis XV at Frederick the Great's court, Casanova and the Venetian doges, Beaumarchais trafficking arms for the American revolutionaries as Malraux did, a hundred and fifty years later, for the Spanish Republicans. Read the memoirs of Anthony Blunt, which were published by Bourgois twenty-three years ago, and also his writings on Picasso, Poussin, or the architecture of François Mansart. In each case, what mines to be tapped for a novel! Literary fodder in its pure state. You'll find there the most radical and therefore the most pure form of the writer's paradox according to *Contre Sainte-Beuve*:[‡] I'm deceiving my world. I'm not who I appear to be. It's marvelous to be taken for another and all the while, hiding behind this mask and this borrowed identity, to take on the features and steal the soul, the heart, the life of my contemporaries.

But let's get back on track.

We're not going to agree about the story of the German

---

*Maurice Garreau-Dombasle, who was the French ambassador to Mexico.

[†]Alexandre Kojève, Russian philosopher and statesman who had a great influence on twentieth-century French philosophy.

[‡]Collection of critical essays by Marcel Proust on authors he admired in which he opposed the biographical approach espoused by the nineteenth-century literary critic Charles-Augustin Sainte-Beuve.

officer assassinated in the metro: you're pretending you don't understand that killing a German officer in the middle of Paris in 1943 is not exactly a "random killing." But let's move on.

Nor will we agree on the question of the poor Chechnyans, who don't seem to interest anyone and in your eyes too should just die without making a fuss. There certainly is, as you say, "something" about them in Tolstoy; that something is indeed in *Hadji Murad,* one of his last masterpieces, in which we see how this small martyred people is also (and the latter may explain the former) a great, proud people, insubordinate and incarnating a spirit of rebellion that the Putins of yesterday and today have always tried to bring to heel. I would so much like you to understand . . . But I know that you'll say I'm pontificating if I insist too much, if I explain that once you get to the point where between 10 and 20 percent of a people have been killed off, its capital city wiped out, and half of its country transformed into an immense ground zero, this is no longer an internal affair but really a matter for everyone. So I'll drop that too.

We won't waste any more time on Barrès, even if there too the question is not as straightforward as you seem to think and is complicated, if I dare to say so, in the opposite way: there is a Barrès other than the one you mock. There's the early Barrès, who is neither the *integral* nationalist of *La Colline inspirée* nor the Catholic drum-roller of *La Grande Pitié des églises de France** and particularly not the protofascist of his notes on the period of the Dreyfus affair. There was that young Barrès, a romantic, a tortured soul who

---

**La Colline inspirée* (*The Sacred Hill*, novel, 1913) and *La Grande Pitié des églises de France* (*The Great Pity of the Churches of France*, 1914), both later works by Maurice Barrès.

espoused the "cult of the ego" and was a resolute enemy of laws, a Venetian by temperament, a lover of Toledo, admired by Malraux and Aragon, a man ultimately rootless enough to relate to what you say about your lack of attachment to the places you live in.

Strangely enough, what struck me in your letter was that story of the stones "cast into the vacuum" and to which our freedom is to be compared, as well as the idea you draw from it, according to which we are temporary guests in this world, condemned sooner or later to "leave the room."

The image is interesting.

It was used as you know by an entire Greek school of thought founded by Democritus and Epicurus.

It's the image used after them by Lucretius, who really conceived the world as a hail of stones thrown into the vacuum along parallel trajectories with from time to time a "clinamen," a minuscule deviation, a swerve that causes them to meet and through meeting to form bodies.

As a parenthesis, this is an image that fascinated a whole series of writers before yourself, from Ovid to Montaigne, Bossuet to Rimbaud and Lautréamont, who saw *De rerum natura* as an extraordinary, brilliant, and in the proper sense of the word a visionary book ("*providens*" is what Lucretius called it; Rimbaud translated it as "*voyant*," seeing).

And, by way of another aside, it's an image that stands up fairly well from a strictly scientific point of view, since there are serious people who some twenty centuries later continue to consider it valid: Marx and Engels, obviously, who saw Epicurus and Lucretius as major thinkers and regarded their theory of "clinamen," this declination of linked atoms deviating slightly from their trajectory to form singular beings, like your stones and comets, as one of the sources of their dialectics. And, apart from them, real scientists like Darwin and

Dmitri Mendeleev with his periodic table, researchers into chaos theory or fluid mechanics, the most specialized astrophysicists and naturally the discoverers of the electron, the proton, the nucleus, the atom, all agree that *De rerum natura* with its rainfalls of particles tumbling into the void, sometimes swerving from their trajectory and becoming unruly, was not too far from the truth.

I've no problem, then, with the image.

But there is one thing. It freaks me out and I'll try to explain why.

Upon reflection—and in fact I haven't stopped thinking about it since I received your letter—I think that there are several things about this image (and the philosophy that goes with it) that I find troubling.

First, the thing about the vacuum through which the atoms tumble. That would make anyone dizzy.

Second, the fact that in this vacuum, this endless, bottomless abyss, stones hit each other, jostle, bounce off each other in a whirl that oscillates between Villon's ballad of the hanged, the jig of the tortured in Dante's circles of hell, and the falling bodies on September eleventh of those who threw themselves from the tops of the towers . . . I don't find it exactly a cheerful prospect.

Third, in this tumbling there's no way back, no possible backward zoom, no way of catching up. Yes, there's the clinamen, the deviations from the trajectory. That's all well and good, but these deviations, as if by chance, all go in the same direction, that is, downward. To quote Lucretius, he says that no body can extract itself from gravity and rise by its own force. He explains that even bodies such as flames, which give the impression that they rise, are only illusions and soon fall down. Once you start falling, he insists, there's no stopping it, all you can do is drop and keep dropping. This is no longer entropy. It's Carnot* writ large. It's not sliding, it's sinking, collapsing, guaranteed 100 percent. There is absolutely no chance of the opposite possibility. It doesn't even allow the hypothesis of a nanosecond in which you might right the helm, enjoy a moment's respite, glide. Damn!

Fourth, there's the other real problem that the adversaries of the Epicureans, from Cicero to Kant to Rousseau, have repeatedly raised. The theory may explain the fall of bodies, entropy, the decline of our flesh, the precariousness of our lives, it may do justice to physical phenomena such as floods, turbulence, storms, or the apparent rising of flames. But there's one thing it leaves out of the equation: the appearance of that very particular type of pebble called consciousness. Everyone must feel that it is problematic to reduce this to a sum of particles, springing up out of nothing or out of the fullness of matter—which comes to the same thing—which met by chance, joined together, aggregated, and formed a block. The one who expresses this best is Rousseau. That so-called naturalist who in reality only loved gardens and music—that is, nature reworked, rearranged, denatured—develops his response admirably in the great anti-Lucretian texts of the Second Discourse or Chapter 9 of the *Essai*† (as you can see, I've been reunited with my books). The state of nature, he explains, is a time of great floods and colossal earthquakes. It's a time when all the world's regions were surrounded by water and portions of the globe fell away like

---

*The Carnot cycle is a thermodynamic cycle proposed by Nicolas Carnot in 1824. The point here is that this is not entropy (or, rather, no change in entropy).

†Jean-Jacques Rousseau's Second Discourse ("Discourse on Inequality") ("Discours sur l'origine et les fondements de l'inégalité parmi les hommes") and *Essay on the Origin of Languages* (*Essai sur l'origine des langues*).

drifting islands. But what was distinctive about that time, he adds, its resultant and essential characteristic, is that the only humans that could emerge from it were stupid, barbarous, and incapable of living together. We don't know which of the "beasts" or "trees" was the most ferocious in that world, but what we do know very well is that it had no place for real humans . . .

Fifth, the fact—to which the opponents of the Epicureans also objected, in particular Nietzsche—that even supposing that consciousness might somehow be formed, that one might—by what mental acrobatics I don't know—manage to allow for the constitution of a soul through an addition of pebbles, this would give rise, whether one wants it or not, to a stony, ossified soul, formed once and for all, as smooth as a shingle, monolithic, with no becoming, no flaws. But we know that it's not like that, that the subject is always in the making, engaged in quite a different adventure, a thousand times more complicated. You are this, you are that. Something else in a different situation. We are a meeting place of multiple identities, broken, contradictory, vying with each other, then at peace, then once again at loggerheads. Each of us is not a subject but an aviary. Perhaps we are not the devil, but each of us is legion. It's this multiplicity, this shambles, that your theory of stones or comets will always fail to take into account.

Finally, this theory has a major fault, one last snag, which is that I would be incapable of using it (and at the end of the day that's what counts), specifically, either as a philosopher or in my everyday life. Even supposing that it could explain how a subjectivity is formed, supposing that this idea of falling in a straight line and of an agglomeration of atoms meeting by chance and not remaining stuck to each other could explain to us the genesis of this complex, shifting, ambiguous object, changing from one moment to the next, which on arrival has the face, voice, and silhouette of Michel Houellebecq or of his Irish neighbor, there is one more thing (of which in this case I'm quite sure) that it is incapable of explaining. That is the mystery of what happens when two of these chances meet, the spark produced when two of these tumbling objects cross and take shape, in a word the moment at which two of your stones come into contact and when the humans make a little bit of humanity . . .

Dear Michel, you'll think that I've made a great deal out of a poor little pebble you threw out in passing, in the course of debate.

That may be.

But it's because I take the author of *The Elementary Particles* seriously.

And therefore I also take seriously this feature of Epicurean philosophy, which I'm sure you didn't simply overlook.

Thus to sum up, I have nothing against the Epicureans.

I'm not denying that they liberated the ancient soul from the nonsense that encumbered it before they came along. (Lucretius may have been mad, clinically mad, writing his *De rerum natura*, like Nietzsche, in the moments of remission between his attacks of insanity, but I still prefer this lunacy to the pre-Socratic theories on love and hatred, to which the four elements of Empedocles were thought to be dedicated!)

Nor do I deny—let's leave nothing out—the positive role that a spiritual injection of a healthy dose of Epicureanism might have today in the face of the return we're seeing to magical thinking, represented in the United States, for example, by a revival of so-called creationist theories or theories of an "intelligent design" and the incredible anti-Darwinian offensive described to me the other day by the essayist Adam Gopnik.

For the reasons I've just outlined, I find this doctrine terrifying, unbearable, and, for myself at least, unusable. And given my idea of what philosophy should be or, if you prefer, the use I make of it, that's a crippling defect.

So, in return for your image, I'm going to propose another.

I'm not saying it's any better or any truer (as if that were the question!).

It's just that in Western tradition it's the great alternative narrative to that of the Epicureans.

It's the one that begins roughly with that other book that is the Bible, and in the Bible, Genesis.

And here, at the point in my reflections to which you led me with your sentence envisaging the stone tumbling into silence (!), its chief merit is that it fits in better with my experience, with the questions I ask and basically with my needs.

You know the story, don't you?

It's the story of chaos, or to speak like another writer, Rabelais, who knew his Bible well, of the original *tohu* and *bohu* in Genesis, within which a mass of whatever composition you like (the biblical text says "brownish soil" but in its place you could put stones, comet, gas, atoms, it doesn't matter) will (1) form small piles, differentiated packages of distinct aggregates, in certain cases similar to idols or statues; (2) have each of its piles impregnated by a force that the text calls *ruah*, meaning both "divine breath" (escaping from the nostrils and injected into the nostrils of the inert statue) and "wind" (real wind, which devastates the land, raises seas, and falls in gusts and whirlwinds from the clouds); and (3) form, in this way, as many unique beings as there are breaths, as many individuals different from each other as there are meetings, instances of compenetration between the packages of earth and the *ruah*.

There too you have a tumult, a great scene, catastrophic and dizzying.

There too you start with a beautiful text, a very beautiful text, poetic in the way sacred texts are, and which masses of writers have been able to and will be able to make their own.

Since the *ruah*, the vital principle, is a material force, strictly material, not any sort of occult or spiritual thing, you do not abandon the healthy materialism that was the good side of your Epicureanism.

And finally, to the extent that the *ruah* comes from outside and is a breath breathed by the one you dare not name Yahweh, you retain the idea of life as a reprieve, something borrowed that you'll have to return, so you can keep your hotel room. This has never been better expressed than by the Jew Luke, some thousands of years later, when he whispered to the dying, "Tonight, you'll be asked to return your soul."

Except that the biblical model contains a number of advantages that may seem insignificant to you but that I consider decisive.

The first is that chaos is not a void. It's true that it's another form of desolation, a state of the earth in which solitude, darkness, the abyss reign (Genesis 1:2). But to me that still seems less dizzying than your big bang.

The second advantage is that certainly the scene is terrible, endlessly bloody, with shadows and dust, underground monsters, snakes, curses, generation and thus corruption, abominations, floods, Gehenna, Sheol.* But all of that is less dark, less ballad of the hanged, less Dante-like than the *De rerum natura* and without going as far as the land of milk and

*In Judaism, Sheol is the general abode of the dead (similar to the Greek Hades) while Gehenna refers to the place of eternal torment for the damned (hell).

honey of the later texts, in the myrtle, cypress, and rose tree of the "plantations of Yahweh" evoked by Isaiah and Hosea, you have this whole landscape of trees that you love and that, since Genesis, has surrounded the tree of life.

The third advantage is that here too tumbling dominates. Here too, to say the least, the tendency is to fall. But it's less systematic. It's a rule but like all rules it permits exceptions. The giving of the law, for example; the word thrown up to heaven by the thousands of prophets scouring the region. And even death, the very moment of death, which is when you have to vacate your room, it is specified that the *ruah*, far from returning to earth and being reabsorbed by it, far from becoming dust like the mortal coil shuffled off, rises to heaven. There's always that.

The fourth advantage is the possibility of a subject. I've already demonstrated that in a book entitled *Le Testament de Dieu*. It's always said that it's the weight of religion that prevents the affirmation of the subject and particularly of the free subject. Well, my thesis at the time was that it is paganism that, by mixing everything up, defining individuals as pure packages of matter, stones, atoms, excludes the possibility of a subject conscious of being a subject, while it is Judeo-Christianity with its *ruah*, the transformation of divine into human breath, in other words the hypothesis of a soul made in the image of God, that makes this subject conceivable and possible. In thirty years, I haven't budged an inch from that view. I still believe that the only way of thinking that distinguishes us, you and me, from the tree, the stone, or your dog Clément is to emerge from Greek thought and as tradition says to play Jerusalem against Athens. This is what allows the second model. This is its other advantage over the Epicurean apocalypse.

Fifth, there's the form of this subject. That there is a subject is one thing, but it's quite another to know how, with what status, in what guise, and in what light it exists, whether it is this lethal subject, this small, completely round sphere, outlined once and for all, detached from the external world, as related to us by the theory of the stone, or if this is a living, moving subject, which keeps on being transformed, even though it is said to be fixed, and of which you and everyone else have had a concrete, lived experience. For that subject, again the biblical model is irreplaceable; in particular, the biblical model as updated by its modern interpreters, its great leaders and exegetes, beginning with Spinoza. What did Spinoza say and what did he have to offer in this debate? His big contribution is the idea of substance, the great one and only substance whose subjects are said to be modes. For Leibniz that was the mistake. In his opinion as soon as you approach Spinoza's intermeshing of substantiality, you begin to lose your way, since creatures are condemned to differ only by degrees, a bit like the way the waves in the sea differ from each other. In reality, the opposite is the case. There are other charges—and what charges!—to be made against Spinoza. But on this point he's right. His idea of the One Substance has something to recommend it. It blasts through the boundaries of the stone. It explodes the membrane separating interior from exterior. It allows subjects that may extend the territory of their subjectivity, contract it, and extend it again according to their mood, circumstances, and stage in life. It's like a polder, an individual. Or like an island, yes, an island, which is always, at every instant, engaged in a struggle with the sea. It advances, it retreats. It annexes portions of the territory, then loses them again. It's not a state, it's a process. It's not rest, it's work. And it's a work that goes on—that's the marvel of it—as long as we live. Yes, that's it, that's what is the brilliant idea. To put it clearly, it means that the subject is no

longer substance. And to say that the subject is no longer substance means that there is no longer an essence to preserve,
pamper, to remove from the space of competing essences, to
harden, to flatten. It is always in the process of constructing
its essence and working toward its individuality. Indeed we
should no longer speak of "individual" but of "individuation."
These are processes, unstable compounds, never completely
finished. Combinations, mixtures. Inside or out? Darkness or
light? Dreamed life or waking dream? A night watched over?
A sleepless night? All of that.

There is a sixth and final advantage to this scheme. It takes
account of that dimension of intersubjectivity on which Epicureanism (and Leibnizianism too, for that matter) founders.
Why? That's very simple. Since the individual is this mixture
and this process always under way, the border between what
is inside and outside is constantly shifting, redefined by the
battle waged without respite by rival individuations against
one another and the rest of the world. Thus, we can deduce
that what is in one today will be in another tomorrow, that by
the end of our exchanges that which forms part of my essence
at the moment of my writing to you may perhaps have
entered yours. In short, there are as many bridges as chasms,
worlds shared as worlds at war or in debate. And it is in that
experience of sharing, that obvious fact of a conflict that is
also always an embrace and an exchange, it is in the flesh of a
world that is at the same time both shared and disputed that
the real refutation of that sense of solitude imposed by the
atomist philosophers can be found. And that is the only foundation, ontologically speaking, for a politics and ethics that
can draw the subject out of an egoism that would otherwise
turn its hard-won singularity into a prison or a shroud. There
too, the Bible can help, and Spinozism with its symbolic/car-

nal spaces. Levinas too, of course, who by decentering his subject, through the way in which he makes it actually cross the border in order, like shadows or like the soul in certain dreams, to peel away from itself, to float above its own name and find a way of entering into the neighboring subject, makes two fundamental contributions. He corrects the egoistical side, the vital, moving force of Spinozism. And this makes him *the* modern philosopher who has contributed most powerfully to making accessible the mystery of what makes the ego the "hostage" and the "debtor" of the other.

We all, dear Michel, have the philosophy of our insomnia.

But in my insomnia there are two things that recur and that terrify me.

The void, naturally.

Like everyone else, the void.

But even more so, a surfeit of being, even where it is the fullness of this confident, self-sufficient being, puffed up with pride and independence, which Sartre called the bourgeois, the mere thought of whom made him nauseated and that ultimately is nothing more than the moral—or immoral—version of this stone-subject.

Well, I have cobbled together a philosophy of resistance to nausea.

First without Sartre, then much later with him, I put together a complicated construct, whose chief virtue is that it can help whoever wants it (obviously beginning with myself) to ward off the double specter of being nothing and of being nothing other than yourself, of having no place in this world and also of having one, but one that fills you with an even more biting embarrassment and shame.

A Jewish monadology.

A monadology not only without God but without Leibniz.*

Or, if you like, with a Leibniz reconciled with Spinoza, so all in the shadow of Sartre but also of another major but unrecognized contemporary of his, Levinas, without whom, I must repeat, Spinozism would be nothing more than a form of antihumanism of the worst kind.

For the moment, I'm pleased with it.

I may not have reformed the French economy.

But I've made myself clear to myself.

And above all I've explained to you the other reasons, metaphysical this time, for my being this "committed" intellectual who in order to exist needs to feel accountable to the other.

Philosophy isn't sorcery.

It's a way of coming to terms with your fears and perhaps escaping them.

It's a way of not giving in to the *tohu* (in Rashi's† translation, the paralyzing "stupor") or *bohu* (in the same translation, a depressing and desperate "solitude").

It's a "montage" that allows you to continue the war that Kafka spoke of and to try not to lose it. Here is your armor, there's a combat machine, over there a way of strengthening your position or recovering another, or digging out your trench more effectively. It involves strategy, tactics, calculation, and, fundamentally, survival.

I'm being quite sincere about this.

Now it's up to you to play.

---

*Gottfried Leibniz's late philosophy, as set out in his text *Monadology*, a metaphysics of "simple substances."

†Rashi (acronym for Rabbi Schlomo Yitzhaki): French rabbi whose biblical and Talmudic commentaries made him the foremost medieval Jewish scholar.

The region of Shannon does not, in itself, have any particular character. A large, sluggish river empties into the Atlantic Ocean. It is surrounded by low hills covered with a patchwork of fields. But sixty-five miles north, you come to Connemara, which is to say you enter into a different world, with a light—alive, almost physical—that it is hard to believe can truly exist here on Earth. If you continue along the road, you go through the landscape, often shrouded in mists, of County Sligo, then one comes to Donegal, with its harsh scenery reminiscent of the Scottish Highlands, where the light is already that of the North. If one decides to leave Shannon and head south, in less than an hour's drive you come to Killarney on the banks of Lough Leane. The banks are so beautiful that, on a state visit, Queen Victoria permitted her servants to get down from their carriages to admire the scenery at a spot that has since been known as Ladies' View. From Killarney, it is easy to visit the jewels that are the Dingle Peninsula, Iveragh (though the Ring of Kerry is to be avoided in July and August), Beara, Durrus, and Mizen Head, the southernmost point, which closes the ring.

Shannon, in short, is an ideal point of departure for exploring the west of Ireland—a series of landscapes that to my eyes have no peer anywhere in the world and that it is unimaginable to think I will ever tire of. So I decided to leave County Dublin and, giving in to a surge of optimism (for if in theory I am a pessimist, in practice in my day-to-day life I demonstrate an enthusiasm, a naïveté that is often surprising), I moved my boxes of books into a house that is not habitable just yet and won't be for several months, maybe until the end of the year.

Here I am, therefore, utterly powerless to respond to your letter in like terms. To be frank, I haven't read Levinas and I've never really managed to take Sartre completely seriously. But I could, I should, be able to dig out what Spinoza, Leibniz, Kant, or Nietzsche had to say on the subject. I am not sure I entirely understood these philosophers, and the meaning of monadism, for example, has always seemed to me somewhat obscure. But the others you mention, I agree, have sometimes given me the impression of an additional clarity; like turning on a light in a darkened room.

I happened to be in Paris to promote this film you haven't managed to get to see when I got your letter. After a moment of panic, my first reaction—symptomatic—was to rush to a bookshop and get a copy of Pascal's *Pensées*.

But first I have to tell you about the language course I took in Germany. No, no, I'm not trying to sidestep or evade the subject; in fact, I am just *putting it back in its context*.

At the age of fifteen I was, surprising though it may seem, a pretty well-adjusted teenager. My education at the Lycée de Meaux was going peacefully (after a disastrous start when I stupidly drew attention to myself by getting ridiculously high marks, I quickly worked out that, to be popular with my classmates, I had to temper my enthusiasm; I therefore did very little work, got acceptable results, and easily graduated from one year to the next). I didn't smoke, I had never touched a drop of alcohol. I was even, to some extent, *sporty*. (Several times staying with my father on holiday, I cycled up to the Col de l'Iseran, half a mile above Val d'Isère, and I scored a number of fine goals for my school football team.) I was listening to *cool* and *trippy* music like Pink Floyd. Girls, for the most part, found me *cute*. Of course, there were a number of worrying signs (prematurely reading Baudelaire, a chronic inability to watch animals suffer), but very few, to be honest.

My grandparents and I probably imagined Germany to be a country constantly shrouded in winter mists, so I set off wearing an anorak, suitcase full of heavy sweaters and thick socks; I think I even had a woolly hat and mittens. In fact, it can be really hot in Bavaria in the summer (and the course was held in Traunstein, in southern Bavaria, practically in Austria).

This was not only my first time in Germany; it was the first time I had ever been abroad.

That summer the weather was exceptional. One radiant sunny day was followed by another just as radiant and sunny. After a morning spent studying German, we had our afternoons free. We could cycle through the half-empty streets of the little town or meet up in the shade of the trees in the park, lie on the grass, or swim in the Chiemsee, which was close by. And the young German girls were—how can I put it?—not very shy.

The upshot: I spent most of the trip, which could have been idyllic, holed up in my room devouring Pascal's *Pensées*.

This, I am aware, may seem surprising, but adolescence as we know is a dangerous and turbulent period; some teenagers

spend their afternoons alone in their bedroom listening to
heavy metal (and in the worst-case scenario then go out and
shoot twenty of their schoolmates with an automatic
weapon). And Pascal, if one takes into context the original
violence of his writings, can produce a greater shock to the
system than even the heaviest of heavy metal groups. The
famous phrase "The eternal silence of these infinite spaces
terrifies me" is too well known and has lost its impact,
but it must be remembered that I was reading it for the first
time, with no safeguards, no advance warnings, and I took
it *full in the face*. The terror of infinite, empty space into
which one tumbles for all eternity. Pure terror. Let's take
fragment 199.

"Imagine a number of men in chains, all condemned to
death, some of whom are daily slaughtered in the sight of the
others; and those remaining see their own condition in that
of their fellows, looking at each other in distress and despair,
await their turn. This is an image of the condition of men."

It goes without saying that there must have been some
secret flaw in me that I tumbled, feet together, offering not
the least resistance, into the abyss that Pascal opened up
beneath my feet; but I don't want to psychoanalyze myself, it
bores me rigid, I just want to note that Pascal was, for me, the
first instigator, the first tempter (because I think that I read
Baudelaire before without really understanding, captivated
by the pure, plastic splendor of those verses, which remain, to
my eyes, the most beautiful things the French language has
ever produced).

After Pascal, all the suffering in the world was ready to
surge into me. I began to close my shutters on Sunday afternoons to listen to France Culture radio (whereas beforehand,
I was more top forty on RTL), to buy records by the Velvet

Underground and the Stooges, to read Nietzsche, Kafka, Dostoyevsky, and soon after, Balzac, Proust, all the rest.

There was another thing, too, and here my story becomes a little curious. At the time I had a friend named Jean-Robert Yapoudjian; we were actually very close, and since second form we had always sat together in class. I knew he was a Christian (and more than just a common or "garden-variety" Christian, his father was a general in the Salvation Army and ran a center in Villeparisis that took care of social cases). With the greatest possible tact, he had always refrained from talking to me about his faith, which, he knew, was completely at odds with my family upbringing.

That year, when we went back to school in September, I asked him to tell me a bit about Christianity. He gave me a present of a Bible in which he had copied out a passage from the Letter to the Corinthians on the flyleaf for me to read. I still have that Bible. I read and reread it for years, whereas I never even opened *De natura rerum*.

Things, in fact, went a little further than that, and I can remember myself—the memories are strange, floating, almost surreal—attending the optional religious education classes at the Lycée Henri Moissan de Meaux. I can see myself later, hanging around with a "Christian discussion group" at the Institut National Agronomique; I can even remember going on a pilgrimage to Chartres with them. (Here the memory is more precise; I remember, for example, that we spent a night away and had forgotten to bring a sleeping bag; I was therefore in a position to judge that famous "Christian charity" on actual evidence.) Mostly, I can picture myself on many Sundays *going to mass*, something I did for a long time, ten years, maybe twenty years, wherever I happened to be living in Paris. In the midst of congregations of BCBGs* and even aristocrats in the Seventh Arrondissement; in the midst of almost entirely African congregations in the Twentieth; with all of these people I exchanged the *sign of peace* at the appointed moment in the ceremony. And I prayed— prayed?—what or who I was thinking about I don't know but I tried to behave in an appropriate manner, so that "our sacrifice may be acceptable to God, the almighty Father." How I loved, deeply loved the magnificent ritual, perfected over the centuries, of the mass! "Lord, I am not worthy to receive you, but only say the word and I shall be healed." Oh yes, certain words entered me, I received them into my heart. And for five to ten minutes every Sunday, I believed in God; and then I walked out of the church and it all disappeared, quickly, in a few minutes of walking through the streets of Paris.

This is something few people know, almost no one in our circle, probably with the exception of Fabrice Hadjadj,† who works for *Art Press* these days, who must still remember his surprise when he came to the apartment I was living in at the time on the rue de la Convention and found bookshelves full of the Christian magazine *Magnificat*.

And then I chucked it in. I eventually chucked it in after one last derisory attempt to follow the preparation for adult baptism (this time in a parish in Montparnasse). You see, dear Bernard-Henri, what led me to tell you all this, what probably led me, as soon as I got your letter, to retrace my steps, to immerse myself in Pascal again, was probably your use of the word *advantage*.

---

*BCBG, an acronym of "bon chic, bon genre," refers to well-heeled middle-class ethics and aesthetics; it is equivalent to the American "preppy."

†Fabrice Hadjadj (born 1971) is a French writer and philosopher, who was raised Jewish, became an atheist, and later converted to Catholicism.

Because it's true that a world with no God, with no spirituality, with nothing, is enough to make anyone *freak out completely*. Because to believe in God, quite simply, as our ancestors did, to be embraced in the bosom of the Holy Mother Church affords certain advantages, though it does not afford *only* advantages. I know you don't really like Péguy, but, even so: "May they come and fall asleep in your outstretched arms." Or what about the man everyone always approves of (and rightly so), Baudelaire:

It is the famous inn set down in the book,
*Where one may eat, and sleep, and sit a while.**

The only thing is, the only problem is, I still don't believe in God.

You, apparently, do. And I should have known, because you've already said as much, though less explicitly in books, but I just pretended I hadn't read them, which is nothing new for me when I have to deal with a believer: for as long as I can, *I turn a deaf ear,* because I have difficulty confronting the subject head-on; I feel somehow dazed (skeptical not only of God but of belief itself). This explains why, the next time we meet, I will probably look at you a little strangely. It is the look I use on such occasions; it's not malicious, though it has seemed so sometimes. Nor is it envious (for one can only really envy in others something one believes one might have someday). It is a look of unease, of surprise. Because even if we are both rather contemptible individuals, as I said when we began writing to each other, this is something that separates us. You have, in some undeserved way, received some sort of *grace;* right now I can't think of any other word. Some-

*Lines from the poem "La Mort des Pauvres," in *Les Fleurs du Mal*.

thing that allows you to take seriously these stories of *ruah*, of God's breath, whereas all I can do in such circumstances is nod my head.

So, the philosophical questions you raise? If I am fundamentally atheist, that does not mean I am *materialist*, and here, too, it was Pascal who brought me down to earth, fragment 70, which is explicitly directed against Descartes (but which also reduces the ideas of Democritus or Epicurus to nothing):

"In general terms one must say 'That is the result of figure and motion,' because it is true, but to name them and assemble the machine is quite ridiculous. It is pointless, uncertain, and arduous. Even if it were true we do not think that the whole of philosophy would be worth an hour's effort."

Once this idea is firmly fixed in your mind, once you truly accept its radical premise, you realize that to explain the world is simply to describe it. To give the most precise, the most broad description. Define its entities without ever losing sight of the brilliant principle set out several centuries earlier by William of Ockham: "Entities must not be multiplied beyond necessity." Define the relationships between these entities— usually, but not always, mathematical. Combine these mathematical relationships to create new relationships by direct proof. Test each of them, unfailingly, through experiment. Where experiment contradicts theory, one must resign oneself to changing the paradigm, to constructing new entities.

But never does one try to "assemble the machine"; one never questions what is *behind* the physical entities one has defined, that one can measure; whether it is matter or spirit or some other mental mishmash that man, on a whim, might dream up. In short, we dismiss, permanently, all *metaphysical questions.*

Positivist from henceforth, we contemplate with a smile (a slightly disdainful smile, I grant) the various metaphysicists, materialists, and spiritualists who make up the belief market.

This attitude of disdain is, at heart, a modest position, a position of submission to the only, not exactly brilliant, principles that have never failed man in his search for truth: experiment and proof. Dull principles, which will never incite a revolution or an emotional attachment. For my sins, they are mine. "The truth is, perhaps, sad"; I think Monod is quoting Renan* in his most famous, equally sad, book, *Chance and Necessity.*

So, playing Jerusalem against Athens? Not at all, I can't, and I confess you worry me a little when you exclaim "any *truer*? (as if that were the question!)." Because, yes, that seems to me to be precisely the question, and the particular merit of Western philosophy is to have placed the question of truth center stage, sacrificed everything for it, going so far as to eventually consent to a form of suicide, reducing its own scope to that of an epistemological complement. It is Nietzsche, I think, that big subtle cat, who first recognized the dangers the sciences—having more or less killed off revealed truths—would have on philosophy itself. But it was he, consequently, who tried to taint the search for truth with suspicion. He thereby opened up in philosophy what might be called *the era of disloyalty.* Because what is philosophy if it relegates the search for truth to the background? We're pretty much back to the sophists.

*Ernest Renan (1823–1892) was a French philosopher and writer, best known for historical works on early Christianity.

. . .

In animal societies, in the most evolved of animal societies (land and marine mammals, certain bird societies), a language appears, which makes it possible for members of the group to exchange information; in parallel an individual consciousness develops. The phenomenon is further developed in the primates, and in man. It is not abrupt, there is no difference in nature; it happens slowly, by degrees.

Or rather (because *ontogeny recapitulates phylogeny*, it's an approximate, classic expression, a *gimmick*): in the brain of the fetus, a number of nerve cells, once reached, form connections, create networks, begin to process the stimuli in its environment, limited at first to the womb. Very early on, images appear, *memories* are created.

And—classic defense mechanism—"we are only beginning to understand these phenomena." It is true that they are among the most complex phenomena we are aware of, but that is not a license to abandon the general framework of the scientific method.

And consciousness will also appear, once they reach a certain stage of development, in machines, those entities made up of circuits, created by man; we need to prepare ourselves for that.

Consciousness, "the ghost in the machine," as certain theoreticians of neurophysiology call it.

An evolutionary consciousness, obviously (new connections are formed every minute; new concepts, new memories; and the neurons themselves, contrary to what was long believed, can regenerate).

Of course this despiritualized conception is not without its consequences. In the first place, I absolutely reject the radical difference you establish between animal and man.

Between animal and man, to state it bluntly, it is the essential that is identical; the difference is of degree but in no case of nature.

In the second place, in some more obscure and more disagreeable sense, this is not unconnected with your *(political) commitment* and my own reservations. It's painful for me to admit, when I think of my atheist, politically *committed* friends, but I've never really understood the root of their *commitment*, it has always seemed to me to have more to do with a Christian tradition than they themselves suspected. I am speaking from pure intuition here, but in all the Christian groups I tried in vain to belong to, one of the things I completely understood was their *commitment*. It was very clear: they had accepted the idea that, being sons of God, all men are brothers, and behaved accordingly. To me it did not (nor does it now) seem obvious. I have a certain compassion for the needy, but it is not really very different from my attitude to an animal caught in a trap; I simply try to open the jaws of the trap because I imagine the pain. And as for the notion of *human dignity*, I have to say I find it completely baffling.

For my part, I don't feel any particular dignity in myself: people could hurt me or mistreat me; they could certainly break me; they could cause me permanent physical or psychological damage. I would complain about the suffering, the mistreatment; I would complain the same way an animal complains, not specifically as a man.

A *dyed-in-the-wool positivist* is a tiresome adversary; as tiresome as and perhaps more disagreeable than a *dyed-in-the-wool materialist*, because unlike the latter he will never oppose something head-on. The Viennese are subtle. A divine breath, *ruah*, a logical positivist will say, of course, of course, let's agree to denote it "R," could you set up a practical demonstration? How would you set about showing it? The entity, the equation, the proof. And psychoanalysis (Popper versus Freud?) cannot be refuted and therefore does not belong to scientific knowledge. *Ite missa est,* to the positivist.

You may, if you like, the positivist would say, deal in metaphorical reconstructions. Man, at a certain stage, needs metaphors and legends. Matter itself was a necessary myth to put an end to God.

We work, the positivist would say, in a nonlegendary circle; a circle of claims that can be attested and refuted.

However many things—and however much of what matters— lie outside this circle. This circle, which will expand and consolidate its empire (there are many discoveries yet to be made about hormones, about neurotransmitters). But one thing remains inviolate in the expanding sphere of the natural sciences, which has to do with the kingdom of the intersubjective. Friendship, affection, love (this was your last objection and it is the only one that I accept). Love definitively articulated by Plato in unforgettable phrases. Love that one can generalize as *liking,* which would allow one to include the sincere astonishment that seized Schopenhauer, that honest philosopher, when he found himself in the presence of phenomena that contradicted his theories, an astonishment he sets down in his book: "It is surprising to see these people run to greet each other, though they have never met, just as though they were old friends."*

*The full quote, from Schopenhauer's *Counsels and Maxims: Our Relation to Others,*" reads, "It is really quite curious to see how two such men, especially if they are morally and intellectually of an inferior type, will recognize each other at first sight; with what zeal they will strive to become intimate; how affably and cheerily they will run to greet each other, just as though they were old friends."

This will probably not lead to a theory of the rights of man but may shed some light on the strange phenomenon of which I have an experimental knowledge, as a novelist, which is that people who are complete atheists and who are therefore convinced of their complete ontological solitude, of their absolute, irremediable mortality, still go on believing in love, or at least behave as though they believe.

And go on believing in moral law and go on behaving according to its tenets.

Dostoyevsky's "If God does not exist, then everything is permitted," though a priori convincing, proves experimentally to be false.

All in all, modern phenomena (since God is not long dead) but unquestionably interesting—and maybe it means revisiting Kant. Or studying a little sociology. At this point, I confess, I don't know any more.

That's the good thing about letters, when you don't know any more, you pass the hot potato. It's a sort of three-card monte for two.

That's rich.

Apparently, you actually understood that I have what you call "faith."

Dear Michel, not at all.

Of course, that's not what it's about.

It clearly can't come down to that *for me either*.

In order to clear up the misunderstanding, I will also have to go back to my early years, first readings, first turmoils, primal family and school scenes, A to Z, all of which, like you, I've never spoken about before. But beyond "passing the hot potato" and the "three-card monte," that's the virtue of correspondence . . .

I come, as I think I've told you, from an atheist family, which had lost its Judaism.

It wasn't the "French-Jewish" background of the bourgeois Jews from before the war.

Nor was it the "low-profile" approach of those great republicans who in the previous generations, at a time of peace, had believed that in order to survive you had not exactly to give up but pretend to give up your origins.

In other words, it had nothing to do with the famous "Marranism," born at the time of the Inquisition, which consisted of giving off all the possible signs of "normality" to the exterior world when necessary, while remaining internally faithful to the lessons of the fathers.

No. It was first and foremost an effect of the war. It was a direct, explicit reaction of horror at the worst things that war led to. And it was an attitude, almost a resolution, that was not too far off that of Heinrich Heine's character who exclaims, "What? Judaism? Don't talk to me about it, Doctor! I wouldn't wish it on my worst enemy! Insults and snubs—that's all it will get you. It's not a religion, it's a misfortune." It was decided internally as well as externally, in secret as in public, that this Judaism thing was a most unfortunate matter that brought all the world's problems in its wake and that we had to do everything we could to escape from this time.

I know this is a caricature.

I also know that my parents would not have liked to hear me put it like this.

But that was the spirit in which they returned to the world in 1945.

That was why we didn't respect the Sabbath or any other religious feast in our house.

That was why until I was twenty-five or thirty years old, I never under any circumstances entered a synagogue.

That was why, until I was that age, I had no idea about the contents—I won't say of the Talmud, but even of the Bible. I can't begin to describe my father's astonishment, his astonishment and dejection, when at the age of thirty I published *Le Testament de Dieu*, which was intended to be a book about the glory, the grandeur, the philosophical content of biblical literature.

What? he seemed to say. All that work, all that effort to break with the past, all that culture, those exams, the École Normale Supérieure like Pompidou, the *aggrégation** like Sartre, the forging of a young Frenchman nourished by the best disciplines and the world's best books, just to fall back, at the end (and worse—if only it was at the end—but no, this was the beginning!). His cherished son had barely had his first French hit with *La Barbarie* [*Barbarism with a Human Face*] before falling into this mishmash of superstition and archaism. All that in order to return to the hut in Mascara—how distressing, what a pity.

I've written books that were more scandalous.

In *Le Diable en tête,* I painted a portrait of the father that might have offended him.

But no.

What shocked him was *Le Testament de Dieu.* It's the only one of my texts about which he—who was always one of my very first readers—never said a word to me.

As if it constituted a major and, even more so, an incomprehensible transgression in terms of the cultural redeployment program, which was basically the family project.

What I've just said applies to him, my father.

But it also applied, in the same way, to my mother.

In fact, her reaction had a type of innocence that made it almost more spectacular.

I remember the day—in fact, it was the day before the publication of *Testament de Dieu,* when Jean-Edern Hallier tried to sabotage the book by publishing an article explaining that my mother was not Jewish, so that by definition I was not either, and that this collection of pages, announced with a

---

*Competitive civil service examinations, which those aspiring to teach at the second or third level must pass.

blaze of publicity as the return of the prodigal son to the fold, was therefore a sham.

Where did he find that story?

What could he have read to give him that harebrained idea about my pretty mother, the daughter of a practicing Jew, who was himself the son and I believe also the grandson of an actual rabbi and connected on the other side, through his mother, with a valiant quartet, my uncles who were humble fishermen of Béni Saf, as attached to the "Tradition" as they were to that stretch of sea, which for their entire lives consti-tuted their horizon. They were four brothers. Their names were Moïse, Hyamine, Maclouf, and Messaoud. I can still see them from when we spent the ends of our summer holidays there, seated in the café in rue Karl Marx, which made up the ground floor of the family home and where they went, dressed in black, wearing their hats to drink their weekly anisette at the end of the Sabbath. I can assure you that for those four there was no doubt as to the ancient origin, the solidity and pride of their identity.

In short, I've never understood where that silly idea came from.

And given the really vicious nature of the man in question, I cannot rule out the possibility that he simply concocted this fable with the sole aim of doing me harm.

The funny thing about this story is, first of all, the propor-tions this rumor took on. (The great rabbi Sitruk,* who had recently been elected, thought there was cause for concern and thus gave it an unexpected echo.) And then, there was my mother's own reaction. I decided to tell my mother, once the matter began to find its way into the community press, which she certainly didn't read, but then, you never know . . .

*Joseph Haïm Sitruk, former chief rabbi of France.

I did so tactfully.

I took a lot of precautions before describing the nature of the offense.

In the same breath I swore that the insult would not go unavenged and that I would not rest until I got Hallier to retract his slander. (Which I had, in fact, already done by calling him out at Lipp's, asking him to follow me down the road, and when he refused, knocking him over at his table beside the cash register, in a scandal that was pretty badly viewed and for which I was barred from Lipp's until years later, when Mr. Cazes* died.)

I kept on like this until, from a cute face she pulled and the slightly too jaunty way she said it wasn't such a disaster and that I'd do better to focus on the book's publication, I understood that in what was now her world, in this value system in which a Stendhal, a Jules Romains,[†] or a Roger Martin du Gard[‡] were worth a thousand prophets like Isaiah, it was not such a disaster to have one's Judaism denied. Or rather, at that moment I understood that part of her, an undoubtedly secret part, unconfessed and perhaps even unbeknownst to her, was in some sense delighted . . .

So, to say the least, there was very little trace of Judaism.

An opaque, unreadable trace, whose code you would need to be a Champollion** of the soul to decipher—that was my situation.

At home I hardly got the type of education that predisposes you to "belief" and "faith" . . . that's the first fact.

---

*Marcellin Cazes, owner of Brasserie Lipp, a Parisian institution.

[†]French poet and writer.

[‡]French author awarded the Nobel Prize in 1937.

**Jean-François Champollion, French classical scholar and orientalist who deciphered the Egyptian hieroglyphs.

And outside of the home?

Did this methodical amnesia mean that exposure to Christianity might lead a Jewish child in the 1950s into I don't know what temptation or substitute allegiance?

Perhaps, yes.

In fact, this has happened.

France is less of a secular country than it is said to be. It's not so easy when you're raised in ignorance to resist the seduction of a Christianity that has become like the air you breathe, air that, as it had to, occupied the entire void. There was Pascal, the beautiful paintings in the museums, that music by Bach and others too, of which Cioran* said that God owed everything to it: the cathedrals, the names of villages, the monuments of the national novel, virtues and sins, this "inner France," this "national novel." You can turn them around in as many directions as you like, but they are and will remain fundamentally Christian in essence.

And I still remember my consternation and despair as a child on the day before school broke up for the Christmas holidays, when, on the pavement in front of school, I was caught up in a joyful conversation about the presents each of us was expecting to get. Crazy with excitement, I mentioned the Teppaz pickup truck I had asked for and saw my best friend, my real best friend (he's still there, he exists, he's a brilliant Parisian banker—I see him from time to time and strangely enough I've never mentioned that scene to him or indeed to anyone else), stare at me, wide-eyed and meaning no harm, and heard him exclaim, "How can you be getting a present? It's not possible! You're Jewish! Jews don't celebrate Christ-

---

*Emil Cioran, Romanian philosopher and essayist who became prominent in France. The comment referred to here is that "without Bach, God would be a second-rate figure."

mas. How could you be getting a present on Christmas Eve?"
And all our classmates, seeing my crestfallen air, burst out
laughing. Fifty years later, the cruelty of their laughter rings in
my ears still; that laughter, which relegated me to the
pathetic, imaginary Christmas that was the inevitable lot of
those families who decided that from Christmas to Easter and
Easter to Trinity they would go all the way, go to the most
absurd lengths, in playing this game of inner France.

But at the same time, it wasn't quite that either.

The situation was more paradoxical than this anecdote
might suggest.

What made things complicated, devilishly complicated,
was that my parents were *also* proud and that this desire to
break, to have nothing to do with the "Covenant" of old, this
systematic shedding of their Judaism, their way of saying
"poor fellow" about a traditional Jew, lost in his superstitions,
or their blank incomprehension when confronted with the
"return" announced by *Testament de Dieu*, strangely enough
went hand in hand in their case with a stony contempt for
anyone they included in the universally damning category of
"shameful Jews."

Who were these shameful Jews?

They were Jews who lowered their voice at table when they
spoke the word *Jewish*.

They were Jews who had changed their names during the
Resistance and kept their new names after the war.

There was a pharmacist, a cousin of Jacques Derrida,
whom I mentioned in *Comédie* and who tried to be stylish
with his overstarched white shirts, his sons in the Polo Club,
and his overemphatic way of saying "Madame Baroness" to
one of our neighbors.

They were families in which you had to have your first dinner jacket at the age of fifteen.

They were those Jews who were so well brought up that they would never say or do anything that could possibly lead their friends into the bad taste of making an anti-Semitic remark.

And even in *our* family there was one character who was the archetype of all that, the real symptom of the illness, a sort of living proof or living stigma of the recurrence, the omnipresence of that Jewish shame. His case would be mentioned indirectly and with a heavy helping of innuendo. He was my father's older brother, Armand Lévy.

Poor Uncle Armand!

I don't know how true it was, but my father said that during the 1930s he was a soldier in the Croix-de-Feu.*

He blamed him for having inveigled his way into it, during the war, in a village in the Cannes hinterland, instead of fighting against the Nazis, as he himself had done.

At the Liberation he had married a blonde with milky-white skin, Paule de X, who was his entry ticket to the France of grand old names. He forced us, his nephews, to speak to her using the formal "vous" form. She wasn't particularly beautiful or especially interesting. And my father always insinuated that Armand had chosen her only in order to join his surname to hers and, like the pharmacist, to make himself more stylish.

Since misfortunes never come singly and since his melancholic wife never, as he put it, "gave him any children," there was a sort of tacit understanding that he would take my brother and me out some Sundays. He took us to places like the Cercle interallié,† the Polo Club, the Bois de Boulogne, at

---

*Cross of Fire, French far-right league during the interwar period. It was dissolved with the rest of the leagues in the Popular Front period (1936–1938).

†Cercle de l'Union interallié, a social and dining club established in 1917.

the mere mention of which my father would give a smile in which his commiseration and disdain clearly also mingled with a certain concern at the idea of the "bad influence" this "shameful Jew" would have on his two sons . . .

If I praised the stained-glass windows in the Cathedral of Chartres after a school trip, this had to be Armand's influence.

If I merely expressed the desire, instead of studying, to attend a "surprise party" at the house of a friend with a handle to his name, that was Armand's influence too.

When I wanted to join the scouts (which was a great dream of mine when I was between, say, six and eight years old), that was also because the same accursed Armand, the former member of the Croix-de-Feu, the husband of Aunt Paule, had put it into my head. In order to get it out, enormous efforts had to be mobilized (setting up a private group of scouts in the village in Seine-et-Oise, where we spent the weekends and school holidays, which was reserved for my cousins, my brother, and me, but was in every way modeled on the official groups, with uniforms, pennants, tents in the garden, animal nicknames, suitable scarves, a flag, and walking in single file to buy bread in the village each morning).

Later on, he certainly never said a word about what he thought he could guess from the type of women I was attracted to and of whom I would say, in all modesty, that I liked them to resemble me as little as possible. We never spoke of essential things, so how much less likely were we to talk about that! But I'm convinced that part of him could only have seen this extension, admittedly somewhat extreme, of Lévi-Strauss's theory of the incest prohibition as the ultimate effect of Uncle Armand's influence.

In short, there was no more Christian influence than Jewish.

Christianity was even more disapproved of than Judaism.

This was not so much a contradictory but a double injunction, which, to say the least, didn't leave any choice.

It left absolutely no room, as you can see, for this religious questioning, this "grace," which, alas, have eluded me as much as they have you.

Let me recall my years at the École Normale.

I'm not even thinking about the Jewish students, who were all or almost all atheist universalists, militants in small left-wing groups and in particular in the working-class left.

But when I remember my fellow students, who were called the Talas (in the École's jargon, this meant the ones who went to mass), I can still see this small group, made up, among others, of the philosophers Jean-Luc Marion, Rémi Brague, and Jean-Robert Armogathe (who became the diocesan curate of Paris, and writes the great editorial on the liturgical significance of the Easter feasts every year in *Le Figaro*), it's quite clear that I reacted to those boys who took literally the evidence of God's existence, not only according to Bach but according to St. Anselm and St. Bonaventure—and that I would react today—with the same stubborn incredulity, the same hardened positivism, as you did to your Jean-Robert, that boy from Villeparisis whose father was a general in the Salvation Army.

But let's get to the bottom of this.

The reason why I'm telling you these stories is to let you know two things: first, that in relation to all that, those old times and the scenes connected with them, yes, it's true that I've taken a "journey back," which hasn't escaped you and which I certainly don't wish to play down. Second, this "return," strictly speaking, has nothing to do with some sort of mystical attraction or indeed religious conversion of the sort you imagined.

The first point is obvious to anyone who reads my work a bit. My unconditional support for Israel. My intransigence, which I hope is unwavering, whenever the old anti-Semitism rears its ugly head. (On this point, I'd like to mention in passing the decisive influence of another comrade, unjustly forgotten: Pierre Goldman, a writer and martyr, a small-time crook and a great wit who used to say that even Jewish jokes were unbearable when told by a non-Jew.) . . . My constant recourse, which I believe has become more insistent over the years, to the texts of the tradition (Bible, Talmud, etc.). Hebrew, which I've learned a little. My reading and rereading of Levinas. The institute of Levinas studies, which I set up seven years ago in Jerusalem with Benny Lévy and Alain Finkielkraut, a quite unexpected development in my life. When I put all that together, I'm forced to admit that they add up to a combination of features that make of me overall a rather "positive" Jew, the opposite of the Jew of negation Jean-Claude Milner spoke of, and whose portrait Sartre painted in his *Réflexions sur la question juive,* and which I was programmed to become by my family.

On the other hand, the second point requires a bit more explanation. What most people seem to find hard to understand is that Judaism is not a religion. The word *religion* does not exist in Hebrew. The only vague equivalent, *dath,* is a word made up by jurists who, very recently, upon the foundation of Israel, wanted to make the new state like other states, to bring it into line with older regimes and therefore to insert something reminiscent of the division between theology and politics found everywhere else. If the word *religion,* as used by William of Ockham or Pascal, does not exist—and you won't find it in any book of the Talmud or in the mouths of the sages or masters who made the great oral law—it's because the thing itself doesn't exist either. Do you know, for example, that the term for synagogue, *beit knesset*, means a meetinghouse, not a house of prayer? Do you know that the Torah refers less to some sort of bible or missal or book of prayers than to a constitution (really a constitution in the strict sense, almost political or at least civil, of the word *constitution*) given by Moses to his people after the receipt of the tablets? Do you know that there is a whole current of European Judaism (the one that flourished at the end of the eighteenth century in Lithuania around the Vilna Gaon* as a reaction to the mystical explosion of Hassidism and then to the great messianic movements that swept through the shtetls at that time and almost swept away their reason) that rates study above prayer? Or, to be more precise, that if it had to choose between blind, ignorant faith on the one hand and Talmudic science, full of detours, scruples, and doubts, it would, without hesitation, opt for the second? Do you know that, once again in the nineteenth century, in the middle of what you might call a world of belief and faith, there were eminent masters (I'm thinking of Rav Kook†) who believed that atheism did not pose any problem for Judaism? They even saw it as a perfectly serious and admissible hypothesis, and in any case preferred an honest and logical atheist, a serious disciple of Nietzsche, someone who had reflected on the possibility of God's death and even its consequences, to some simpleton who merely believes in the "existence" of the unique One? And what can one say about those texts by Levinas that

---

*Vilna Gaon, otherwise known as the Rabbi Eliyaha of Vilna (1720–1797): a Talmudic scholar and Kabbalist.

†Rabbi Abraham Isaac Kook (1865–1935), a Latvian-born rabbi, scholar, and Zionist who became chief rabbi of Jerusalem in 1919.

also flirt with atheism and tell us that Judaism is not a way of seeing but a way of living, that what's at stake is transmission rather than revelation and that its great, its real concern is man's relationship not with God but with his fellow man?

So naturally there are Jews who are believers. But there are others, no less Jewish, who would not even understand what you meant if you asked them whether or not they believed in God. I know something about these "returns" to Judaism. And I can tell you that for every Franz Rosenzweig* who has returned to the law of the fathers after one mystical night, you have a thousand cases for whom it's an ethical adventure, an experience of life, language, thought, or even art that dictated this *teshuva*. Arnold Schoenberg, for example, who had converted to Protestantism and who on July 24, 1933, went to tell Rabbi Louis-German Lévy of rue Copernic that out of hatred for Wagner he was returning to the Covenant. Then there's Benjamin Fondane, that pure poet and out-and-out Baudelairean, who at the door to the gas chambers recited poems from *Les Fleurs du mal* in order to give courage to his companions in martyrdom. Ten years earlier, he had returned to the Jewish scripture, in his case for poetic reasons, out of loyalty to Rimbaud, Baudelaire, Tzara. Or Benny Lévy, another case in point, who has always insisted that, at first at least, in the days when he was still called Pierre Victor and was emerging from his Maoist season, it was a need for thought, interrogations that grew out of his reading of Plato, at the same time as he encountered the dead ends of the "political conception of the world," that led

---

*German-Jewish theologian and philosopher who grew up in a minimally observant Jewish family and considered conversion to Christianity but then made a committed return to Judaism after undergoing a mystical experience.

to the storm that he called his "turning." And then there's myself, if you allow me to say so, who came to a reading of the Jewish text at the end of an intellectual—I almost said conceptual—journey, whose major stops were philosophical ones . . .

So you understand, don't you? When I talk about *ruah*, when I contrast the narrative of Genesis with that of *De rerum natura*, when I say that I'm more a follower of Jerusalem than of Athens, I'm not juxtaposing faith with reason, spiritualism with materialism, a "legendary" revelation with your "set of rebuttable assertions"—I'm merely juxtaposing one book with another, beyond all that, in that zone that's very vague and yet decisive and in which, for each speaking being, the philosophical and life choices we make are located.

At the end of the day, there aren't many "fundamental" books.

There are very few "universal" books in the sense intended by Borges when he spoke about books that contained other books, indeed encompassed the whole library.

There's Homer.

There are the Old and New Testaments.

There's Lucretius's poem, and I feel that I'm honoring him by placing him in this company.

There are also, depending on each person's inclination and language, the *Divine Comedy*, Shakespeare, Dostoyevsky, or the *Summa* of St. Thomas Aquinas.

And I'm saying simply that for me, this is how it works. I know that there's nothing better than the *Iliad* to see what war is really about, the extermination, the destruction of cities. I know that Greek thought, in particular that of the Epicureans, can be very useful in thinking about free will. I'm certain that there would be no human rights without the highly audacious Christian hypothesis of man as a creature in

God's likeness and therefore inviolable. But I also believe that in order to think about what makes me a human being and connects me with other humans, to understand what, to use your own words, distinguishes people from animals and is the reason why my compassion for a rabbit caught in a trap will never be of the same order as what I feel for the inhabitants of Sarajevo under siege, to provide a foundation for that idea of human dignity on which I've staked my belief and so needed the philosophical resources to defend and illustrate, I've found nothing to match the lesson of Rabbi Akiva and Emmanuel Levinas.

It is there, at a level that goes beyond (or is perhaps more basic than) the question of whether or not we're living in the "truth."

It is there, in that region of the soul where positivism (or what you call that) is bound to lose its footing.

And none of this has anything to do with either "disloyalty" or "metaphysics." It's axiomatic, truly axiomatic: these are the first principles of thought, indemonstrable, or, as in arithmetic, irreducible and from which, for each one of us, everything else proceeds.

Your letter ends so abruptly, dear Bernard-Henri, that at first I wondered if there was not a paragraph—or indeed several paragraphs—missing, but maybe not; we are on such difficult terrain that I feel as though I'm boring a tunnel, in total darkness, and I can hear you drilling on the other side, a few feet away; but we can hope for a stray pickax to burst through the seam of flint, for a sudden dazzling light. And if we are not yet equal to the task as *intellectuals*, we have at least broached the one subject on which I believe we can shed some faint light for our contemporaries. Because, as both you and I are aware, the *return of the religious* that looms today looks about as friendly as the Incredible Hulk; but we are no less aware that it is nonetheless inevitable. Obviously, it is impossible for me to *establish* that for a society to cut itself off from the religious is tantamount to suicide; it is simply an intuition, but a persistent intuition.

We approach the subject from very different standpoints, at least as far as I understand from what you wrote about those Jews who broke with the religion of their forefathers and refused to become members of the Catholic Church in their host countries. What did they have left? Very little, apart from the communist faith. And when that too crumbled

beneath the weight of evidence? Well, it must have been difficult. Go *back to their beginnings*?

What was the point of all the effort preparing for the *École
Normale*? I can understand why your father took it badly.

There are, of course, the Jewish texts; but if you'll permit
me, there is something else. I very much like the way you talk
about your maternal uncles, Moïse, Hyamine . . . I can picture them, these Jews dressed in black, when the Sabbath
was over, drinking their weekly anisette; in a few lines you
manage to make them sound infinitely touching. "God of
Abraham, God of Isaac, God of Jacob; not of the philosophers
and of the learned." It was Pascal's "Mémorial," too, that
brought me to him; a devastating poetic thunderbolt, unlike
anything in the French literature of the time.

It's like in Dostoyevsky—"a single beautiful childhood
memory, and you are saved."* But what you have to understand now is that, when it comes to childhood memories like
this, I do not have a single one. You are right, France is much
less secular than people claim; in certain regions (Brittany
being the most obvious), you need only scratch the surface
and you find yourself in profoundly Catholic territory. Other
regions, like Burgundy and the Southwest, on the other hand,
have long since been dechristianized; and the most important fact (it is its historic failing) is that the Church never
managed to regain the confidence of the working classes. The
last time I was in Paris, I was passing that little church in the

---

*Houllebecq is referring to a passage in Dostoevsky's *The Brothers Kara-
mazov*: "People talk to you a great deal about your education, but some good,
sacred memory, preserved from childhood, is perhaps the best education. If
a man carries many such memories with him into life, he is safe to the end of
his days, and if one has only one good memory left in one's heart, even that
may sometime be the means of saving us." (From the translation by Con-
stance Garnett.)

Sixth Arrondissement where Ozanam* and Lacordaire† once preached. They at least understood that if the Church did not break the unnatural covenant it had made with the bourgeoisie and the employers, if it could not forge ties with the working classes, it was signing its own death warrant. They tried, they preached in the wilderness, they failed, and by the time the Church finally woke up from its long sleep, it was too late.

So, in my family, no matter which way I turn, no matter how far back I look, I can see nothing akin to a religious tradition. I can, on the other hand, see a certain communist faith. I have occasionally read in a newspaper that I was "brought up by communist grandparents." This is both absolutely true and absolutely untrue. My grandparents hadn't read Marx or Lenin or anything like that. He hadn't even read Maurice Thorez‡ and I'm not sure that they ever flicked through the Party's election program. But they voted communist at every election, that much is true, and I don't think they ever thought of voting anything else. It was exactly what is called a *class vote*.

Such faith, not fed by an intimate knowledge of the texts, is fragile; and my father, as soon as he got rich, as soon as he found himself *out of his class*, it disappeared in the blink of an eye. When I think about it, I never saw him show any real, genuine interest in it. When I think about it, I never saw him

---

*Antoine Frédéric Ozanam (1813–1853) was a French scholar who founded the Society of Saint Vincent de Paul. He was beatified by Pope John Paul II.

†Jean-Baptiste Henri Lacordaire (1802–1861) was a French preacher, journalist, and political activist and is considered to be one of the founding fathers of modern Roman Catholicism.

‡Maurice Thorez (1900–1964) was a French politician. He was a leader of the French Communist Party (PCF) from 1930 until his death and served as deputy prime minister of France from 1946 to 1947.

take a real, a genuine interest in *any* political issue. This is slightly frightening, because it means that with me, we are dealing with second-generation *absolute atheists*—not simply religious atheists but political atheists. When you get to this point, atheism is not joyous or heroic or liberating; there is nothing anticlerical about it, nor is there anything *militant* either. It is something cold, something desperate, lived like a pure incapacity; a white, impenetrable space where one advances only with difficulty, a permanent winter.

And the feeling, exhausting in the long run, that one is a vague organic hodgepodge whose controls are gradually failing.

No *Dionysian laugh* to enliven things; these days, Nietzsche's philosophy seems to me like futile provocation, a joke in bad taste.

Nothing, therefore, would give me greater pleasure than to venture into this "region of the soul" where positivism, you may think, is bound to be out of its depth. The fact remains that the Judaism without God you outline still seems rather mysterious to me. Nor am I convinced that it is likely to elicit much sympathy from Chief Rabbi Sitruk, but I'll let you worry about that.

The first thing would be to give up the idea of linking Man to the Universe. Man would go on being this fragile, medium-size object somewhere between quarks and spiral nebulae.

Such a philosophy (let's call it that, if you prefer the term to *religion*) would merely connect men to one another, afford them common values. In terms of ambition, this is limited but I grant that at least it would be a start.

In passing, I have to say that your position is the exact antithesis of a rapidly expanding spiritual movement (the only expanding spiritual movement in Europe these days) based on ecological fundamentalism mixed in some cases with left-wing alter-globalization [the global justice movement] and in others with half-witted New Age cults. This movement does attempt to connect Man to the Universe, to give him a place in the "balance of nature" (and in particular to keep him in that place); but it also has very little to say about anything that might connect men to each other. Deep down, it's a sort of neopantheism. It's comforting to know that the Jews will be there to oppose it.

At heart, you're not all that far removed from positivism. At least from the positivism of Auguste Comte (who is, after all, the founder of the movement). But when he tried to found his "religion of humanity," there was an immediate schism and he lost half of his disciples—including all those who had any intellectual weight in France at the time. I think he managed to marry two or three working-class couples (in spite of his attempts to gain the sympathies of Napoléon III and later Tsar Alexander I, the working classes remained his *target market*); the "religion of humanity" had some fleeting success in Brazil. And then, sometime around 1900, it all fell apart.

Saint-Simon, Pierre Leroux, in fact a whole host of social reformers in nineteenth-century France, had also envisaged founding a religion without God; they had even less success.

And yet Auguste Comte had a number of fine ideas. I remember a conversation I had once with Philippe Sollers (it's been a while since we mentioned him; we've missed him) in which we agreed on the fact that prayer could have immediate psychological benefits, independent of the existence of the addressee. I didn't tell Philippe at the time, because I didn't want to traumatize him, but that it's a typically Comteian idea. I even find it surprising to find Comte, who could have had no knowledge of Eastern meditation techniques, talking about posture and breathing control. A truly original mind who drew much from his own resources.

Chesterton, always shrewd, notes that the most reasonable aspect of the positivist religion is what, at first glance, might seem the most baroque: the creation of a calendar. With a starting point and its markers, annual, weekly, daily. Everything is good that sets man in an ordered, meaningful time frame; one distinct from the physical time of his old age and decline.

In spite of all this, Comte, as I said, failed; failed totally and miserably.

A religion with no God may be possible (or a philosophy, if you prefer; something that carries in its wake, like so many delightful corollaries, a code of ethics, a sense of "human dignity," maybe even a political theory, *if compatible*). But none of this seems to me to be conceivable without a belief in eternal life, the belief that in all monotheistic religions acts as the great *introductory offer*, because once you've conceded that, and with this as your goal, everything seems possible; no sacrifice too great—viz., Islamic suicide bombers.

Comte wasn't offering anything like that; all he proposed was one's theoretically living on in the memory of mankind. He gave the concept a slightly more high-flown twist, something like "incorporation into the Great Being," but it didn't change the fact that what he was offering was a theoretical perpetuation in the memory of mankind. Well, that just didn't cut it.

Nobody gives a shit about living on in the memory of mankind (not even me, and I write books). So why do I spend so much time *correcting my proofs*? I don't know, Proust was surprised that he did. I suppose it must have something to do with the idea of a *job well done,* which doesn't necessarily have anything to do with a Protestant work ethic; the Protestant work ethic simply opportunistically seized on an age-old propensity in man, who is essentially an animal that *makes*— tools or machines—which, to my mind, includes books, and perhaps this is at the root of our inability to understand each other. I don't confer on books a sufficiently lofty, sufficiently *sacred* status; for me books are something to be remade generation after generation, none of them gifted with eternal status, and take my word for it, this is something that does not suit me because I've been lying through my teeth since the start of this paragraph; as an author, of course I want to *live on,* but on the other hand I haven't lied at all, since it's true that I would rather really live on, to live on physically, as physically as possible.

One of my favorite parts of *The Genius of Christianity* is probably the bit where Chateaubriand launches into a stylistic comparison of Homer and the Bible, his goal being to show that if Homer's writing is extraordinarily beautiful, the Bible is even far superior. He deploys all the insight and the analytical acuity one has every right to expect from a writer who is himself a phenomenal stylist, and he carries it off; I have to admit, it is an astonishing victory, he is completely convincing. Carried away by his enthusiastic apologia he seems unaware of the danger that gradually mounts with every page: by heaping praise on the literary qualities of the Bible, one comes to think of it as a literary work—one of the finest in the history of mankind, it's true, but nothing more. Exalted, at times extraordinarily moving, but at heart a fiction, and nothing more than fiction.

There you are; this, at the end of the day, is what my reading of the Bible led me to conclude. Oh, it happened gradually, over a period of years. But by dint of comparing translations, choosing the "best one" (my criterion was not accuracy, but purely aesthetics), by continually rereading my "favorite passages."

And it's true that I persist in separating the discussion of literature—however intensely emotional, however symbolically profound—from the discussion of truth. In saying that, I feel rather narrow-minded, an old Calvinist stick-in-the-mud.

(But that is possibly exactly what I am.)

(There are worse things, it has to be said; all you have to do is consider the famous Proposition 7 that concludes Wittgenstein's first work: "Whereof one cannot speak, thereof one must be silent.")

The fact remains that I find myself in exactly the same position of philosophical uncertainty.

So, to sum up. The rights of man, human dignity, the foundations of politics, I'm leaving all that aside, I have no theoretical ammunition, nothing that would allow me to validate such standards.

This leaves ethics, and there, I do have something. Only one thing, to be honest, luminously identified by Schopenhauer, and that is *compassion*. Rightly exalted by Schopenhauer and rightly vilified by Nietzsche as the source of all morality. I sided—and this is hardly news—with Schopenhauer.

It does not allow for the establishment of sexual morality, but that is something of a relief.

It does, however, allow one to establish justice and law. Quite easily, but without the picturesque elaborations of Kant (I use the word *picturesque* in the strongest sense of the term; one could compare reading Kant with a hike through the Alps. It's very curious that he never left Königsberg,* an area that is quite flat. Much more than Nietzsche, he gives me that intoxicating impression of rarefied air, of gazing out to the farthest distances . . .).

It remains a mystery that Schopenhauer alludes only with a vague terror to the *origin of compassion*. For after all compassion is merely a *feeling*, something fragile on the face of it, although it seems to be reborn, naturally, from generation to generation.

Not to mention the question that is the logical corollary: What if compassion disappeared?

I think, in that case, humanity too would disappear.

And that the disappearance of such humanity would be a good thing.

And that we would have to wait for the arrival of another intelligent species, more cooperative, better adapted by its original tribal organization to ascend toward moral law (by which I mean a species rather superior to primates).

To break with humanism, therefore, does not imply breaking with morality, which stems from the apparent organization of the world into separate beings—whether *or not* these beings are mortal.

In short, I've just been won round to a sort of absolute. I think that's rather good news.

It is a limited absolute (moral law is rigorously applied but in a limited domain). What can be said of what remains out-

*Königsberg: now Kaliningrad (Russian Federation).

side? *Free will?* Yes, I'll go for that; I'll assume it has some meaning. So, free will for everything that is morally indifferent (which, it has to be said, represents rather a lot and the great tragedy of our overpoliced societies seems to me excessively limit the domain).

It's not that I really believe in this notion of *free will.* Spinoza's argument (conscious of desires but not of their cause, hence the sense of freedom) still seems to me irrefutable. And if I gently nod my head when I hear the phrase used around me, it's so as not to *make things worse for myself;* so that the discussion doesn't *get out of hand.* Because I've noticed that people in general are very attached to the fiction of *free will* and that, maybe, it is a useful fiction.

Human beings, in general, are possessed of a surprising ontological self-importance.

But they can have their *free will,* since they're so keen on it; it's like a decoration, it doesn't cost much and people seem to like it.

On condition you don't think it through too clearly, it's no problem.

No problem at all.

There I go, I realize I've started writing "human being," slipping into the third person.

It's not that I feel *superior;* please, don't think I mean it like that.

It's more a sort of disparity, the persistent impression I'm playing a role.

As you know, for years now I've lived abroad. There are certain clichés associated with the French (fine wine, fine food . . .) and more than once, to grease the wheels of social communication, I have found myself *overplaying my role as a Frenchman.* I have launched, apparently enthusiastically, into extravagant eulogies about Madiran wine or some food or other I've only just heard about.

For similar reasons, though more rarely, I have found myself *overplaying my role as a man*—manifested a passion that I did not feel for Aston Martins, Pirelli calendar girls, and Michel Platini's* free kicks.

And I feel more than capable (I would undoubtedly do it if I were ever faced with an audience of aliens) of *overplaying my role as a human.*

Even in the absence of an intergalactic audience, I cheerfully accept that aping human behavior in everyday life can be signally helpful. It is only in my books—the only things that really matter to me—that I insist on maintaining a certain *critical distance* with regard to humanity.

Given this preoccupation, which is important to me, I'd like to stress that I have always been on exceptionally good terms with Jews. I am happy to listen to people talk about what it is like to be Jewish (as though this had a particular relevance to being human). In doing so, I implicitly recognize a certainly validity in the Jewish destiny.

I've been a great deal more impatient with Russians when they try to talk to me about the "Slavic soul." I have been very quick, believe me, to send them packing.

Not to mention the Celts or the Corsicans, but now we're just getting ridiculous.

It is really quite frightening, this affectation peculiar to

*Michel Platini (born 1955) is a former soccer player, and current president of the Union of European Football Associations; he was a member of the French national team that won the 1984 European Championship, in which he was voted the best player.

middling-size mammals, interchangeable on the face of it, to form specific species. This is in stark contrast to the attitude of my dog (a middling-size dog—his legs are a little stubby, but he's middling-size nonetheless), who recognizes dogness in Chihuahuas and Dobermans alike.

I think, in dealing with humanity, it's important from time to time to take a *bacterial point of view;* I specifically use bacteria because some are toxic while others are beneficial (the ones you get in yogurt, for example).

And ask yourself, from a point of view that is as detached as possible, whether humanity is an experiment worth pursuing; weigh up the merits and the drawbacks and, based on the results, try to make the necessary adjustments.

I don't know much about the history of philosophy, but it seems to me that, after a certain point, there was a regression; that Kant managed to elevate himself to a viewpoint independent of the contingent conditions of humanity, yet valid "for all reasonable beings"; and that since that point we have curtailed our ambition a little too much.

This is a pity, since, having created characters in novels, I know that humanity is treacly; it's like putting your hand in a jar of molasses, you start finding excuses for everyone and you get bogged down in a senile sickly-sweet niceness.

I don't know, maybe I'm just a bit pissed off at the moment.

Dear Michel, I'm back in New York, in a hotel room, which at the moment is the place in the world where I feel best (nothing can be truer than Proust's saying about hotels, in Cabourg and elsewhere, being the only places where you don't get "jostled").

I am thinking about your last letter and how to reply to it, as I do each time.

I don't know how you do it.

We don't talk, so I have no idea how you go about it.

When I receive your letters, I always take a day or two.

I read and reread them.

I look for a way in, a handle.

I watch out for the things that connect us, the things that separate us, the things that appear to connect but that in reality separate us—our "correspondences."

I wonder ultimately what characterizes someone the most, what they show or what they conceal, what they say or what they don't say, which may not, after all, be the most interesting thing about them.

I try to anticipate as far as possible how you will reply to my reply and how I'll respond to that.

In other words, I wonder what will tighten the exchange

without constricting it, refine the game without closing it off, what will allow me to go forward while allowing you to bounce the ball back and move forward as well.

I've already mentioned that I've played a lot of chess.

But—and I don't think I've told you this—I've played a lot in just this way, by distance, what we used to call "by correspondence," as opposed to games said to be played "by the clock." I was a member of a club associated with my high school, in the days long before Internet and e-mail. You would ponder your move, put it in an envelope, and wait for your partner's move by return post. The games went on for weeks, sometimes months. Marcel Duchamp, who liked nothing better than playing this way, was involved in games that might go on for years, and at that time I was lost in admiration for everything Marcel Duchamp did. (In the last period of his life as an artist, he sent his "readymades" from New York, also by correspondence, with instructions to Suzanne, his sister, who still lived in Paris and assembled them for him. And it was the same with chess! He battled out his best games, some of them with Man Ray, Henri-Pierre Roché, Francis Picabia, like this, without any contact, apparently not touching, another way to avoid being jostled.)

In short, I loved those games of distance chess.

I loved them the way, I believe, Duchamp saw them: less as a match than a game, less of a competition than a way for two people to invent and produce together a work of the mind, with questions, answers, frustrated passions, sudden revivals, shared or hidden flashes of understanding, virtuoso performances, the setting of traps.

I think there's a remnant of that in the pleasure I derive nowadays from our correspondence. Naturally, there's also the enjoyment of debating, confessional writing, and the way we push each other to rummage through heaps of secrets.

There's the secret side to this adventure, the fact that up to now we've managed to stay in disguise and that nobody knows what we are up to. (By the way, as an aside, in connection with this stealth, about what I was telling you the other day, that practicing secrecy can be equated with the occupation of writing, about this "taste for dressing up and disguise," which our dear Baudelaire made the core of his literary ethics, I rediscovered a poem by Brecht, written toward the end of Hitler's rise to power, entitled "Praise of Illegal Work." It's about covering your tracks, hiding, multiplying identities, forgetting, losing everything, even your name, and, as if that were not enough, like a literary Mr. Arkadin,* going so far as to recruit paid biographers to discover the last witnesses to a life that can only be misunderstood and must therefore be erased.) Of course, all this counts, but in the growing happiness our correspondence gives me, in the pleasure I experience in reflecting, each time, on my next "strike" and then my impatience in waiting for your "counterattack," I also have the feeling of going back to the old times of those interminable chess games, which were some of my greatest thrills as a child and adolescent. Their champion in all categories, Jan Timman, a Dutchman, described them as a form of "mental boxing," but a form of boxing—he insists—in which you confront only yourself and the limits, constantly being pushed back by your ruses.

I have your last letter in front of me and am in the middle of going slowly through your arguments one by one and wondering where I can find a point of entry.

Perhaps a way in would be the question of a "religion

---

*Mr. Arkadin: film by Orson Welles in which the hero pretends to suffer from amnesia and employs someone to investigate his past with a view to locating and killing anyone who knows about his former criminal activities.

without God," although that is not at all what I am calling for. At best that would be Voltaire, at worst Maurras. In any case, it's not me.

Or perhaps your vision of Kant who you say never left the rarefied, sublime air of Königsberg. First, that's not true. It's a legend invented by Germaine de Staël in the pages she devotes to him in her book *De l'Allemagne* [*On Germany*], which are, to say the least, rather inaccurate. It's not at all the case in fact, since even in his youth, when he was a tutor at the home of the pastor Andersch and later the Keyserling family, he went to live in Judtschen, near Gumbinnen, then Osterode,* and then lived in other places. What's more, this image of Kant as immensely uptight, as regular as clockwork, frozen in his discipline, with his obsessive austerity, his corset of imperatives and abstractions, leaves out a whole dimension of turmoil, madness, even schizophrenia. This was just as much a part of him and explains, or is one of the explanations for, this need of his to lock himself up in a cast-iron system of thought. The "categories of understanding" are also a verbal straitjacket, a bastion against his spiritual tempests, the antidote to the theosophy, occultism, and spiritualism that—we tend to forget—were the first temptations to beset the young Kant. Indeed, he spent the rest of his life trying both to allay his obsessive fear of them and to avert their return.

More generally speaking, there is this "philosophy" about which you say you "don't know much" but that you are able to make free with in a way I really envy—this way of saying with such assurance "Schopenhauer thinks that . . ." or "Nietzsche replies that . . ." or "Spinoza's argument about this or that is,

---

*Judtschen: later Kanthausen, now Veselovka, Russia. Gumbinnen: later East Prussia, now Gusev, Russia. Osterode (am Harz), Germany.

in my view, irrefutable because . . ." It would be unthinkable for a professional philosopher to express himself in this way. It's difficult for an old fogey like myself, trained in the idea that philosophies are systems, coherent and closed entities, and that there is nothing more perilous than to take a piece, isolate it, give it its own particular destiny, appropriate it, in short quote it! This was Jacques Derrida's first lesson when he met with the new arrivals at the École Normale, who, as in the army, were called "conscripts." Without being at all face-tious, I would pay to unlearn that lesson of no floating philosophemes, never any philosophical utterances uprooted from their page of origin! On principle, never say "Hegel or Heidegger or Heraclitus says that . . ." because, unmoored from its context and, still worse, from its original language, this statement no longer has the same meaning and some-times no longer has any meaning at all! (You may object that this is exactly what I did myself the other day when I was put-ting forward my flimsy, labyrinthine construct inspired by Levinas and Spinoza, my monadology without a monad, my concept of the subject. Yes and no. I was tinkering about with something, piecing together a contraption of my own. In doing so, I'm afraid I was skating within the forced patterns of compulsory figures. Whereas quoting freestyle is quite a different approach . . . It's utterly different, in fact, being the phenomenal power of someone who sees the field of philos-ophy as an expanse of divorced utterances and a game of free association . . . And I repeat, I really wish I could dare to seize that power.)

Then there's Auguste Comte, who seems to really fascinate you, whereas I've always been not only suspicious of his "we're going to reconstruct society using science" side but was never actually interested in him. (Well, no, I'm mistaken there. As I said that, I realized that there is a bridge between

Comte and myself or, to be more precise between my generation and that of Comte, and that this bridge is Althusser.
Althusser, who in his famous text *For Marx*, in which he
denounced the "lamentable history of French thought in the
hundred years following the revolution of 1789," found only
one name to exempt, that of Auguste Comte, describing him
as "the only mind worthy of interest that French philosophy
produced." In the "fury" that was always directed at Comte,
Althusser sees proof of the "incredible lack of education and
ignorance" that is forever "our lot." And then there's the other
Althusser, who particularly resembles Comte, Comte the
man, in so many of his characteristics—his madness; his high
doses of neuroleptics; his analyst, Diatkine, counterpart to
Comte's doctor, Esquirol; his stylish and frantically penned
books without notes or readings . . . There's religion too—
that early religiousness and again at the very end, after the
death of Helen for Althusser, that of Clotilde de Vaux for
Comte. There's their inability, even greater than Kant's, to
move, to travel, and then the flow of their correspondence,
all those letters—feverish, on edge, paranoid—to the great
minds of the time whom they considered to be tormented
souls awaiting the true, positive faith. Death in life, books as
a prison, scientism as another straitjacket . . . If there's anyone Althusser resembles it's obviously Auguste Comte, the
inventor of the law of three phases. How was this not noticed
at the time? How did we, his disciples, manage to overlook
the evidence?)

Finally, there's your misanthropy . . . There's this idea,
which is very close to me but which I nevertheless find repugnant, of "drawing up a statement of account" for mankind—
which, you say, we should dare to write "from the point of
view of bacteria"—as to whether or not the "experiment" has

succeeded, whether or not it deserves to be "continued," if it's all that it's made out to be, if being human has such a proud ring about it.

What's repugnant about it? Well, I don't need to spell it out. You can well imagine that, particularly presented like this, your question is bound to make anyone uneasy who has spent their life attending to the fate of the Bosnians, the shattered memories of the Afghans, or the minuscule victims, lost without a trace, of Africa's forgotten wars.

How is this idea close to me? That's a bit more complicated. What I mean here is that there is a culture that believes profoundly and takes to its limits, indeed to frenzied, absurd lengths, this idea that humanity is a failed species and that we should consider making a fresh and better start on other bases, using the same materials but put together in a truly new mold. That is the culture I came from, the one that shaped me when I was twenty years old. To be more specific, it's revolutionary culture in general and Maoist in particular. It's that whole body of thought, inspired by Althusser, no less, whose project was to "split history in two," to "change man at the deepest level," "aiming right at his soul," in other words at the core, to "correct our aim," as you put it, to subdue our grotesque, slimy "ontological pretensions," to envisage nothing less than the "disappearance" of mankind as it has been understood up to now. What has caused this idea, once so close, to become distant? What caused people like me to turn our backs on this idea after envisaging it in a concrete form? (And when I say concrete, I do mean concrete, not only out of a kind of dandyism and as a literary experiment; I really did wonder, in Bangladesh, faced at every step with unspeakable poverty, whether it was worth being a human being in this way and whether the Naxalites, the local Maoists, might not be right with their project—which was crazy, Cambodian before the event but radical—of sending it all to the laboratory and bringing back out in test tubes a product that was a little improved.) Maybe that was the point at which to take up the debate. Maybe that was the real question. That's what I was just thinking—that this was the right angle, the right mix of philosophy and biography to kick-start the discussion around what Karl Kraus called "the last days of mankind" in his endless play of the same name, which inspired me to write *Le Jugement dernier* [*The Last Judgment*] two weeks ago. And just then, they brought me in *Le Monde* (there's a new system in the American hotels that allows you to get the French papers in real time on lovely, brilliant white paper that doesn't mark your fingers), and on the third page I saw that crazy article about your mother and the book she's apparently about to publish.

My first reaction, I must admit, was to think the whole thing was too crazy to be true. I thought, this is just not possible. It's some trick of Michel's. He was the one who instigated this farce with his mother or some extra that he's passing off as his mother. The ultimate hoax. Gary/Ajar times ten. Without saying so, we all, especially since Gary, dream of the ultimate mystification, the one that will render speechless those of our contemporaries who have been the least deceived and will allow us, poor clowns tired of our own comedies, to be reborn in a new guise, a new skin, another family novel, another novel period. And then the mother strikes. It's the maximum provocation, the most outrageous audacity. After all, isn't the mother question the most central one archaeologically for every writer? Isn't it true that the moment someone becomes a writer is that moment—and not an instant sooner—when they find the correct distance between their own language and the source, or matrix, that is, *the mother* of that language? It had to be done. He did it! You've got to hand it to him . . .

Then, once I understood that it was true, that this really was your mother, that she was really talking about you like this and that she was actually giving interviews to announce to all and sundry that she would like to break your teeth with a stick, I tried to think of other bad mothers in the history of literature. I thought of Vitalie Cuif, the "Widow Rimbaud," that violent "poison," as her son called her, a frightening creature "more inflexible than seventy-three administrations of numbskulls." Naturally, I thought of Bazin's *Folcoche** and of Nerval's mother. Then, there was Mauriac's mother in *Génitrix.*† I thought of the horrible Madame Aupick,‡ officially good, indeed dripping with niceness, sickly sweet, yet overjoyed, after his aphasia in Brussels, to find her little Charles quite senile, diminished, totally hers. I recalled "Bénédiction," that terrible poem in which the poet's mother is "horrified" by what she has given birth to, shouting that she would have preferred to give birth to a "nest of vipers" than the filth that makes up a writer. I vaguely remembered that Beaumarchais's trilogy ends, after *The Barber of Seville* and *The Marriage of Figaro*, with a play that I've never read called *La Mère coupable* [*The Guilty Mother*] and is supposed to tell a

---

*Folcoche (translated as *Viper in the Fist*): novel by Hervé Bazin portraying the hate-filled relationship between a mother nicknamed Folcoche (from *folle*, "crazy," and *cochonne*, "pig") and her children, inspired by the author's own childhood conflicts with his mother.

†François Mauriac's novel *Génitrix*, in which a middle-aged man makes an unhappy marriage in order to escape his domineering mother.

‡Name of Charles Baudelaire's mother after she remarried. She is usually criticized for failing to appreciate her son's genius.

similar story. So I ran through it all again in my mind. I tried to think of the most obscene offerings of this kind in the history of literature. But even then, this is extreme. First, because I'm not sure that there is any greater harpy than your mother, the now famous Lucie Ceccaldi (perhaps in Greek literature—those monstrous mothers, part ogre, that you find in Ovid eating their offspring in a stew or on a skewer, but in modern times, among normal humans, nowadays, no, really, I can't think of any examples). And then, having a bad mother is one thing, but learning from the press that she considers you a parasite, a phony, a good-for-nothing, human scum (less offspring than outcast) is obviously something else again, and, as far as I know, it has no precedent in any literature.

Finally, I thought about you. Just you. About the fact that you must be suffering, that you might be overwhelmed, grieving, you yourself horrified, enraged, in despair. I remember that you've spoken to me of your father, a lot, in fact, and in a way that, as I told you, I found moving. But you've said nothing about her or at least almost nothing. Suddenly I was annoyed with myself for not having noticed this, for never asking you about it, for thinking this was normal. I thought of my own mother, such a charming woman, more like Romain Gary's mother or Albert Cohen's. I realized how lucky it is—if not for a writer, then at least for a man—to be blessed with a mother of this kind. I tried to put myself in your shoes, to imagine the effect of having this block of violence and hatred at your origin. I thought about calling you. That's not one of our habits. But I felt like calling you. Just like that. For no reason. Just to hear your news, chat, tell from your voice how you're getting through this earthquake, so intimate yet public. But then, it was late. In fact, with the time difference, it was very late. I didn't do it. And here I am writing to you. This is what I feel like writing to you. This story is so staggering, so unprecedented, this Oedipal murder in reverse and put on display is so unheard of, that I prefer to forget about Comte, Kant, Althusser, the misanthropic generation, Karl Kraus and really let you talk. In chess, that's what's called a waiting move.

It's true that talking about Comte or Althusser these days seems faintly ridiculous to me; worse still, it seems slightly frightening, like the people who count telegraph poles as they're driving to the hospital trying to forget the fact that their wife has just died, and then spend the rest of their lives counting the slats of the venetian blinds in their nursing home, the tiles in their bathroom . . . It frightens me because I have witnessed this mechanical intellectual activity that the brain becomes engrossed in in order to repress the central horror; I have witnessed it in old people but I know that it also happens to younger people.

Almost exactly a week ago, my dog, having set out on his own, came back from a walk in a pitiful state; I don't know how he managed to crawl as far as the door, because his hindquarters were paralyzed and his paws very painful. He was vomiting a lot. He spent several days at the clinic, where the vet gave him cortisone, unsure whether to perform surgery.

At the same time rumors started to circulate, then there were articles on the Internet, about my mother's book.

I started to get oozing red spots all over my forearms and my legs.

Today my dog is back from the clinic, he is sleeping a lot;

from time to time he opens his eyes and looks at me. For the time being, the vet has advised complete rest. I hope that he will completely recover but I'm not sure. I could say much the same thing about myself.

You're right, dear Bernard-Henri, to note that the affair of the "now famous Lucie Ceccaldi," as you call her, evokes a maleficence greater than that of bad mothers in modern literature; of course it is possible to cite repulsive creatures from the darkest depths of Greek mythology. Others might think of the monstrous Baba Yaga in Slavic folklore, who smashes the skulls of newborns to feed on their brains. There are a number of similar tales among African tribes too. The same things must exist in most cultures as long as you go back to the point before patriarchy took over, where the right of life and death over one's progeny, the right to carve up, to devour one's children, belonged to the mother.

What I simply wanted to say to you is that this ancestral age, the prehistory of humanity, we are living it right now in our postmodern civilizations. The conflict between mother and child is absolute, uncompromising, from the moment of conception: it is the mother and no one else who decides whether or not to have an abortion. One of the questions I'm most often asked by people who know about the business is: "But why didn't your mother have an abortion? She was a doctor, she would have had the contacts." I don't resent the question, it occurs to them spontaneously and obviously a few seconds later they feel embarrassed. I'm not questioning the right to abortion, I'm not questioning anything, I'm just explaining.

Not only did my mother not have an abortion, but, a few years later, she *reoffended;* she had another child with another man, then off-loaded her daughter in circumstances rather worse than she did me (I think she literally abandoned the child or something, one way or the other the name of

Ceccaldi was wiped from the records of my sister, but I'd rather be vague about it; I don't think she would want me to talk about it).

At a certain point during pregnancy, women are often good-humored and in excellent physical condition. That's what it must have been, I suppose; she *got a kick* out of being pregnant, but the breastfeeding, the diapers, no thanks.

I haven't seen my mother many times in my life, fifteen at most, but the day she truly disgusted me was the day she told me that, in La Réunion, she had run into my old Malagasy nanny who had asked after me. She thought it was funny, inappropriate, that my old Malagasy nanny should ask her about me after thirty years; I found it incredibly touching, but I didn't even try to explain it to her.

One senses that there is in the chaotic, absurd life of Lucie Ceccaldi something terribly, appallingly *contemporary*.

If only the spiritual channel-hopping; just think, in the space of a few years, I watched this woman convert from communist to Hindu and then Muslim (not counting some minor Gurdjieff-style bullshit); but even so, I got a shock in her interview with *Lire* to hear she now refers to herself as an "orthodox Christian."

And most of all, of course, her absolute inability to sacrifice anything for her children; her inability to accept the fact that people die and their children live on. Anyway, things like that are pretty common nowadays, which means that Europe's demographic decline doesn't exactly come as bad news; but back in her day they were pretty rare.

She is, all in all, an absolutely self-centered creature of real but limited intelligence, and someone that I can't even bring myself to hate. She's right, for example, when she says that I was much better off with my grandmother, a woman she else-where calls a "hateful prole" (something that cast an interesting light on her own communist affiliation). I owe both my grandmothers many happy years of childhood; my sister, I believe, was not so lucky.

To this premature abandonment I also owe the fact that my earliest childhood was filled with images of women other than the rather repellent one of my mother. There were my grandmothers, of course; there were also my aunts, my father's sisters, with whom I spent much more time than I ever did with my biological mother. And before words, before memories, there was my Malagasy nanny, and maybe others. People are not very particular about love, I think, we take it where we find it.

So you see the situation, in a sense, is not as serious as you imagined (I can understand that she might appear to be a monster to someone who had a tender, loving mother; but that's not something that appears on my mental landscape). What is absolutely despicable, on the other hand, and you're right, unprecedented, is that the reams of threats and insults from my mother come to me *through the press*.

For this there is no excuse; this goes beyond banal self-centeredness and becomes pure spite. A few months ago, I got an e-mail from my sister in which she told me our mother wanted to meet with both of us, so we could talk, could forgive each other, something like that. I accepted, though I wasn't really keen on the idea; there was talk of meeting in late January or early February. And after that I didn't hear anything. I was a little surprised. Now I understand: in the meantime, my mother had found a publisher.

I can quite easily imagine what the book itself is like. She recounts her journey "through the century," as some journalist at *Le Monde* called it. (I don't know this Florence Noiville, but she seems incredibly stupid . . . that perky, hackneyed tone—"Lucie Ceccaldi is certainly a hell of a character!" and so on.) I am sure she reveals (it is over four hundred pages, after all) how adventurous, how fascinating her life has been, sometimes difficult, but always fascinating, in every country in the world, with the most extraordinary characters from all walks of life. Given that the book was revised by the journalist Demonpion, it's bound to be a piece of shit.

It's pretty scary that the old cow found a publisher; but where I might start to *somatize* is when I see the way the journalists, like vultures, swoop on the most putrid, the most sordid passages. It will go on for a while longer. And when they're bored with it, or rather when they're worried that the public are bored of it, they'll hold their noses and say, "This whole Houellebecq thing is really rather sordid," and it will be as though I set the whole thing up.

On every level, the relationship between me and the quasi-totality of the media in this country has reached the point of all-out hatred, in the same sense as your talk about "all-out war" (rather a strange war, incidentally, given that I am unarmed; it would be fairer to say *an all-out war of extermination directed at me*). Obviously, no one is actually interested in my mother, except maybe Florence Noiville, assuming she is as dumb as she seems. It is *me* they are trying to bring down through her, and from now on, I shouldn't have any illusions: they'll stop at nothing, there will be no quarter given. The separation between private life and public, between the author and the work? It's all too complicated, nobody worries about scruples like that these days.

I think what I am going through is something similar to what medieval criminals did when they were pilloried. The word has been so overused that we've forgotten the horror of the thing itself. The condemned man was exposed on a public square, head imprisoned in a wooden frame, hands fettered, face exposed, and any passerby could slap him in the face, spit at him, or worse.

Three years ago, wounded at hearing Demonpion on the radio repeating the story that I "lied by telling *Les Inrockuptibles* that my mother was dead," I tried to set the story straight. I had had the information from my sister, who had heard it from her father (who still lives in La Réunion). So I went to the effort of asking my sister to write a letter explaining all this, and it was published in the readers' letters section of *Les Inrockuptibles;* the story got almost no publicity whatever.

Much more recently, persuaded by your example, I thought that it might be interesting for me to find out what people were saying about me, "to know my adversary's position." But in my case, there's no point anymore: my adversaries are everywhere.

Oh, of course there are a few exceptions; but the exceptions are strange and difficult to understand; in fact, that is exactly what they are, *exceptions*. It's curious, for example, to think that *Paris Match* is the only general-interest magazine that has so far refrained from commenting on my private life. It's also notable that women's magazines (with the exception of one or two) have always shown enormous tact on the subject.

All of this, of course, runs contrary to the standard clichés. Because women are supposed to be "chatterboxes, gossips," et cetera. I'm happy to believe it, but it's the reverse of what I have observed. Similarly, it might seem surprising that *Le Monde* would print vulgar, foulmouthed articles while *Paris Match* is being delicate and restrained; but what can I do, that's the way it is.

Behind every cliché there's a theory, however rudimentary.

But when a fact contradicts that theory, we don't know what to do; we just set it down and wait around for a new theory (we're always trying to come up with theories, and maybe that's the problem; it would probably be better to admit that we are quite simply dealing with different human qualities).

However, there's nothing to stop me from taking the facts into account. And I would, if I could find the energy, feel a certain satisfaction at the thought that with most of the media I no longer have anything to lose. Except that's not true, the situation is unequal. They have nothing to lose because they know I will never speak to them again. I still have a lot to lose and they know it. Things could get worse; things will get worse.

I am not claiming that my physical existence is being directly threatened. Although people like Assouline, Jacob, Naulleau, or Busnel surely would feel a thrill of joy to find out I'd committed suicide (something which is possible, after all; I more or less fit the profile people associate with suicide; it wouldn't really surprise anyone).

But, failing a real suicide, what they would like, at least, is for me to stop writing. Or, if I really have to go on writing, for no one to talk about my books. For people to talk about whatever they like, about my advances, my tax returns, my political opinions, my taste for alcohol, my family history; but never, under any circumstances, about my books.

Naturally, they are going to win.

What is curious is that I foresaw this a long time ago. I remember it was when I was awarded the Prix de Flore* in

*The Prix de Flore is a French literary prize founded by Frédéric Beigbeder in 1994 to acknowledge young authors. Michel Houellebecq won the prize in 1996 for his collection of poems *Le Sens du combat*.

1996 (at that point I was in my ascendant phase). In the middle of a conversation, for no apparent reason, I remember saying to Marc Weitzmann,* "You'll see, you'll all end up hating me." He stopped what he was saying, and gave me a strange look and suddenly I realized that what I had just said without really thinking about it was an *insight*, a precise, dazzling perception of the future shooting through me. I don't really believe in intuition, or rather I believe in it absolutely, but I can see nothing mysterious or alchemical about it: I think moments of intuition are simply unpredictable moments of great tension in the brain, a burst of ultrafast reasoning where nothing has time to skim the conscious mind (neither the proofs nor the premises). I was, in a moment of particular lucidity, simultaneously conscious of the fact of being a writer, of what I intended to write, and of the intellectual capacities of the time in which I lived; and I came to the conclusion that I was, that I would soon be, deemed *unacceptable*.

In 2005, when I did my interview with Sylvain Bourmeau for the *Inrockuptibles* DVD, I had already had time to think about this and was able to explain myself more analytically. And my conclusion, on that occasion, was clear: the group always wins.

In Western societies, an individual has the right to stay on the sidelines of the group for a few years and attempt to gallop freely. But sooner or later the pack wakes up, the hunt starts, and eventually they corner him. At that point they take revenge, and their revenge is terrible. Because the pack is scared, and that might seem surprising because they have strength in num-

---

*Marc Weitzmann (born 1959) is a French writer and journalist and a former literary editor of *Les Inrockuptibles*.

bers: but it is made up of mediocre individuals who are conscious of and ashamed of that fact, and furious that, even for a second, their mediocrity is exposed for all to see.

That is where I am; the pack has caught up with me. It won't let me go and this will go on until I am dead, and for a little while after that (my death will give rise, I think, to some *lively controversy*).

And then, obviously, everything will calm down; skeletons.

Okay, I think it's not a bad thing to have talked about these things, that it's interesting to note that in some sense nothing has changed, and it's true, for example, that it's amusing to see *Télérama*,* that deathly dull rag, every time there's something organized about van Gogh or Artaud portraying them as victims of the bourgeois, narrow-minded, obscurantist societies of their times, the whole shtick with the implication that such a thing couldn't happen these days because we're all so much more open, more intelligent.

What is new is the obscene way they go about it these days. The incredible lack of tact, of humanity. For example, I can't bear the smug way the journalist Demonpion, when he's called on, professes to be an expert on the subject of me. It's like vomit, I can't deal with it, I don't have the stomach.

By comparison, I can tolerate the sight of blood; and of hatred. Maybe not having had a mother makes you *stronger*, but if so, it does it in a way you wouldn't wish on your worst enemy. You never take love for granted; to be honest, you find it difficult to believe in love at all. You remain a sort of *feral child;* never completely at peace, never completely domesticated; always ready to bite.

Télérama is a weekly French magazine of television and radio listings, with occasional feature articles.

. . .

Never having had a mother? At least I knew she existed; I could situate her genealogically speaking (even if, most of the time, I didn't know where she was geographically). My sister saw even less of her than I did; to her, our mother was an almost ghostly presence. But it's striking to note that even children who have lived their whole lives with adoptive parents, often in happy homes, still feel the need (usually late in their teens) to find their "real" parents.

When asked, they all say that they "need to know." Need to know what? A few of them are happy to know the genealogy, to have a few brief biographical details. But most of them, if it is a possibility, want to meet up with their parents.

There are the pathetic ones who have an idealized image of their parents, who imagine they are going to find a princess (this usually happens when the adoptive home was not a happy one). But most of them are clear-sighted; they realize that someone who abandoned them like an old piece of furniture is unlikely to be a particularly admirable human being. They expect, quite reasonably, that they may encounter a human wreck or a complete shit. And still they desperately want to meet this person, they track them down, often expending considerable effort in the process.

It rarely results in a long-term relationship. Often, they're happy to meet up just once. A few hours to make up for a whole life. What happens during those few hours is obviously a great mystery; one that, it seems to me, I am better placed than most to imagine.

Curiously, they hardly ever feel hatred; no, what's at stake is something colder, something sadder.

Nor is there any *forgiveness*, and I confess that I take exception to hearing my mother say, "We should all forgive each other," and so on, when she comes on like Dostoyevsky at his most infuriating. To me, it's just another sham, and a cruel one at that.

What is at stake is recognizing that a wrong has been committed, a wrong whose consequences are still spreading like ripples. It is the recognition, too, that this wrong is permanent, that what is done cannot be undone. Finally, it is the recognition that the wrong is limited; it is the transformation of a limitless, ignoble wrong into one limited in space and time. It is an attempt to halt the indefinite uncoiling of causal chains, the endless propagation of misery and evil.

Some go a step further: they attempt to define themselves in terms of the wrong done to them; they use their unfit parent as an anti–role model. Some go much, much further, and I know that my sister (I hope she will forgive me for citing her) went so far as to refuse to work so she could devote herself to her vocation as a *housewife and mother;* and I know that she did so successfully. One in a thousand, maybe, might succeed; but there is nothing inevitable about it. It is possible to break the chain of suffering and evil.

But everyone, even those who do not have this strength, learns a great lesson from their encounter. It is, in a sense, the dark face of the *Tat tvam asi,** the "Thou art that," that Schopenhauer posits as the cornerstone of all morality. The radiant face is compassion, recognizing one's own essence in every victim, in every creature subjected to suffering.

The dark face is recognizing one's own essence in the crim-

Tat tvam asi is the Sanskrit expression of the relationship between the individual and the absolute in the Upanishads.

inal, in the executioner; in him through whom evil has come to pass in the world.

You are faced with your own essence and at the same time you are its chief victim.

What happens at this point is difficult to describe, but it has nothing to do with Christian forgiveness. It is more akin to an understanding, a light; a knowledge of both good and evil and of one's own nature. And a wish, which may take the form of a prayer, to be delivered, as far as possible, from the wrong path.

Maybe I have come back to somewhere not far from philosophy. I hope so; to be honest, the detour was rather painful, and I hope it was simply a detour, and I hope, though I can't be sure, that I have come through it *once and for all*. I would very much like to discuss the status of philosophy, if you'd like to, but I don't feel up to starting it, and besides, I want to send this letter to you as soon as possible, and I'm already waiting impatiently for your reply; our letters have become one of my few joys.

Dear Michel, I know all that.

I knew it from day one, even though you had, I think, a sort of reprieve when your first books were published.

And I know how slander, malicious gossip, and lies can leave indelible traces.

You tell yourself, "It will go away, one image will displace another, one piece of information will replace the previous one." But no, it takes root. It's like a background noise that you know you'll have to live with until the end of your days. And there's no point in rebelling, revolting, protesting. I've lived through thousands of stories like the one of your sister's letter of denial published by *Les Inrocks*, which made no impact. I know by heart the golden rule of the literary nuclear war, according to which there is never, absolutely never, the possibility of a second strike. And if I never take action against that bullshit or look for compensation, it's not because it "costs a lot" or because I don't want to provoke the newspapers. It's, first and foremost, as I think I told you in one of my first letters, because ultimately part of me couldn't give a damn about any of this and is well "fireproofed." But even more so, it's because it doesn't make any difference. Not one iota. You could bring all the legal actions you wanted and for some people you'd still be only a nauseating matricidal killer, a racist and an Islamophobe. I could attempt to set the record straight in every possible and conceivable way and I would only strengthen their case that I'm a bourgeois bastard who knows nothing about social questions and takes an interest in the world's disowned only in order to promote himself. Kant said politics is destiny, but he was wrong. It's your reputation that's your destiny. In our Ubuesque societies, rumor is one of the faces of fate. And I've paid for the knowledge that there is nothing you can do to combat a rumor, gossip, or false information that spreads like a virus.

I'm going to relate an anecdote, one that's minor but telling. It was at the time when a series of atrocious books about me appeared. They were dashed off, contained almost an error per page, and were nothing more than a tissue of malevolence and invention disguised as biography. Among the pile, there was one that said that, on top of being a bad writer, a show-off, a liar, an uninteresting narcissist—the only cause for surprise being that so much had been written about me—I was an actual villain, who had been denounced as such by some British NGOs (*sic!*). Allegedly I had thousands upon thousands of slaves working for me in obscure African shipyards. Then, one morning I opened *L'Express* and found a review of that book, entitled "BHL Does Good Business." The article was brief and not malicious. I even remember that the journalist was sympathetic and felt a real curiosity for my "case." Except that what the article basically said was "This guy has some good points. He wrote a very respectable book on Sartre but now we know that this humanist, this character constantly prattling about human rights and the fate of the oppressed, is himself a slave-owner, denounced as such by some British NGOs, etc. Isn't life strange? Writers are mysterious. It's a fascinating mystery . . ." I must emphasize again that the journalist had nothing but goodwill toward this man who was complex enough to be the author of a good book on Sartre and yet also to exploit people. The paradox was presented just like that, as a fact, without the least note of outrage and in the cold analytical tone of someone who has added his little contribution to the great and eternal reflection on the oddities of literary history. "Why didn't you attack the book that information came from?" asked the paper's editor, Denis Jeambar, dumbfounded, when I met him by chance and explained that this story was absolutely untrue and that it was regrettable that his paper had endorsed it. "Because it wouldn't have changed anything," I replied. Because once that type of information has been printed, it will be repeated, whether or not there has been a trial. Because there's no second chance, ever, when someone launches that kind of missile at you.

So I know about slander.

Having the pack at your heels—I think I know about that too.

The demolition of the boundary between public and private, the pursuit of the man beneath the writer, that way of setting the dogs on him, after instructing them to rip off his mask, all the better to retrieve his store of secrets. I'm afraid that I also have had that experience.

I've known even physical aggression, extending to assaults on the face (those famous *"entartages"** that have entered into our customs and certainly into our language and whose real violence, not only physical but also symbolic, nobody

---

"Entartage": peculiar practice that has become a part of French public life and has led to the coining of this new word. It consists of throwing a pie into the face of a well-known personality. Under common law this would probably constitute an assault or at least battery, but in France it is the source of endless raucous laughter.

seems to appreciate). In fact I've had more than my fair share of them.

Where we differ is in our reaction.

Where you are wrong, in my opinion, is about the outcome.

I don't agree, indeed I profoundly disagree, with the idea that in this struggle, in what is intended to be an out-and-out war, in this physical set-to between writers and those who can't stand the sight of them, the pack will always win. I'll try to explain why in precise terms.

First of all, the pack is afraid.

That's easy to forget when you see it advance with such fury and ferocity, so hungry and driven.

But, as you say very aptly, it is afraid.

It is much more afraid than we are.

More afraid than you, me, or any other writer who has been in its clutches.

It's Bernanos's* theory about the Nazis.

It's Malaparte's† theory in the dreadful scene with Hitler in the sauna in *Kaputt*.

I think it's true that people would not be wicked if they were not first filled with a basic, uncontrollable, animal fear.

Of course, we shouldn't mix everything up here. Let's not compare the people who are taking advantage of your mother's book, in order once again to spit in your face, with actual Nazis. All the same, I think we can always conclude

---

*Georges Bernanos, a French author and ardent Catholic, initially supported Franco in the Spanish Civil War but became disillusioned with the Francoist cause and was violently opposed to the Nazis and the Vichy regime.

†Curzio Malaparte: Italian journalist and author, initially a Fascist, then an anti-Fascist.

that those who are wicked are first and foremost frightened. This is true firstly because that's how it is. They have an all-encompassing fear of life, death, of their specters, their fantasies, the child in them who has died and whose corpse they are carrying, the spitefulness of others, each person's loneliness, their desires, what they don't desire, their hidden weakness whose depths no book has ever plumbed, their element of madness, their conformism, their inescapable mediocrity and their ruined ambitions, the war of everyone against everyone, and the eternal rest to which they know that they will one day be condemned. But this conclusion is also correct because once you've grasped it, once you've understood that spitefulness is always born out of panic, a pathetic fear that has found this way out of having to expose itself, then you yourself are less afraid and better armed to resist and fight.

I'm going to tell you another story.

It dates from the same period. Although I thought then, just as I believe now, that you should not take legal action afterward, as the wrong has already been done, equally I believed and believe that you have to do everything you can beforehand, in the run-up to the publication of this kind of "book," to limit the damage, clear the minefields, ensure that the worst lies are not all engraved in this wretched marble. So when I am asked to, I meet most of the authors of such books. I tell myself that there must be a speck of honesty in each of them that cannot resist my demonstration, with the help of hard evidence, that I am not a pedophile, that I didn't kill my father or goodness knows what else. To be quite frank, I also think you shouldn't miss an opportunity to have some fun and in fact (even if it is too soon to tell you more), I've had a lot of fun in misinforming that lot of idiots and making sure that even if their books were successful, they could only be ridiculous. So I agree to meet them when they are wise enough to request it for two good reasons, first the pleasure of misinformation and what almost amounts to a hoax and, second, an attempt to cushion the blow. One of them struck me as particularly vicious and I sensed him sniffing around some private matters that I really didn't want him poking his nose into.

One day, after bolstering his ego in a suburban bar off the beaten track, I told him in the kindest, most honeyed tone, "Do you remember the conference of Helsinki and its famous baskets in the 1970s? Well, when I think of the slander, which I understand from your questions that you're getting ready to publish about me, it's the same kind of thing. There are some things that I can't prove are lies. Let's say we'll put them in the first basket. There are some others where my keen lawyer Thierry Lévy will be able to make you eat your words and I assure you that he'll do so mercilessly. And then there are some that I wouldn't like to give any extra publicity to in a trial, even if I won. If you mention those you'll lay yourself open to other types of revenge, such as getting beaten up, little accidents, minor and major frights. I know it's not nice to talk like this, but isn't it better, among good companions, to say this kind of thing before rather than afterward? Isn't it preferable for everyone to reach this sort of understanding before it's too late and while matters can still be rectified? Let's call this the slander for the third basket, and I'm going to tell you exactly what it is . . ."

At that point, the guy got up. Very angry, his face purple with rage, he shouted, "That's blackmail, sir. I won't accept blackmail. There's nothing left to say. Good night."

So there I was on my own, like a fool, at the table, thinking, "I tried and failed. He might even—as I would do in his place—put the scene in his book and use it as an introduction.

Too bad; it's a good lesson. It's never a good idea—and I knew that—to speculate too much on human baseness . . ."

I was at that point in my reflections when I saw the bar door open and the purple face reappear, a timid smile on his lips, his expression still antagonistic but a bit more pleasant. "OK," he grumbled, sitting back down and taking out the policeman's notebook he had been writing in before the incident. "I see that you're not in your right mind and to some extent I understand that . . . your father, your wife, your children, yes, that I understand. But tell me, what exactly do you put in your third basket?"

The problem was solved. The pack member was afraid. And it was a banal fear, the most stupid fear of the coward who, as in a bad detective story, doesn't want to have his skull smashed in and negotiates. In the end, none of the stuff I was afraid of appeared in his masterpiece.

Second, the pack is weak.

Why is it weak?

Because it's afraid—see above.

But also because it's driven more than anything else by fear, mockery, resentment, hatred, bitterness, spite, anger, cruelty, derision, scorn, all of which Spinoza called the negative emotions and which, as he definitively established, make you weak, not strong, are a sign of impotence, not power, which diminish the ego and reduce its capacity to act, indeed profoundly debilitate it, making it unworthy and unintelligently aggressive.

There's nothing moralizing about that. Still less is it wishful thinking. It has nothing to do with a vague and sugary "You can't build on what's negative, everything that's extreme is insignificant, etc." It's just physics. The mechanics of the body and its emotions. It's what we're beginning to see in France, for example, with the misadventures of Sarkozy. If he's not succeeding, if he remains fairly low in the opinion polls, if there is something out of joint in his relations with public opinion and those who elected him, it has nothing to do with consumer power, exposure of his private life, his ostentatious interaction with the world of money. It's because his campaign was based on resentment, putting the bad Frenchman in the pillory, fantasies rehashed from the National Front, stories about insecurity and immigrants. In other words, it's because he built his campaign on the typical "negative emotions." And Spinoza says that with the negative emotions you may succeed in the short term but, by definition, in the long term you'll lose. A despot, the author of *Tractatus* specifies, shares with the priest the desire to instill in his subjects as much as he can of the negative and therefore servile emotions in order to dominate them more effectively. But he'd better beware of letting himself be contaminated, used, guided by these emotions—he may need them in others but he himself must avoid them like the plague. Otherwise, he'll commit a fatal error, he'll be unable to govern, his sovereignty will be ruined and impossible to restore, the pact will be broken . . . I won't go on inflicting Spinoza's demonstrations on you. But if you would like to take a closer look, I have my books again and it's in *Éthique*, Book IV, propositions 50 and following. I've been reading those pages and have just faxed them to Olivier Zahm, who has started a philosophy column in the magazine *Purple*. They're inexorable.

What does this mean specifically for a writer? It means we should aim at what Spinoza called a "selective organization" of our emotions (transition from emotion to action, from passive joy to active joy, from the external cause of this joy to

consciousness of its internal cause, common concepts, etc.). I
don't know about you, but I never think of getting revenge. I
forget almost immediately the details of the wrongs that have
been done to me. It has happened so often in Paris and elsewhere that I meet someone and remember vaguely just as I'm
shaking his hand that he wrote something awful about me.
But so what? I've forgotten. Sometimes my wife is there to
remind me. Sometimes she isn't, but that's all right . . .
Because I have to tell you something about the relations of
strength between those who live in resentment, intoxicated
by their bitterness, alienated by their melancholy and their
bad blood, and those who, not so much out of virtue as
through their makeup, self-discipline, or just because they
have something better to do (e.g., a new book to write), manage to escape this merry-go-round of poisonous emotions. It
is the second lot who, once again, for reasons of pure emotional mechanics, will triumph over the former. Joy makes
them intelligent and strong, whereas spite is a poison and
sooner or later poison kills.

I'll give you an example: that Internet site answering to the
name of Bakchich [Baksheesh], which specializes in spreading so-called information that in reality is pure defamation
and where, as it happens, we both have a real nest of common
enemies. Yesterday, or the day before, I read in *Libération*
that they can no longer afford to pay their "informants" and
that they are about to go bust. Obviously, that's not imma-
nent justice. It's just that their tone, the hard toil of their derision, their hatred of others and themselves, their way of
wishing so fervently for your death as a writer or mine, in
short their immersion in the negative emotion of rank bitterness, intoxicates them and reduces them to idiocy, making
them uninteresting, fossilized, weak and, in this case, mortal.
Strength pitted against strength. In this game the writer will

always win. In any case, he will have the last word. *Bakchich*, that insignificant rag, which, by some slip you couldn't even invent, took as its title the same word used for the bribes paid to police informants, will not only have failed but will be forgotten, while the writers it tried to bring down in issue after issue will continue to write and be read.

Third, the pack is stupid.

I'm not saying we're particularly intelligent. We have our foolish areas, of course, beginning with the temptation to give in to the paranoia, which casts its shadow, among other things, over this correspondence. But the pack is stupid, so unbelievably stupid. It's like a great lump of an animal that can't see beyond the end of its nose. And fundamentally it takes so little to disturb it, to make it lose its head, its radar, to disorient it, to get away from it.

A mask, for example. A borrowed or made-up identity. A minimum—our friend Sollers would say—of comedy, the art of fleeing and evasion. A false lead. A decoy that all of a sudden throws the big animal's detectors and those of its manipulating master off the scent. An art of hiding by revealing yourself or revealing yourself by hiding. What Heidegger would call a technique of disappearing into the shadows of Lethe, or the opposite method, which amounts to the same thing, of making yourself *lanthanonta*, literally "inapparent," but under the lights, with all shadows dispelled. The trick that always works is that of complaining you've lost when you've won. The shrewdness of the Chinese tactics of giving the command to attack openly but always conquering in secret. And then moving, just moving. When the pack attacks, the tendency is to curl up, bury yourself in a hole, to freeze. But you need to do the opposite. You need to spread out—I nearly said *go astray*. Move as much as you can. Put the greatest possible distance between yourself and the pack. Increase your sidestepping, springing forward, strategic withdrawals, surprise attacks, pincer maneuvers, counterattacks, or simply diversions and avoidance.

Of course, it's possible to build a refuge.

Some sort of internal niche that will shelter you from the oil slick of the negative emotions.

You can make yourself an island—Kafka spoke of "cellars" or "caves"—that would be not a space shuttle but a sort of land shuttle that would give you a little shelter.

But please, only mental islands!

Concentrations of space or time that will be like new internal coordinates, adapted to each one of us.

Niches are all well and good, but you must be able to take them with you on your travels, and equally—although this also comes down to the same thing—they must be able to take you on their travels!

Please note, there's no need to go too far. It's enough to travel in your own town—see Debord's *Panégyric*. Or even a journey around your own room, like that of de Maistre, the other de Maistre, Xavier, who, alone with his dog (him too!), was able, within his own four walls, to undertake the longest, most exciting, and most perilous of odysseys. A journey from one identity to another, even to a multitude of identities, like Gary and Pessoa. Or from one book to another, one genre to another—Sartre, Camus, all those hunted and hated writers who, like good warriors, like tightrope walkers on the taut rope of a work that was a prism through which all the possible disciplines were refracted, outwitted their pursuers by always managing to be where the pack wasn't expecting them.

I must remind you that it was Baudelaire, no less, who described this program best with the two new entries he pro-

posed to add to the list of human rights: the right to contradict yourself and the right to leave . . .

I would also like to point out that this strategy I'm talking
about is the one recommended by antiterrorist police to those
who, like my friend Salman Rushdie, have been objects of
death threats. Bodyguards, police protection are all well and
good, but they all say that the best tactic of all is movement,
running forward, staying in your place or in one position for
as short a time as possible, the art of swerving, taking
detours, surprise effects . . .

So Baudelaire and Rushdie were caught up in the same
struggle? But of course.

Finally, the pack is never entirely a pack. Moreover, you
know this. You yourself mentioned Bourmeau, Beigbeder,
and others who, come hell or high water, have never stopped
defending you from those vicious dogs, which must be as different from your nice dog, Clément, as, according to Spinoza,
the "barking animal dog" is different from the "celestial con-
stellation dog." And I too could name my antidogs, my comrades in guerrilla literature, my fellow chess players, without
whom I could never have emerged intact from thirty years of
debates, fights, blows given and received, the clashing of
swords.

To mention only the dead, I'm thinking of my kind Paul
Guilbert, whom I met thirty-five years ago when the *Quotidien
de Paris* was starting up and who wrote about my books—all
my books, including those like *L'Idéologie française*, which
he wasn't sure he agreed with. But he knew there was a pack;
after a childhood under Vichy he was able to recognize its
characteristic smell. And like one of the great musketeers,
with his helmet of golden hair that turned white with age but
right up to the end never lost its gleam, as a writer without
books but who was brilliant and had decided to let his life's

work be absorbed into that of his friends, he simply decided, immediately and once and for all, that what I was doing should be defended.

I'm thinking of Dominique-Antoine Grisoni, also dead, who died so young, even younger. His work was barely started, he had his books, his disciples, his women who took up his time, his Corsica that he loved, as did Jean-Toussaint Desanti, known as Touki, the mathematical philosopher who taught us both. He led an unusually intense life full of joy, despair, sensuality, suffering, frenzied anxiety, a taste for war and erudition, sarcasm and admiration, multiple and mingled temporalities, lucidity, passion, something of Artaud's madness poured into a mold with a rigor to rival Althusser's. Until the end, that man took the time to provide me secretly with ammunition, information about the enemy camp, wise advice, invaluable suspicions, rescue plans, castles in the air, articles supporting me, critical readings of my manuscripts.

I'm thinking of all those nameless people who write to me when my books are published or when I appear on radio or television or even for no reason, without any particular occasion, just to encourage me, to talk to me, to tell me that they liked such-and-such an article but they didn't like some other one as much, but that I must continue, not give in, stay the course. I remember Elsa Berlowitz, a woman without position but not without qualities. I ended up eagerly awaiting her faxes after each of my contributions (the day when a handful of friends went to scatter her ashes in the rosebushes of the Jardin de Bagatelle, I felt I had lost a support as mighty as Bernard Pivot or Josyane Savigneau,* just to give you an idea!). I remember another woman—I never met her and all

*Bernard Pivot: French journalist and host of a cultural television program. Josyane Savigneau: French journalist and writer.

I knew was that she was called "A," perhaps Aline—who wrote to me every day, literally every day, for twenty years, just to comment on my acts and gestures or to say a few words about a page in one of my books, to send me a laundry note, a four-leaf clover, or an article she had cut out. (Once, on my return from a vacation, and already cursing the pile-up of thirty or forty letters that would be waiting for me as at the end of every year, one for each day, I didn't find a single one. A little later, I learned in a message from someone close to her that she was dead. And that death of someone I had never seen, whose first name I hardly knew, the only thing about whom I knew was their written voice, got me down as much as the death of a friend.)

And since you mentioned the Internet, isn't there for you as much as for me an entire region of the blogosphere that refutes the unkind image of those who see in it the world's garbage can? There's the Australian blogger who sent me a quasi-thesis on my Baudelaire that I wrote twenty years ago. Or those students at Hofstra University, on Long Island, who, with their professor, have been keeping an archive of all my speeches that for decades have been cast to the four winds. Or the Chinese guy who kept the notes of the seminars I gave on April 12, 1986, at the Institute of Foreign Languages in Beijing and who woke up today to discuss them on an equal footing. That fan of Romain Gary who listed the occurrences of his name in my texts. That defender of Sarajevo under siege who recognized himself in a shot of *Bosna!** and then began to read my works . . . That unknown community of allies who have appeared from nowhere and everywhere, those friends who save our lives, that little army of light and shade, reading a line here and there and then another and another. And in

*Film by Lévy (1994).

the end it all adds up, and I can assure you that it outweighs the pile of shit that our enemies would like to bury us under. It too can give us courage, can restore our confidence. And it's the ultimate reason for the responsibility we have, you as much as I, not to stay alive but to win. War again. Chess. I don't know how you see it, and yet . . .

So there you go, Michel. I realize that, despite having said so much, I didn't reply to your question about evil, its philosophy, its coils, and how we can escape getting stuck in the wrong track. (If I had, I would have told you first that I don't believe it's possible to "break the unlimited chain of the causes and effects of evil" and second that, instead of using your image of the coils, I prefer that of the Möbius strip where, even if you have the impression that you're getting away and rising, you never escape from the surface, the plane, the continuity of evil. Third, what's at stake is not to "undo" evil but to "make do" with it and to limit its power—all propositions to which I may return the next time.) But I felt like telling you these little things without losing any time. Perhaps I'm naïve or overemotional. But there was a tone in your letter and especially a couple of words that made my blood turn cold, and that's why I wanted to reply right away. There's no reason to be afraid. I really believe that. You know the story of Hobbes, don't you? Do you know the joke that all-round champion used to make to his friends about fear and its effects? That unrivaled theoretician of fear, the man who founded his theory not only of states but also of societies on it, said that he believed his affinity with fear came from the fact that his mother had given birth to him prematurely as the result of a shock. So you see, another story about a mother. Really, there's no getting away from it . . . But there's no reason to be afraid of our mothers, or of fear itself.

Dear Bernard-Henri, your letter this time led me to a long period of unproductive thought, as usually happens when I try to think about issues of strategy (I would love to have been fascinated by Sun Tzu and the game of Go; or at least by chess and Clausewitz; sadly, when it comes to games, I never got much further than *belote*, Mille Bornes, and Tarot* at a push; I don't know where I get it from; it's strange given that I liked math, I was even good at it).

To tell the truth, I suspected that you were probably pretty experienced on the subject of slander; but I only *suspected* as much, and that bears out your success, but also its limitations. What I knew was that various unpleasant rumors had circulated about you; but I would have been incapable of recounting a single incident (although I have been known to read the newspapers in recent years).

So, you're right, they are crap; they can't even make up a memorable story, something even a third-rate novelist can manage. But it still leaves a trace, a taint; and it works, you know it does, and you have been a *natural target* for considerably longer than I have. Someone has a little bile, a little

---

*Three common French card games familiar to children.

sad passion they need to vent? Well, there are people you can dump on; Bernard-Henri, for example. And Houellebecq, yeah, not bad, a lot of people are dumping on him these days.

When we started this correspondence, it occurred to me that I was likely to make new enemies—yours. Then, emboldened by your example, thinking to myself that it probably would be useful to "know my adversary's position," I went back to Googling myself. And gradually, but increasingly plainly, I realized a fact, a small but significant fact: *we already have the same enemies.* This is much more obvious on the Internet, where people rail against everything without any sense of decency, where everything is exaggerated, insulting, crude. But aside from the additional vulgarity (and after all, it's probably normal that, in creating a "global village," the Internet has brought back some of the cheerful brutality of village morals), it has to be admitted that the Internet adds little in comparison to the traditional printed media—in fact, it's depressing the mediocre use humanity makes of this extraordinary tool.

Among our most constant and most bitter enemies are first and foremost all those Web sites (bakchich.info, for example) that adopt the same editorial approach as *Le Canard enchaîné** or of *Voici* (I am unable to find any significant difference between those two magazines; the only thing that might be said is that when Frédéric Beigbeder was literary editor at *Voici*, it was a lot better than *Le Canard*). I regularly read pieces about myself in sections like "Indiscrétions," or the "Téléphone Rouge," the sort of gossip columns that have sprung up in most of the papers in recent years; these pieces are generally untrue, sometimes grotesquely so. But the prize

---

**Le Canard enchaîné*, founded in 1915, is an influential satirical magazine published weekly in France.

for barefaced lying in any medium goes to *Le Canard enchaîné*. Not once have I read an accurate story about myself in *Le Canard*. And more often than not, it wasn't even a case of exaggeration or a biased reading of the facts, but out-and-out fabrication. It's staggering, when you consider that the people who read *Le Canard enchaîné* think they are reading secrets that most people don't know, unearthed through hours of patient investigative work. It's much simpler than that: they just make it up, they write the first thing that comes into their head, pure and simple. It's also staggering the impunity these people enjoy, and go on enjoying: justice has the reputation for being complicated and slow, and very few victims (apart from politicians and those who have legal teams to deal with such things) take the effort to sue. And of course, no one wants to turn everyone in the media against them; it's simpler and more sensible to *keep your mouth shut*. To which one might add the shame one feels from constantly having to justify oneself to people you despise . . .

Among our most constant and most bitter enemies are the Web sites, the loathsome, terrifying proliferation of far-left sites that might model themselves on *Le Monde diplomatique* or *Politis* but which, in keeping with the maximalist logic of the Internet, go much further and, where people like us are concerned, almost go so far as to call for us to be killed. It's here that you realize that the unholy collusion between the far-left and radical Islam is not a fantasy dreamed up by Gilles-William Goldnadel, but is something that is increasingly becoming a reality. I leave the accountability of those who find excuses for Islam because it's the "religion of the poor," or who look for points of agreement between Marxist thought and Sharia law, but I will say that every anti-Semitic attack or murder in the French *banlieues* owes something to them.

. . .

When all this has calmed down, long after we are dead, some future historian will be able to draw some great lesson from the fact that we both, and at much the same time, have comfortably fulfilled the role of *public enemies*. I don't feel able to expand on the idea, it's just an intuition, one that still seems strange to me: but I believe that the person who manages to work out why the two of us, so different from each other, became the chief whipping boys of our era in France will, in doing so, understand many things about the history of France during this period.

The fact remains that, right now, while we are still more or less alive, the situation is difficult. I'm grateful that you haven't tried to persuade me that "things will get better." Because things won't get better; so what is there that can help? Well, the most crucial are the encounters with anonymous readers (anonymous or famous, it doesn't really matter, what matters is that they are *readers*), whether on the Internet or in the street. Such encounters are neither self-conscious nor awkward. The readers know there are many of them and they assume (rightly or wrongly, it depends) that I have a hectic schedule so they need to *get straight to the point*.

The first thing they say to me, and the most important, is to keep on writing. They usually put it as simply, as brutally as that. The phrase they most often use is "Keep on writing."

But why, first of all, do they say this to me? I don't think my writings bear the mark of any particular suffering. When asked if writing is painful or pleasurable for me, I've never known how to answer; the truth, I think, is that it is something else and can take either of those forms. An extreme nervous agitation, an exaltation that can be rapidly exhausting. In a long article that appeared in that curious publication *La Revue des deux mondes** (a magazine, it is strange to think, that has existed at least since 1830, which saw and supported the rise of the Romantic movement in France!), a writer named Marin de Viry made an interesting analogy between writing and cycling. People tend to praise the mountainous stages, he said, where each new sentence, like each turn of the pedals, seems to display superhuman effort; but the stages of flat open country where nothing seems to be happening but where, at any moment, things can change dramatically have their own charm; the long stages along flat stretches, or stretches that only seem to be flat. The writer, I think, was comparing me to a flat stretch; it was kind of him, but not, I think, entirely true. What my novels make me think of above all are the *downhill stages* (people know little about them, in general; there are no spectators on the downhill stages, the exercise is too abstract, even the motorcycle cameras seem to hesitate, for fear of going off the road). I feel that I am writing a novel when I have put in place certain forces that should naturally lead the text to self-destruct; to an explosion of flesh and spirit, to total chaos (but they must be natural forces which give the impression of being inexorable, which seem as dumb as gravity or destiny). My job, at this point, involves keeping it on the road, allowing it from time to time to skirt the void without allowing it to fall in. It can be exhausting, if you like, though not in the usual sense; mostly, it's dangerous.

My readers, in any case, are not supposed to realize this. I brake gently from time to time, I adjust the handlebars, but these are microadjustments, in principle imperceptible to

---

La Revue des deux mondes (Review of the Two Worlds) is a magazine devoted to literary and cultural affairs.

those watching; the result should give the impression of a perfect, geometric trajectory inscribed since time immemorial.

My readers probably guess this and were they to pore over the text they would quickly realize everything. But I think most of them simply read and enjoy the pleasure, both intellectual and sensual, of a successful downhill run (on a bicycle or on skis, the principle is the same; Formula One is a little less interesting, there is the overtaking, the accelerating, there are artifacts). And if they tell me, in a tone that is almost commanding, to keep on writing, if every time they suspect that I am *the kind to give up*, it is for other reasons.

I expect it is because they have *seen* me, on television or at some public event; or that they've read one of my interviews. And each time, they realized that I bore easily, sometimes to the point where I seem to be struggling not to nod off; that I was not, in any case, terribly brilliant or terribly talkative; that, all in all, I played the role of author very badly.

I am about as ill adapted as it is possible to be for a public role. I spent my school days trying to avoid calling attention to myself and my professional life in much the same frame of mind. As a child I dreamed of subjugating humanity, of captivating or of vanquishing it, and leaving my mark on it; but I also dreamed of staying in the shadows, of hiding behind my creations.

I think it can be said that that's been a complete washout.

Philippe Sollers has managed to be a constant presence in the media for more than forty years and people have learned nothing, or almost nothing, about his private life. That's what you call success; of course he began his career in an era infinitely less brutal than ours, and people maintain certain habits; even so it is a stunning achievement.

You, and I apologize for saying this, have been rather less successful; but it's true that you started later and on territory that, from the first, was much more dangerous.

As for me, well, I don't need to draw you a picture.

During certain encounters with certain readers, I have sometimes been weak enough to complain, to deplore the hostility, even the hatred that greets every book I publish. Their response has always been the same (and I mean in absolutely 100 percent of cases; I cannot remember a single exception). It amounted to saying, "I don't understand . . . you should be *above all that.*"

I could tell they were a little disappointed. To be honest, I was a little disappointed in myself. Because it's true, I remember a time, though it's a long time ago now . . . it must have been around 1990. I had already published a number of poems and articles in *La Nouvelle revue de Paris,* but my book about Lovecraft hadn't yet appeared in the collection *Les Infréquentables.* I must have been unemployed, because I had the time to go to the weekly meetings of the magazine. Michel Bulteau had just published his own book (about Frederick Rolfe, Baron Corvo) in the same series. That day, there had been an article in *L'Express* by Angelo Rinaldi,* seriously panning the book.

It may be useful, in order to appreciate the anecdote, to know something about our future positions. Well, Angelo Rinaldi has invariably given my novels mixed reviews, in

---

*Angelo Rinaldi (born 1940) is a French novelist and literary critic and the literary editor of *Le Figaro.*

which the negative has eventually won out; he has never, however, lowered himself to personal hostility, never reached the level of vulgarity of an Assouline or a Naulleau. At the end of the day, Angelo Rinaldi does not like my books, which, obviously, is his right.

There were quite a lot of people at the meeting that afternoon (the press officer, the publishing director, a number of the writers for the magazine), and they all commented on the review, dissected it, discussed the possibility of a *counterattack*. I was astonished. At the time, I didn't know who Angelo Rinaldi was (for younger readers, I should point out that he was an influential French literary critic in the 1980s and 1990s). I couldn't think who would read *L'Express* (I still can't). After a while, I sensed that I was starting to rile people, dumbly repeating in various forms, "But it doesn't matter, it's just an article in a *maga-ziiiiiiiine . . .*"

Michel Bulteau glanced at me irritably; he must have been thinking that *I would understand in time.*

In short, we *decline,* that's what I mean to say; we start off placing the book on a pedestal, on a very high pedestal, and everything else (newspapers, magazines) doesn't exist, has no importance whatever, they are simply a teeming mass of parasites who disturb the unique and perfect relationship between an author and each and every one of his readers.

And then eventually you come to realize the reality. What got me, my personal Achilles' heel, was money. For me, everything was played out in the few days surrounding the publication of *The Elementary Particles.* In those few days I realized that I had a chance, a small chance, of escaping from the world of work. It was wonderful, it was unhoped for. So, yes, I moved heaven and earth to widen the crack through which the light was streaming. I did all the media, absolutely all of them. Because it has to be understood that while I had perfectly nice work colleagues (especially at the Assemblée Nationale), office work was a complete waste of time for me; from the first it was only ever a job that paid the rent.

And, at the time, I thought that book sales had some connection with the media coverage they got. Actually, everyone around me seemed to believe it too. For PR people, that's normal, it's their job. For a publisher, it's a little more curious; you expect him to be a businessman, you assume he looks at the bottom line from time to time, that he should have worked it out by now. But publishers, like producers, are probably not really businessmen; they too are hoping for a certain *cultural recognition*, which, curiously, they associate with the media rather than, say, with university work.

Deep down, I was never really interested in celebrity. If, for example, I had had a small private income, I would certainly have written books (I might well have written more), but I would never have set foot in a television studio.

Be that as it may, after the sensational success of *The Elementary Particles*, I was caught up in the system; and I had also become the *man to bring down*. At first, in the hands of old codgers like Angelo Rinaldi and Michel Polac,* things were relatively calm, they remained within the bounds of the *literary polemic;* but I would quickly experience much worse. I would quickly realize that in interviews, just like on an American cop show, everything I said "could be taken down and used against me." And even things I didn't say. Demonpion, a specialist on the subject of me, quickly defined how my statements should be treated. Either I express a reprehensible opinion, in which case it's very simple, I'm a bastard;

*Michel Polac (born 1930) is a French television and radio presenter, filmmaker, and writer.

or I don't express the required reprehensible opinion, in which case I'm a bastard and a hypocrite.

An example taken from an interview with this creep:

"Do you think he's an Islamophobe?"

"Yes, yes, absolutely, I can prove it, his own statements prove it."

"Do you think he's racist?"

"Here, you have to be careful, *because he's usually very cautious.*"

(I can't guarantee I'm quoting word for word, but I have scrupulously respected the spirit, it can easily be checked.)*

(It's important to point out that this did not happen under some fascist dictatorship, or during the period of the Moscow trials, but in France three years ago.)

You are completely right, I shouldn't lump these things together. On the one hand, the scum I've just mentioned are no better than those who officiated during the Nazi dictatorship; in human terms there is no progress, there's no point deluding yourself, only the historical circumstances are different. But in present-day France, I am not running the risk of extermination or torture or even being imprisoned (although, if memory serves, one of the Muslim organizations that sued me called for a sentence of one year in prison; though in that case it was generally considered that the summing-up was ridiculous and had no chance of succeeding). In fact, I risk rather less in an interview than I risked during the multiple

---

*In the interview to which Houellebecq refers, Demonpion actually says: "Is he racist? Well, if he isn't he's not far off. When you reread his biography of Lovecraft you feel an extraordinary sympathy for this American author who, for his part, was profoundly racist."

oral exams and the *concours* that punctuated my career as a student (in which there were *bastard examiners* and *trick questions*). I am risking no more than I did during the annual career assessments that were rituals of my professional life.

So there is nothing to be really afraid of; there is something to be *a little afraid of;* and to be honest I don't share your absolutely negative attitude toward fear. Psychologists, in general, consider that a moderate level of fear, producing a reasonable level of stress, improves a candidate's intellectual performance, at least where it is not a case of being truly creative, but of giving someone else the minimal social satisfaction, the feeling of being worked up one expects at an exam or an interview.

I took the whole "unauthorized biography" thing a lot more badly. Because, after all, *what gave him the right?* And why should I even have to complain about something so obviously immoral? Why is it that such a work is not banned by its very nature? Where are Demonpion's search warrants, his police powers? What gives him the right to violate the confidentiality of private letters? There is clearly something in the very functioning of our societies that I can't bring myself to accept.

How did I proceed in this case? Pretty stupidly, I think. I did not, as you suggest, *act in advance,* and it's true that I regret not having, like you, attempted a little *physical intimidation* of the author. It would probably have worked and, given the evident shortcomings of the legal system, would have been absolutely legitimate. And, contrary to what he claimed, I did not even try to put "a spoke in his wheel." To anyone who phoned me and asked if I wanted them to cooperate, I said of course not, but that's about all.

Some people cooperated without asking my opinion, some of them long-standing friends; I felt, I admit, very sad about that, but I didn't think twice about deleting them from my address book.

It was much easier for me to deal with the media that had published information, without my consent, whether true or false, which I believed concerned my private life. This simple operation sorted out a lot of things and the results are slightly farcical. To my mind, the only French dailies I can deal with now are *l'Humanité* and *La Croix.** Among the weeklies, we have *Elle, Les Inrockuptibles, VSD,* and *Paris Match.* Things look much more positive with the monthlies. I've never had any issues with *Le Chasseur Français* or *Chiens 2000 . . .* Okay, I'm joking, but most women's magazines, like I said before, and most upmarket men's magazines have demonstrated exemplary propriety.

To be honest, from the very beginning of my career, I've been struck by the fact that the most interesting interviewers did not necessarily come from what one might think of as the most respectable magazines. Clearly, in our strange society, it's not only the reputations of people that are often inaccurate . . . One sometimes feels Orwellian in the face of the accumulation of diametrical, performative lies, what one might precisely call *antitruths.* I find it interesting though not fascinating; Philippe Muray died too soon.

At the time, all this was painful, but I had certain resources; not least my *hatred* for the journalist Demonpion. As with fear, I don't share your entirely negative view of hatred. It is a

---

*l'Humanité is a French communist newspaper founded by Jean Jaurès in 1904 *La Croix* is a French Catholic daily newspaper founded in 1880.

feeling I have rarely felt; but I remember that I found something refreshing, something bracing, about it.

With my mother's book, it's a very different matter. In this case, none of my readers think I should *"rise above it"*; they all realize that what has happened is serious.

I realize, and this is very strange, that I still cannot bring myself to hate my mother. Perhaps it is difficult to hate one's mother regardless of the circumstances; perhaps one always feels that in doing so one is hating oneself, disowning oneself. Right now, I feel a sort of numbness, a stiffness; I feel terribly sad and demoralized, but, even now, no hatred. I feel as though I've been bitten by a poisonous spider and am waiting for the moment when I will be devoured. I hold my mother no more responsible than the spider, left to her own devices, in accordance with her nature; she cannot help but bite and inject her venom.

More than anything, there is something that I had never felt, and that is *shame*. Ashamed of my mother, ashamed to be her son, ashamed to be myself. Nietzsche had some powerful, beautiful words to say on the subject. (*"Whom do you call bad? He who always wants to put people to shame,"* etc.)* The thing is, Nietzsche was a good writer, a very good writer, but maybe not quite good enough, and what I most remember, what first comes to mind when I think of shame, is Kafka. I rarely mention Kafka when I talk about my first great literary emotions, although I read him when I was sixteen, the same age as I read Dostoyevsky and Nietzsche, whom I mention all the time. But in those writers (and even in Pascal), there was what Lautréamont called a "positive electricity"; you wanted to talk about them, to talk to them. Kafka is different; very close to what I'm

---

*Houellebecq is referring to *The Gay Science*, §273.

feeling right now—a numbness, a stiffness, a cold, physical sensation. I remember the first thing I read was *The Metamorphosis and Other Texts* (published by Livre de Poche) and straight afterward *The Trial* (published by Folio). The last sentence of *The Trial*, immediately after Joseph K. has been caught and stabbed by the two killers: "... it was as if the shame of it should outlive him."

There has been something in my literature, from the first, that goes hand in glove with shame. To be honest, when I published my first books, I expected to bring a certain shame on myself (even though, as I said before, I've always *hated putting myself forward*). What actually happened, and it was a wonderful surprise, was that readers came up to me and said, "Not at all, what you describe are human things, some true of human beings in general, others specific to human beings in modern Western societies ... In fact, we are grateful to you for having the courage to expose them, for having shouldered that part of shame ..."

This, I think, is what some people couldn't stand, why they constantly try to portray my books as being not the expression of a general human truth but the product of a personal trauma; and in a bitter war like that, the *biography*, the crude, stupid *biography*, is unquestionably the most effective weapon; the conflict having reached, in recent weeks, its highest point. The simplistic approach, effective by reason of its very brutality, of reducing all literature to *evidence;* all this was predicted, long before Nietzsche, by Tocqueville.

Because in our societies, it is important for people to feel ashamed of themselves; it may even be the case that shame has become the fundamental tool for taming people. You were complaining in an earlier letter, dear Bernard-Henri, of being thought of as having *no sense of humor;* this may be your rarest quality. What is humor, after all, but shame at having felt a genuine emotion? It is a sort of tour de force, a slave's elegant pirouette when faced with a situation that under normal circumstances would evoke despair or rage. So, yes, it's hardly surprising that these days humor is rated very highly.

But I'm preaching to the converted. I said earlier that I "don't believe in Jews." Well, in general terms, that's true, but there are certain things . . . Because unquestionably, long before anyone else, Jews developed the sense of humor that, sadly, makes it possible for them to endure almost anything. And it is a fundamental change, and a real joy, to see *Israel fighting* these days.

Am I in the process of contradicting everything I've told you since the start of our letters? Am I saying that, in the end, I would rather fight? No, not exactly. What I mean is that, up until now, in my life, the refusal to fight (or sometimes flight) was the result of a *choice.* I chose to go to trial rather than make the "public apologies" the Muslim organizations would have been happy with. On the other hand, I chose to ignore Demonpion. I chose not to retaliate but simply to break off all relations when any newspaper or magazine published the sort of details about my life that normally would be made public only if a man were on trial for a serious crime (and even then, many trials are heard in camera).

Now, for the first time in my life, with my mother's book, I feel as though I no longer have a choice. No more choice than a man stumbling into quicksand who knows that any movement he makes, by stirring up the mud, can only hasten his entombment.

Dear Michel, how about if we stop with the mud, hatred, whipping boys, slander?

We've said it all.

Naturally, we haven't said everything about this thing with your mother.

Or about this question of Islamic-leftism, this new great alliance between new Reds and new Browns, of the axis that runs from those cretins at *Le Monde diplo*[*matique*] to the death squads of the jihad variety. I also believe we've seen only the start of it (where we disagree is about Islam itself, which I always take care to distinguish from Islamism, not out of prudence naturally or any concern for what's politically correct but because I believe sincerely that Islam as such is not at all alien to the spirit of enlightenment, democracy, and freedoms).

But as regards the rest, your enemies, mine, their shared interests, this secret of the times that will begin to unravel when we begin to understand their unspeakable alliance, the reasons that make writers more hated than anyone else, I really believe that we've said everything there is to be said about those pawns, those paid biographers who are quite stupid, writers of poison-pen letters, snitches, vultures attacking living flesh, total nonentities.

I'm only going to say one more thing about it. I don't get too upset, I never reply to those people, and I would suggest that you do the same. The reason why—apart from the whole question of negative emotions, having to bother with strategies and replies, apart from Spinoza and Hobbes—is that they're just not worth it.

On the other hand, there were two things in your letter that led me to what are also probably useless reflections, but no matter . . .

First, your narrative of your beginnings: your lack of desire, you say, to be the center of attention; this essential timidity that made the young Houellebecq the man least prepared for "playing a public role"; in a word, this misunderstanding that was the beginning of it all.

I was also struck by what, a little earlier, you called the "strengths" that hold or fail to hold your texts together, your problems of "steering" and "braking," your conception of literature as a variant not of bullfighting but cycling, and what this reveals about your way of working and your passion for writing.

The first point interests me because, even though this may seem even more surprising in my case than in yours, I was not at all prepared to become what I am either.

I'm not saying that I found it hard to play my role of "author" once I'd stumbled into it.

Or that in my childhood and adolescence I had that shy, unassuming nature, perhaps solitary, certainly fleeing from the footlights, that I sense behind your description.

But what's clear is that I was perfectly happy with my local fame, local and tiny, in my classes and in the small groups and cliques that I moved in.

I'm equally certain that when I imagined my future, when, like all young people, I dreamed about my future, I saw adventures, combat, perhaps great books, and through all this a sort of luster, but a rare, local luster that would never take the form of that celebrity that has become my lot and yours.

At the École Normale there were boys who dreamed of becoming ministers or, like a former pupil, Georges Pompidou, presidents of the Republic.

There were some who saw themselves as and wanted to be "great writers" in the style of other former alumni, who had hung around the École Normale for years and who were now enjoying the fullness of their glory, like Sartre or Raymond Aron.

There were some, like my namesake Benny Lévy, who were shooting ahead and were already living in the moment, like the reincarnation of Lenin haranguing the Soviet people.

I wasn't of the same disposition as any of them.

I don't remember ever being tempted in May '68, for example, to take the floor at a general assembly.

Nor—indeed still less—do I remember ever going to dream about my destiny in front of the columns of the Pantheon, the way Jules Romain's pupils of the École Normale did.

In fact, what I remember is quite the opposite. On the first day back to school in 1966, a classmate held forth to a gathering that had formed in the covered-in hall where the pupils of the two first-year and two second-year classes in the preparatory section for the École Normale's arts course met between classes. He gave two juxtaposed portraits, favoring the former, of that alumnus Pompidou, who had been enrolled at the École for so many years, and his obscure fellow pupil, the Latinist Pierre Grimal. I see myself without the shadow of a doubt adding my voice to the protests against this boy who was foolish enough to think of comparing the failed life of a future president, seen on television every night, with the great life, eminently desirable and wonderful, of a translator of Seneca the Younger, Plautus, or Terence and whom we met only in the reading room of the École Normale.

If I had a yearning, it was not for any of those great destinies under the stage lights that the École might prepare you for.

When I think of the people I admired and dreamed of one day resembling, I wanted to be like that specialist on Plautus and Terence, or to be a philosophy professor who, like Jean Hyppolite, had translated the *Phenomenology of Spirit,* or even—sticking with the great Hegelian plotters, the mysterious Alexandre Kojève, about whom a few of us, just a few, were aware that he was master of our masters. There was also Louis Althusser, hidden away like the Minotaur in his office on the École's ground floor, who was the greatest saint of Marxist modernity. And in a quite different vein, there was a playboy, quite unknown really, named Paul Albou—I'd read once that he was Brigitte Bardot's secret lover and had been mad with jealousy.

To use your word, I didn't believe that it was possible to "subjugate" more than a few people at a time.

I believed that influence, like concepts, lost in comprehension what it gained in extension, that it lost in intensity, incandescence, and power what it appeared to win by being exercised over a large number of people.

I liked to seduce and indeed spent a crazy amount of time at it but I too believed that the natural place for seduction, its correct wavelength, its source, was not light but shadow.

And I'll say it again—if I'd had to choose between the life that has become mine and that of some clandestine head of a proletarian left-wing movement uniting those who— whoever they were—would have been the undeniable "aristoc-

racy" of the time, I would have chosen the life of the clandestine head.

So those are the facts.

They can say what they like, but those are the facts.

When I wrote what for me was my *Lovecraft, Les Indes
rouges,* I decided to give it to François Maspero, who was certainly the appointed editor of that far-left to which I was
close ideologically, and whose anti-TV, antimedia, anti-
show-off stance in particular seemed to correspond to the
ideas I had about thought and its influence.

When, four years later, I handed in my *Barbarism with a
Human Face,* whose success I'm sure you know all about,
there are two other facts that say a lot about my state of mind.
First, I wrote it out of love for a woman I'd taken away from a
cinema producer and who, I feared, would be bored in this
literary world I was plunging her into without any notice.
That gangster Jean-Edern Hallier had the fortunate notion
of employing her in his publishing house on the express condition that I should at the end of each month give him a new
chapter of the philosophy book he would get a chance to
gamble on before anyone else. Then, when I had written it,
Hallier went bust and when I approached Grasset to get him
to take on my poor book, abandoned by the wayside, I found
it perfectly normal that he should begin by turning it down
and then publish it unwillingly, just to keep me happy, with
the ridiculously low circulation of 2,700 copies—this can be
verified from the publisher's archives.

And then, finally, came the famous *Apostrophes,* where the
book's destiny was made, as was my own, hot on its heels. The
fact is, I did not go into it exactly reluctantly but rather
with closed eyes, blindly, in absolute innocence not only of
what was going on but of the stakes involved in this kind of
platform. I was far, very far, from aiming at, calculating, or

even wanting some sort of entry into the spotlight for thirty years.

I'll admit that I made up for it afterward.

And I didn't make much of an effort, to say the least, to return to that obscurity from which, as I've just told you, that book plucked me.

When I'm feeling self-indulgent, I imagine that this triggered a sort of trap, a chain reaction, or indeed a clinamen that was hard to resist.

When I'm very self-indulgent and don't hold back from seeing myself in the most flattering light possible, I tell myself that I'm hardly the only one, for crying out loud. There has to be more at stake than the problems of a writer contemplating his navel and worrying about his position in his times! The Burundians, the Darfuris, the Bosnians would hardly have benefited from my return to obscurity. Look at all the good and great causes I've devoted myself to, which needed this constant media racket.

There are also times when I think that you're right, that we do become diminished, that sooner or later we give up on our desires, dreams, ambitions, youth, and that it's at most dubious to dress up this backing down, these small acts of cowardice or major deviations, as I do, in the favorable guise of "friend to humanity."

All of which is true, I suppose.

It's all concurrently true and I myself don't even know in what doses.

Although . . . I hardly dare to say this and yet it's also true.

Strangely enough, deep down I haven't really changed my opinion about the hierarchy of influence.

I am as fascinated now as I was when I was twenty by those great, inflexible figures who provided a sort of background music through the history of my generation and who as a joke I call our "hidden imams"! Benny Lévy, after his political season and his ascent to Jerusalem; Robert Linhart, who preceded him as the head of the *Gauche prolétarienne*, and whose daughter has just described in a novel how one fine day he simply decided to stop talking; Jean-Claude Milner and Jacques-Alain Miller, those two precocious geniuses who, in the corridors of the École on the rue d'Ulm, argued about the origin of the concept of "suture"; or Sylvain Lazarus, who hardly left any books, whose work is known only through the constant references to his "unpublished" or "apocryphal" theses (!) made by Alain Badiou, with his strong media presence. I sometimes wonder whether Lazarus exists, like some character of Borges, only in the imagination of a handful of crazy dreamers, still caught up in the leftism of our youth, in fact precisely that of Badiou.

As for television, that permanent show, one of whose symbols I fear I've become, perhaps when I'm on it I look less "terrorized" or "bored" than you, but I can assure you that I don't enjoy it much, and that I do so less and less, certainly less than at the beginning when at least I had the good fortune to be unaware both of the rules of the game and the posturing it involves, and the effects it can have on the rest of your life.

I've told you all this in order to say three things.

First, it's not at all a given that you become what you are, as proved by both your case and mine, in which misunderstandings triumph and reign.

Second, when the idea of leaving that light-flooded stage in some way or another crosses my mind, far from worrying me, it gives me a slight and quite delicious joy. This departure may be forced or voluntary or result from an excess of comedy, as in Gary's case. Any of these is possible and I don't mind which.

Third, these tales of celebrity are far more complicated, far more determined by chance and unknown quantities, than generally believed in this post-Warhol world, where the thirst for recognition has reached such a pitch of intensity that everyone wants to be a star and does not doubt for an instant that if they provide the goods, they'll make it. A word to the wise is enough. And sorry if by saying this I seem to be slamming the door in the face of some of our nasty little terriers . . .

Now to the next point.

These minor or major secrets of production are always exchanged by two writers—this is a rule that permits no exceptions—once they reach a certain level of intimacy in life or, as here, in a correspondence.

The fundamental question is *why* (write)?

The eternal mystery, and I mean a real mystery, more impenetrable even than that of "commitment," is why certain people like you and me, who could be doing anything else, or even—it must be said—nothing, really doing nothing, just lounging about, traveling, dreaming, seeing friends, reading, should choose to spend so much time in what is really quite a strange activity, which consists of tinkering about, modeling, manufacturing, adjusting, overheating, this other material—words.

You could say that it's more interesting than a normal trade or being a ghost writer, as I was in my early days of "books" by Inspector Borniche or the duchess of Bedford. But we both know that we're beyond that stage and that this point can no longer be relevant.

You can be flippant, as certain writers are, and hide behind

one of the great canonical answers given in 1919 to the survey
in *Littérature*.* The question those three magnificent young
people who were Aragon, Soupault, and Breton asked their
public was "Why do you write?" "Out of weakness," answered
Valéry. Out of weakness! What nerve! Excuse me for being so
direct, but I've never heard anything more affected, insincere,
tacky, and really weak as that reply.

For me the truth is infinitely more simple . . .

For as long as I can remember, since adolescence in any
case, there have been two things—not three or four, just
two—that I felt were worth living for: first, love, and I mean
that in the strict sense, in the sense of loving women, and,
second, writing, just writing, spending nights, days, and
more nights at my word-kit, striving to make the dough rise,
to form a shape, to keep my little columns of signs upright, or
almost . . .

The combination of these two passions is not at all surprising. I believe that they come down to the same thing. Deep
down, fundamentally, they are the same thing, the same kind
of energy, the same drive, the same force—reined in, building up—the same mix of sensual pleasure and pain, sudden-
ness and patience, scrupulous searching and effortless
finding. Why do you write? Because you can't make love all
day. Why do you make love? Because you can't write all day.
When and in what circumstances could you give up writing?
On the day—if it happens—that the other passion, that other
fervor, shows signs of abating. Would the opposite be true?
Would the same correlation apply in reverse? Of course.
These things always cut both ways. What can a body do?
asked Nietzsche. What can it do, what does it want, and in the

---

Littérature: review edited by the Surrealists Louis Aragon, André Breton, and Philippe Soupault from 1919 to 1924.

name of what overriding interest? It can do all sorts of things. I'm not like Beckett, who, to the same question, "Why do you write?," replied half a century later with his famous "It's all I'm fit for." If I will it to, my body can do any number of things that are apparently unrelated to my two essential passions. It can work, for example. It can move from one place to another, heal, sustain itself, live somewhere, sleep, do battle, make noise, toss and turn. But my nature is such that all these activities serve only to underpin one or the other of my two essential passions. My constitution allows me to do practically nothing that is not in some way or another, directly or indirectly, linked to these arts of loving and writing, the double climax that I derive almost equally from both. Truly, there are only two things that my body is "able" to do, in the sense of being equipped by nature to do; two things that are really one and the same; loving and writing, writing and loving, drawing sustenance from the first for the second and tapping in the second the wellspring of the first. That's how it is.

That this passion for writing should occupy the position I've mentioned in someone's life, that it should outclass others, all others with the exception of love, with which it competes or of which it forms a part, derives from a neurosis, which is also quite a banal one—see the irrevocable demonstration given by Sartre in *The Words*, which is really his farewell to books, a cry of hatred and revolt against bewitchment by literature. Except that first off, I like that bewitchment. I don't dream of freeing myself from it. And why would I? In the name of what? I repeat, I have no substitute passion. I don't have a third passion to put in its place . . . Besides, this exasperated quixotism, this passion for words and their echo, this life within and through words, this way of literally seeing the word as the beginning of the world, takes in my case—and this is nothing to be proud of . . . once again, that's just how it is, neither good nor bad, it is what it is—extreme forms verging on the burlesque.

Ideas . . . I haven't written any novels in twenty years and thus, unlike you, I'm a man of ideas and should see ideas as the ultimate rulers. But the more time passes, the more sure I am that even when it comes to questions of truth and ideas, what is decisive are words. It is believed that a philosopher is someone who says, "Look, I have an idea, all I need now are the words to express it." Not at all! Experience, my experience, has proved that it's almost always the opposite. It's words that ignite concepts and not the other way around. The shaft of light thrown by the work of words is the bright spot in the dark that finally nails down the idea.

As for life, I'm not bad at it. I'm not melancholic or depressive, still less a depressionist. But the fact is, the further I go into it, the more life, its joys, its everyday happiness, its meetings, interest me only insofar as they will or can be transmuted into words (not necessarily right away but one day in one form or another, perhaps in a novel, perhaps in a film or in my false novel, the diary I've been keeping for more than thirty years and that I'm sure I'll get into some shape or another one day). It was Althusser who said that you never emerge from thought to get back to reality. Never, once you go into the concept of dog, can you find your way back to the sweet animal of flesh, bones, and barks of which Spinoza said that it had definitively stopped biting. So that's where I am. I haven't changed my opinion or my disease, and on this point, as on many, I'm forced to admit that paradoxically I've remained faithful to my old and disavowed master.

As for art, film, beautiful objects, books even insofar as they are also objects (think of that passion, which I find unintelligible, of what's called bibliophilia, which I sometimes discuss with one of the masters of the genre, Pierre Leroy), the truth is regrettable. The real truth, which I've never dared to say to anyone before, is that none of that interests me unless, once again, it provides a pretext for writing. I am capable of spending an enormous amount of time at Perugia, Monterchi, Borgo San Sepolcro, the National Gallery, the Staatliches Museum in Berlin, the Frick, or Arezzo if the Éditions de la Différence ask me for a book on Piero della Francesca. I can go to the worst flop that Lauren Bacall ever starred in, if I know that I have to use her lovely face in another book, this time in images and sounds, which will be *Le Jour et la nuit*. But to do it for its own sake, without any reason, for the love of art and pleasure . . . What pleasure, for God's sake? I couldn't give a damn about that pleasure. I realize with horror that it's been years since I sacrificed a day or even an evening of good writing for the mere pleasure of going to see a film, to admire a painting, go to the opera unless I know I'm going to use it in a text. And with an even greater horror I realize that when it's finished, when I've completed the text I've been asked to produce, when I've translated into words what I've understood of Mondrian, Macau, a great contemporary novel, the plays of Thomas Bernhard, Warhol's collages, the photographs of Richard Avedon, the ruins of Lagos or Kabul, the heart of America, the last nights of Baudelaire, the films of Coppola or Woody Allen (the only thing that has saved me and because of which I am nevertheless interested in a certain number of things is—and we keep coming back to this—my insatiable appetite for writing, which over time, just as in love, has had to vary its situations and positions somewhat), I realize and not without a certain shame that once they have been put into words, stored in some book or analyzed in an article, things cease to concern me, I lose interest in them, they are so to speak deactivated. I can spend the rest of my days without ever going back to see *The Duke and Duchess of Urbino* by Piero della Francesca, although it enchanted me when I went to see it for my book at the Uffizi in Florence.

Naturally, I try to keep this in check.

There are cases—in which, in order to speed things up, what's at stake is not only art or cinema but politics or morality and the actual destiny of actual men and women—where I'm particularly aware of this rapacious, predatory side, which is the correlate to my belief in the virtues of departing from syntax, the imperceptibly new use of a punctuation sign, of a word catapulted beyond its usual usage, an unshackled sound that rises beyond the realms of silence and noise . . .

And it's the reason why I spend so much time in organizing safety devices for myself to protect me from myself, such as the radio I'm helping to set up in Bujumbura in order to make sure that I'll go back there, an irregular correspondence with some old, young people I met eight years ago in Vienna, knowing that part of me might well be tempted to see them only as bit players in the report I wrote at the time on the "anti-Haider resistance,"* a somewhat forced friendship in N'Djamena to maintain the link with Darfur, a brotherhood kept up with a Pakistani "fixer," or my *Nouvelles de Kaboul,* which I carry around, so that I won't be able to look away.

But that is the truth.

That is the underlying logic.

Words or things? I can't even understand how the question can be formulated.

Literature or life? Life because of literature; for me life

*Haider: Jörg Haider, controversial Austrian politician famous at home and abroad for xenophobic and anti-Semitic comments. He created a new political party and led it into parliamentary elections but died in a car crash shortly afterward.

does not "live," it is not profoundly and carnally life unless I know that I can snatch words from it.

At the risk of imprisoning it? At the risk of locking it up in those little paper coffins of which Sartre said at the end of his life in his interview with Madeleine Chapsal that they were the real subject of his *Critique de la raison dialectique*? It's certainly not that. It's exactly the opposite. I can think of nothing more antifunereal than words well used. By contrast with Sartre, who confused putting into words with placing in a coffin, I can imagine no happier place to stay in life than in a page of literature.

Moreover, I must tell you that in my humble opinion this is precisely why Baudelaire will always be more admirable than Rimbaud: *life is elsewhere*. What a mistake to think that real life is elsewhere! What unforgivable madness when, without leaving Charleville, he was this wonderful poet, to set off for Harrar to plumb language and give expression to its ever more dizzying depths. A season in hell? Why only one season? How I love, by comparison, Baudelaire's exultation of litera-ture, spewed out up to his last cry, of "For God's sake, no!"

When I think about it, this was also the belief of the rabbis who stated that it was words that gave worlds their sub-stance.

And I must say that when I'm down, when I feel like a real prick, when I'm ashamed of all the tricks and reminders I need to make sure I don't forget the Darfuris or the Afghans, I can tell myself that at least I'm faithful to the great and lofty lesson of those sages.

There is no life outside of words; that's the basis of their doctrine.

In order for there to be life, you have to get the right sparks from the white-hot stone of words—that's the heart of the Talmud.

The true logic of living, its real constitutive element, is not the cell, DNA, and so on, it's the pale tissue of the signifier, the fine intrigue of words that is the root of my literary neurosis as well.

I believe.

Of course, if we take this route we must take it all the way to the end.

And if we say that words are living, that they are more alive than living beings, that they are life par excellence, that we are really alive only in proportion to the quantity of words we've ingested, we can't stop halfway. What is inherent to living beings is that they die. We must accept the idea that words, like all living beings, and indeed even more so than ordinary living beings, are earmarked for death, one of their intrinsic properties being that, sooner or later, they are destined to perish.

How soon? How late?

And for these living beings that are words, what is the specific system of their mortality?

And there you have it—the difference between good and bad books. For someone who is interested, as both of us are, in the machinery of literature, its abysses, its chaos, and the complex of forces that allows it not to implode, the only question that needs to be asked about any writer is what is alive in their writing and what is dead. In a given text, which are the words that are already dead, those that have one foot in the grave, those that are alive still but for how long? Which are the phantom words, the ghosts?

The answer is clear.

It can be seen with the naked eye. Your ear will detect it. There's no need to be a great critic. Or rather, to be more precise, that is the principle of all criticism worthy of the name.

In the great writers, the ones that practically discourage us from writing in their wake, almost everything is alive. For a long time, a very long time after the words were written, the power of the drama that took shape through them lives on.

In the bad ones everything is dead. The ink is barely dry and already the words it formed are disappearing. These are books without a footprint, books that leave no traces. It is sometimes said, and you said it yourself about the false books that have been written about you, that they are so bad that they dirty your hands. But it's not that, it's not even that, since the sign of their poverty is that they leave no trace at all.

In the in-between, uncertain ones, the minor or second-tier writers, or in those books by great writers that half failed or half succeeded, death and life mingle; there are areas that stand up and others that fall flat. In the same chapter, the same page, sometimes even the same sentence, you can find a mix of living flesh and dead meat, burning coals and embers, a part that still shines and a part that has faded, the sparkle of literary matter versus the black hole of words that have self-destructed.

Carry out the test.

Carry out this test of "living" or "dead" on the books you love and those you hate.

Do it with your own books, when you're in doubt.

I do it sometimes. It's the only test that doesn't let you down—you'll see.

June 3, 2008

As it happens, dear Bernard-Henri, just before your letter arrived I received an invitation from Matthias Vincenot, who organizes a poetry festival every August in Corrèze; and I almost accepted. I felt a distressing yearning, a brief, pathetic illusion, as though I could go back to the years of my youth when I was known as a poet, and only a poet and only by those interested in poetry in this country. To know again these modest little events, organized by some local council, with the support of some departmental council or a local branch of the Crédit Agricole. To go back to the days when, actually, I was happy.

But of course you understand the difficulties. My notoriety would make the situation awkward not only for me, but also for the other participants and for the whole event. Joys like this are forbidden to me now. And there is another thing, something that is perhaps worse; it is difficult for me to imagine taking part in a public reading in France now. For a long time, I avoided paranoia, in particular, I think because I read Rousseau's *Reveries of a Solitary Walker* when I was very young and was terrified by the growing madness one can feel worsening page by page; I swore to myself that I would never fall prey to it. Today, I have to face the fact that I have not come through completely unscathed. I recognize the symptoms, the tachycardia, the mind racing, the mental block.

Of course, I've got my reasons; if anyone in France right now has the right to be paranoid, it's me.

Rousseau had his reasons too.

When you say this kind of thing, at best, people give you a knowing, mocking look. I remember the interviews with Kurt Cobain where he said he was happiest when he and the band could tour in their camper van playing small venues without attracting the attention of a single journalist. People say, what, you're rich and famous now, what the fuck are you complaining about? It usually isn't long before they start accusing you of *biting the hand that feeds*. Usually you have to put a bullet in your head before they realize you were serious.

So you see, Bernard-Henri, the extent to which it resonates with me when you talk about "local, tiny fame"; because I had that kind of fame; for years, that was my life. The sort of fame where you are read and recognized by your peers and almost no one else.

Not only have I experienced that fame, it still exists. A few months ago I received an anthology of French poetry that Jean Orizet* compiled for Larousse. In the biographical note he writes about me he mentions, almost in passing, that aside from poetry I have published a number of novels that sparked a lively controversy.

Please understand, Bernard-Henri, this is not some affectation, some pose. In Jean Orizet's universe things other

---

*Jean Orizet (born 1937) is a French poet and essayist. He co-founded the magazine *Poésie 1* and the publishing house Les Éditions du Cherche Midi.

than poetry do exist, but their existence is tangibly less important.

Another time, I ran into Lionel Ray.* I'd just been buying personal hygiene products at Italie 2 shopping center. We talked a bit about health, he was worried about some things, had some tests he had to have. He also told me that he had just retired (he worked as a teacher at the Lycée Chaptal). Otherwise, he asked me what I was doing; I told him I was working on a film. He found this funny, entertaining; he already knew I had written a number of novels. But still, he remarked, it had been a while since I'd published a book of poems. The reproach was subtle but real; in his view, it was time I *got back to serious things*.

And William Cliff,† whom I ran into on a train from Paris to Brussels, had much the same reaction. After a little small talk, he launched into a discussion of Villon and on my use— rather too free in his opinion—of the alexandrine.

It is extraordinary, and I find it terribly moving, that such people exist. I feel like saying—actually, I don't feel like saying it at all, but I almost feel obliged to say—that such people *still* exist. People with a system of values so distant, so incommensurable with that of their contemporaries.

How long will they go on existing? Oh, I don't doubt that Gallimard is conscious to some extent of its cultural responsibilities; I'm sure the company will make it a point of honor to publish its old poets until the day they die; but I doubt they will put much energy into looking for their successors.

---

*Lionel Ray (born Robert Lorho, 1935) is a French poet and essayist.

†The pen name of André Imberechts (born 1940), a Belgian poet who won the Grand Prix de Poésie de l'Académie Française in 2007 for his life's work.

Besides, it would be unfair to *cast the first stone* at publishers; when was the last time I saw a poetry section in a bookshop?

And what can the bookshops do, if there are no readers? Maybe we live in a world (this was Ghérasim Luca's* conclusion just before he committed suicide) where poetry simply has no place anymore.

And so something precious is disappearing, disappearing before our very eyes. I can attest to it, I have watched it fade away in my lifetime, even during my modest career as a writer, I have seen the poetry sections in the bookshops get smaller, seen the poetry collections gutter out.

I have also seen the annual, Soviet-style displays of enthusiasm by those in charge; congratulating each other on the incredible success of *"le Printemps des Poètes,"*[†] on the extraordinary and growing appetite of the public for poetry, oh, it makes me tired just talking about it.

In *l'Auteur*, Vincent Ravalec[‡] is viciously funny about the years he spent on another parallel circuit that is culturally subsidized and almost as pathetic as that of poetry: the world of the *short story*.

Before coming to the *true business* of writing novels (in 1994, he with *Cantique de la racaille*, I with *Whatever*), both of us had published (he, short stories by Les Éditions Le

---

*Ghérasim Luca is the pen name of the Romanian poet Salman Locker (1913–1994), a theorist of surrealism whom Gilles Deleuze called the greatest living French poet."

[†]An annual national poetry festival launched in 1999, involving some twelve thousand events across France each year.

[‡]Vincent Ravalec (born 1962) is a French novelist, essayist, short story writer, screenwriter, and film director.

Dilettante; I, poetry with Les Éditions de la Différence). Like him, I experienced those improbable cultural encounters where the cultural attaché from the local council wonders aloud whether the *côte de veau* is included in the *prix-fixe*, where you're never really sure where you'll be staying (he was once put up in an old people's home, I in a disused caravan).

There is, however, a difference—minor but crucial—which means that if I had to recount my years on the *parallel circuit*, my story would be less funny, and less scathing, than his. Publishers consider the short story writer to be immature and lazy; I mean, after all, these little stories have characters, they have plots. What's stopping the writer from doing the same thing on a bigger scale in a novel (which, at least, might find a readership)? Whereas the poet is considered to be an utterly irresponsible misfit; or, more straightforwardly, is not considered at all.

This is why poets, who are *out of the squad completely* in any case, have warmer relationships with one another than short story writers, who are *sitting on the bench*.

And this colors the entirety of their relationships.

Now I am *in the game*, to say the least; I'm desperately looking for a way to get *out* (while continuing, to some small extent, to be in).

Because it requires something to remain in touch with poetry, a certain innocence. Technically speaking, that's all it requires. There is a very beautiful word to designate a man who has discovered treasure; it is the word *inventeur*. Whether he stumbled on it by chance while lost in the forest or after fifteen years poring over old maps dating back to the *conquistadores* doesn't matter. And this is exactly the same thing you feel when you write a poem: it doesn't matter whether you've spent two years or fifteen minutes writing it. It is as though—and I know this sounds irrational—it is as though the poem already existed, has existed for all eternity, and that all you have done is *discover it*. Once it has been discovered, you stand at a certain distance. You have loosed it from the earth where it lay buried, dusted it off, and it shines, for all to see, a gleam of unpolished gold.

A novel is something very different; it entails a lot of grease and sweat; it requires a ridiculous amount of work to hold everything more or less together, tightening the wheel-nuts, stopping it from running off the road; it is, when all's said and done, a piece of *machinery*.

I don't disown my novels, I'm very fond of my novels, but it's not quite the same thing; and with my head on the block I would argue (against Kundera, against Lakis Proguidis and all my friends, against all those who supported me when times were hard) that the novel (even in the hands of Dostoyevsky, of Balzac, of Proust), in comparison to the poem, remains a *minor genre*.

(I realize this is an old debate and one that doesn't concern you personally; but, when all is said and done, this is what I spent my youth doing; it is the sort of conversation I used to have in Le Lucernaire with Benoît Duteurtre and Lakis Proguidis.)

I don't know whether I had *a gift* for writing novels, I don't know whether the question means anything, can one have a gift for something so complex?

I certainly had no gift for stories, I've always found telling stories a pain in the ass, and I have no talent as a *storyteller* (to use a word recently adopted in French).

As for *style*, I wish people would stop bugging me with this shit. Where do words play their most direct part, where do they gain power from how they are arranged? In poetry, first and foremost in poetry. Compared to a poet, no novelist has or can ever have a style. You try, oh, you try to achieve certain harmonies; sometimes you find, you're delighted to find, in a sentence something that would not seem out of place in a poem (it often happened to Conrad, sometimes to Flaubert); but in general you keep your mouth shut about such moments, you let others discover them, you rely entirely on your future readers.

I had a gift for something, for one thing related to writing novels, creating *characters*. They kept me from getting to sleep, woke me up in the middle of the night, Bruno, Valérie, Esther, Michel, Isabelle. And now they are alive, yes, they won.

This can be disturbing about the novelist; he has the power, a power that is normally the preserve of God, to give life.

Lord Jim is alive.

Kirilov is alive (perhaps the most surprising example in all of literature, because he comes to life so quickly in a few short pages).

General Hulot is alive.*

And this is why actors, when they come face-to-face with a novelist, look at him so strangely; because they too try to *give life* to characters; they try with their own means, using their bodies, their faces. And they know, or they sense, that the novelist for his part, using different means, succeeds.

(Thinking about it, it is actresses who really look at me strangely; it's perfectly understandable. When they haven't tried, people always assume that it is more difficult to give life

---

*Houellebecq is referring to Alexei Nilych Kirillov in Dostoevsky's *The Possessed* and to Maréchal General Hulot Comte de Forzheim in Balzac's *Cousin Bette*.

to a character of the opposite sex. In reality, I can tell you, that it doesn't matter; the gender isn't the issue.)

But in poetry it is not simply characters who come to life, it is words. They seem to be surrounded by a radioactive halo. They suddenly find their aura, their essential vibration.

Give a purer sense to the words of the tribe.

"Purity" is truly one of Mallarmé's obsessions, whiteness, snow; I would certainly not have written that, because I am a sentimental little cretin, because whiteness and snow frighten me, they evoke Schubert's terrifying *Winterreise.* Nonetheless, it's very beautiful and perfectly precise.

Few people have penetrated these mysteries by means of their intelligence. Personally, I know only one. His name is Jean Cohen; he was a theoretician, a linguist. He wrote two books, the first entitled *Structure du langage poétique,* and the second *Le Haut Langage,* both published by Flammarion. He does not concern himself with the notion of *literariness* (by which certain texts among the immense body of texts in the world can be called *literary*). He interests himself in the issue of greater magnitude of *poeticity* (why certain texts in the body of literature can be said to be *poetic*).

It would be difficult for me to overstate the shock I felt reading *Le Haut Langage.* Because I hadn't read (and still haven't read) the theoreticians who came before him, Genette, Todorov, Greimas ... But I had the pretension to know for myself, in a very secret place inside myself, when I had produced something that could be called a *poem;* or when, on the contrary, it had missed the mark (often the case with texts written under the influence of alcohol). And here I had stumbled on someone who also knew . . . I felt as though he could read the very depths of my soul.

I mention this because I think he would agree with you on the word *living*. Except that he, unlike us, was not in the media; the dangers he faced were of a different kind. He knows he is being watched; knows his linguistics colleagues are waiting round the corner for him; in short, he has to *produce theory*. And what is most extraordinary is that he succeeds. He succeeds in giving a convincing theoretical elaboration of what quite clearly came to him by pure intuition. In a word, in a hundred words, you have to read Jean Cohen.

Unlike you, Bernard-Henri, I have never sought to join the ranks of the "intellectuals," something that, from what I know of the careers of Jean Cohen and a handful of others, and from what Rachid Amirou (a university professor who specializes in the sociology of tourism and whose work I greatly admire) told me recently, I do not regret for a moment. There too there is slander, polemic, base jealousy, plots . . . And maybe I am idealizing, maybe it is the famous "magic of memory" at work in me, but I don't remember anything of that kind in the little world of poetry. When I published my second collection of poems (which, coming after a novel that had had some press coverage, consequently had the dubious honor of being exposed to the broad mass of literary critics), some journalists saw fit to appear surprised that I use the alexandrine, a form they considered antiquated. In fact, they were rather simplistic (although I sometimes use the alexandrine, I more often use the octosyllabic form, or free verse). Well, whether you believe it or not, in all my time in the little world of poetry, I *never* came across a criticism like that.

That sort of criticism was considered completely outmoded. Whether a poem was written in alexandrines, in free verse, in prose, in anything you liked, made not the slightest difference in the little world of poetry. The alexandrine, I agree, was considered to be one of the possible forms of French poetry— a form that corresponded to the general structure of the language, which had made possible some beautiful works and could still do so.

All this to say, Bernard-Henri, that I have no trouble believing you when you tell me that your fame was in no way *premeditated*. It is all the easier to believe since almost nothing in my life has been premeditated (or, to be more precise, everything I premeditated failed). The only things I have ever managed to plan, more or less, have been my novels (well, at least the beginnings; after the first hundred pages, it goes downhill). And moreover, it was because I never *wanted* fame. It is true that I wanted to earn money through my books; fiercely wanted it, for the reasons I've already given, as soon as I realized it was possible (which is to say sometime around September 10, 1998). Perhaps, had I been rich, I would have wanted fame *as well;* but that is not the way things went in my life. I became famous in September 1998; I became rich in May 1999 when the royalties arrived. Well, I say rich, it's all relative. Let's say, rich enough to be able to think about giving up a job that simply paid the rent—but that, in any case, always seemed to me the only meaningful benefit of being rich.

The fact remains that, now, we have fame. And that we cannot easily get away from it. Even less so on my part since, unlike you perhaps, I have never felt the least temptation to try the *Romain Gary ruse*.* I don't know why, to be honest; I think I would feel I was disowning myself, disowning my previous writings. I know some artists have done so.; but in those cases I think it was a *genuine* disavowal. Stupid maybe, or at least that is how it sometimes appears from the outside after a few centuries have passed; but at the time, from their point of view, entirely genuine.

There is also the fact that I have, over the years, established with my readers a relationship of trust (and that those readers, whether or not I know them, are the only people in the world to whom I feel a certain duty). I would feel, I don't know, as though I were betraying that trust. And, in betraying that trust, I would feel that I was giving in to the pack.

And I do not want to do that. No, I do not want that.

So, there you have it; I will have to put up with *being Houellebecq* to the end, with all that that entails. Of course, the whole thing might be over the day after tomorrow; but let's leave that hypothesis to one side.

It is true that there are those who have succeeded. Yes, yes, I've finally found something positive to say, it's taken a bit of time, but I've found something! Certain poets, some of the

---

*"Romain Gary ruse" and other references in these letters to Gary and to the pseudonym Émile Ajar refer to the fact that, late in life, Romain Gary embarked on a hugely successful second career using the nom de plume. Émile Ajar was awarded the Prix Goncourt for his "second" novel *La Vie devant soi* and Gary had his nephew Paul Pavlowitch pose as the author. (According to the rules, an author is precluded from winning the Prix Goncourt twice.) The actual identity of Émile Ajar was the subject of much speculation, but was not definitively confirmed until Romain Gary admitted to being Ajar in the note he left when he committed suicide in 1980. His account of his deception, *Vie et mort d'Émile Ajar*, was published posthumously.

greatest, have managed to survive a substantial dose of celebrity; and managed to produce, in the throes of that fame, some of their most beautiful poems.

Well, when I say "certain poets," the only name that really springs to mind is Victor Hugo.

Maybe Aragon, too, but I wonder: Are Aragon's later works really as good as his early work? I don't know, I'd have to look into it; but in the case of Victor Hugo, it's certain.

So, how to become Victor Hugo? How does one develop that inner strength? This will make you smile, but I have managed to derive a certain comfort from the fact that, like Victor Hugo, I was born on February 26 . . .

(The analogy, I admit, stops there. In the famous poem "This Century Was Two Years Old" in which he talks about himself, he describes himself a few lines later as "Abandoned by all, save by his mother.")

(And I suspect I'm off to a bad start when it comes to the state funeral.)

You have every right to smile—here I am, prepared to drift into the consolations of astrology, to believe in auguries and omens, when ever since we began writing these letters I have been posing as a rationalist, a freethinker . . . But maybe that is precisely my mistake. After all, Victor Hugo, after his daughter's death, went through a terrible period of depression; what if it was spiritualism that brought him through it?

Maybe it is time for me, too, to say my *"farewell to reason."* Reason, which has been useless to me, which has never helped me write a single line; reason, which, all my life, has done nothing but torment me with the desolate nature of its conclusions.

And whether I say my "farewell to reason" in the manner

of Pascal or of Hölderlin makes little difference. As long as I do not do so in the manner of Nerval or Kleist.

It was Nietzsche, I think, before he said his own farewell, who suggested that in the future, man should have *two brains*, one for science, one for all the rest.

The rest to include art, and love as well.

It would also include, if I understand you correctly, philosophy as an exceptional case within literature.

It's strange how hard I find it to give up the illusion that there might be a place, just a little space, for philosophy next to science.

Just as, deep down, I have trouble accepting Nietzsche's phrase, even though I understand precisely what he means.

Just as I have trouble accepting that, somewhere, there is a unity, an identity of a superior nature.

Just as I have trouble, in short, in going without *metaphysics*.

In my defense, it must be said I'm not the only one. Even in Aragon I can find it, this belief in a unique, mysterious core from which all else stems. I can find it in his own answer to the question he and Breton posed in 1919; well, in what I have always taken to be his answer:

> *I know not what possesses me*
> *And forces me to say aloud*
> *Neither for pity, to redress me,*
> *Nor as one might his sins avow*
> *What haunts me, what obsesses me.**

*Louis Aragon, from the Prologue to *Les Poètes*, 1960.

So there you have it, the answer to your question. I don't know. I don't know any more than you do. But I do know there is something that cannot be compared to any project and that seems to me to be above desire.

On this point, I do not agree with you, because I remember reading, reading with a passion, long before I ever suffered the confusion of love (and I know that I will go on doing so long afterward, though that's less amusing). Does this mean that I was already writing, I don't mean compositions, I mean writing *for me*? In all honesty, I think the answer is yes, but I couldn't swear to it; in any case I have not kept anything. But I was already reading with such absorption, such intensity, I reacted so powerfully to the words I found in books that I think I was already caught up in the system—that my fate was already sealed. We write because we have read, that seems obvious to me; it is, in a sense, a sort of conversation across the centuries. Except of course that Pascal or Dostoyevsky or Baudelaire is not going to rise from the grave to answer me. I know it, but do not know it; because I behave exactly as if they were about to do so. It goes without saying that we are never as rational as we think we are.

That it is a good life, a beautiful life, I confess, I have my doubts. What kind of life is it where you can't walk three steps without taking a notebook? Where a couple of hours working on a text can leave you in a state of nervous exhaustion that requires several bottles of alcohol to get out of? I remember an interview with Patricia Highsmith where the interviewer asked what would happen to her writing if she fell in love again, fell hopelessly in love. She said nothing for a moment, then smiled, and said softly, "But there's nothing to be done about that. Absolutely nothing."

In Paris at the end of the seventies there was an English bar, slightly kitsch, with fixed tables and moleskin seats, called the Twickenham. It was at the corner between the rue des Saints-Pères and the rue de Grenelle.

As it was opposite Grasset, and since I loathed office life as much as you did, I spent most of my day there, meeting my authors, plotting, phoning.

It was also the meeting place for the pretty sales assistants at Maud Frizon and other boutiques like Stephane Kélian's, which had already set up in this part of town. So I saw this as a wonderland for picking up women. I was accompanied in this by the night barman, Jacques F. Béarnais, who was a joker, master of entrances, double exits, and vaudeville, whom I had made my Sganarelle.*

Because at that time I was leading an odd sort of life, without any real fixed residence, sleeping over at one woman's or at another's, depending on my mood, whom I happened to meet, and the willingness of the parties in question, there were evenings when I was out of luck or had been given to understand that I wasn't welcome. So I would wait until

*Don Juan's valet in Molière's play *Dom Juan ou le Festin de Pierre.*

Jacques had done the till and stay there, locked up for the night with no electricity, no real heating, breathing in the odors of stale tobacco and cooking that had accumulated during the day, lying like a guard dog on a bench that was too short, where I would sleep until dawn, when the day crew arrived to prepare the first coffees and croissants.

The Twickenham was not only my second office.

It was my main residence, where I stored my toothpaste and shirts in a cupboard among the piles of dishes.

I received my mail there.

On the weekends that I had custody of my daughter, Justine, I set up my logistical headquarters there.

It was the time before mobile phones, and eventually I even managed to wrangle the notable privilege of having a more or less concealed landline at the table in the back, where I spent my evenings.

On the other hand, it was there too that the members of the Committee of Resistance to the Jewish Occupation in France, some tiny group of Palestinian extremists, some jealous husband, member of the Groupe Union Défense, or some exasperated Serb knew they could find me, so some bloody battles took place there, usually outside, on the pavement of the rue de Grenelle.

And it was there too that one evening in February 1976, while I was alone at my table, daydreaming, that Louis Aragon suddenly popped up.

At that time I had not published anything, apart from my report on Bangladesh.

I had no sort of literary existence worthy of any writer's interest, far less his.

But he explained that he had spotted me at the Saint-

Germain Drugstore bookshop, which was the last local book-shop that stayed open late in the evenings. He had observed me several evenings in a row, wandering among the new publications and, on the days when I had no money, reading on the spot, standing there, silently devouring without taking notes, forced to develop a photographic memory, in a fever, with the sales assistant turning a blind eye. That day he had decided to follow me and approach me about the televised adaptation of his *Aurélien* that Michel Favart was getting under way and about the idea they had of offering me the role of the poet, Paul Denis.

I can still see him, pushing open the door to the bar, his tall silhouette, the wide-brimmed hat, the Moroccan cape over a very elegant gray linen suit, which even eight years after Elsa's death gave him an air of unconsoled mourning.

I see him parting the small crowd huddled around the wrought-iron bar that formed the center of the room, as if the crowd didn't exist, and the crowd itself, which, without realizing it, made way for him as if for a strange being, one who was extraterrestrial or had been transported from a museum.

He was imperious and courteous, his hands trembled slightly, there was something tender, almost pink about his face, but his eyes were severe like two pieces of blue Delft sunk into his sockets and shone with a sparkle that was at times unbearable. "Am I disturbing you?" he began, as he sat down and without waiting for my answer ordered a lemon-ade with no ice, then continued in a more familiar tone, "How would you like the role of Paul Denis?" Taken aback, I replied that yes, of course, I kept *Aurélien* on my bedside table but . . . "Well, you are Paul Denis. I want you to play him."

There was no irony in his tone, no sort of second degree. Just Louis Aragon and his formidable presence. He seemed like a great lord, unarmed but terribly impressive.

Old?

Not really that old.

Not the tipsy old man that some people these last years have chosen to describe and ridicule.

On the contrary, he makes me think of a sort of golden mask through which that incredibly intense blue stare emerged.

His forehead was high and narrow, the shape of a crown, which made him look like those kings in disguise who at nighttime mingle with their subjects in order to spy on them more effectively.

There was something Christlike too in his posture, but a dry, tearless Christ who has given up on salvation.

And when he left me, two hours later, that silhouette, still just as straight, moved off with a steady step on the narrow pavement leading to the boulevard Saint-Germain. He stopped only, though several times, to examine the façade of a house by the light of the moon, perhaps the house of a famous fashion designer, perhaps Chateaubriand's house on his return from exile. I watched him but was too far away, so I couldn't tell . . .

Why am I telling you this?

First, because you mentioned his name and the scene came back to me as a chunk of memory and images.

Because I consider the author of *Défense de l'Infini, Les Voyageurs de l'impériale,* and *Henri Matisse roman* as one of the great writers of the twentieth century and I'm happy to take this opportunity to remember him.

And also because, on referring to my notes (once again that diary that I have been dictating every evening into my secretary's answering machine for so many years), I realize that the ground we covered in our conversation that evening was, strangely enough, not too far from the matters you and I have been discussing.

We began with that matter of *Aurélien,* which—and I'm not in the habit of saying these things just to be polite—was truly one of my cult books. So you can imagine how I jumped at the offer, and how I took the opportunity to ask some of the questions that had been torturing me for years! Whether Crevel had inspired Paul Denis, whether Denise Lévy had been the model for Bérénice . . .* about Aragon's relations with Drieu, with Breton . . . whether he regretted not seeing those old accomplices again now that they were dead. And how was it possible that, having started out as those tempestuous young people, brothers in apocalypse and pyromania, they could have ended up like that, two worlds ignoring each other, two strangers, completely cut off . . .

We also talked a bit about politics. It was impossible to avoid talking politics, at least a little, when face-to-face with this great French intellectual (at the end of the day, there haven't been too many others of his stature) who, despite the crimes, the shame, the crushing of the Prague Spring, which he himself had described as a "spiritual Biafra"; who, despite having been called "Stalinist scum" by a certain Daniel Cohn-Bendit† in the middle of May 1968, remained loyal to the party until the end, to his party, the French Communist Party which, alongside the Portuguese Communist Party, was the worst of the communist parties in Europe. So I interrogated him about this hideous loyalty, which caused his support-

*Bérénice and Paul Denis: characters in Louis Aragon's novel *Aurélien.* The suggestion here is that they may have been inspired by René Crevel, a French writer involved with the Surrealist and communist movements who committed suicide in 1935, and Denise Lévy, a cousin of André Breton's wife.

†German politician active in both Germany and France, known as "Danny the Red," currently copresident of the European Greens–European Free Alliance in the European Parliament.

ers to despair, and his answer was strange, unexpected, and rather beautiful: that all he expected from the party was an "honorable decline."

I had the unfortunate thought—hoping to impress him—of mentioning François Mitterrand, saying that I happened to have met him and liked the way he wrote. At that point he glared at me with those icy blue eyes, made the gesture of covering his ears as if I had sounded a false note, stared at the ceiling for a moment with a theatrical, incensed air, then gave me a long, very long smile, mingling first with the wrinkles on his face before transforming into a burst of laughter that I was sure was the laugh of his Montparnasse period. "Mr. Mitterrand's writing? You must be joking! There's nothing to like or dislike in it, it's simply indecent, a patchwork of words and clichés. Could we talk about something less repugnant?"

But the truth is that what we talked about most that night was style in general: appealing, detestable . . . necessary and ridiculous; that you can never write as you speak but that there is nothing more grotesque, false, and therefore grotesque than the posing, ornate voice of a writer who wants to write in a great style . . . Whether it was a matter of the voice or the ear? Which was the writer's organ, the vocal cord or the tympanum? And hadn't Hemingway said it all in the line, which I quoted to him but which I believe summed him up, about a writer without an ear being like a boxer with no left hand?

We spoke of a writer's strategies: covering one's tracks, disguising oneself, lying as you breathe, writing the way you play roulette, chess, poker, hiding your hand or revealing it, turning your cards up or down, the art of the mask and the lie . . . bad faith as an aesthetic and a moral decision . . . the law of counterfeiters, inventing the world rather than parodying it, hatred too and how to overcome it, of the long-lasting war to which he had committed himself when, like Breton—but with what talent!—he declared that he had broken with Europe. After that, he became a merciless adversary of a society of "dogs," "pigs," and "succubi," yes, merciless, hating this world and never abandoning his—hopeful—scrutiny of the signs heralding its death knell. There's a man, dear Michel, who for his whole life was one of those "public enemies" we've been talking about . . .

Victor Hugo—we spoke about him also. At the time my prejudice in favor of Baudelaire (I couldn't forgive Hugo for that "new thrill" business, still less for the unbearably paternalistic tone he used in his letters to the black prince of Kamchatka and in his "stylish and tormented kiosks") put me off him.* But Aragon's opinion seemed to be closer to yours, which is not far from what I think myself today: the absurd failure to recognize his greatness, his magnificent bad taste, his mischievous, surrealist side pre-Surrealism, that masterpiece *Les Châtiments* . . . *Les Misérables* and the "will of the novel." And what about Gide's line, I asked. His famous "Victor Hugo, alas!"—wasn't that the killer line? How do you

---

*Baudelaire and Hugo had an odd relationship, both lurching between admiration and hostility toward each other's work. Baudelaire criticized Hugo's bombast and romanticism, while Hugo disapproved of Baudelaire's "decadence." Lévy sees Hugo's apparent compliment to Baudelaire, when he famously congratulated him on having created a *"frisson nouveau"* (translated here as "new thrill"), as rather condescending. "The black prince of Kamchatka" refers to Baudelaire himself—"black" because he was seen as a Satanic poet, while Kamchatka, a peninsula in far east Russia, like Timbuktu, conjures up somewhere remote, the ends of the earth. There is also a reference here to a famous remark about Baudelaire, which appears in several variants, one of which is *"Ce petit pavillon* [elsewhere *kiosque*] *que le poète s'est construit à l'extrémité du Kamchatka; j'appelle cela 'la folie Baudelaire.'"* This quote comes not from Hugo but Sainte-Beuve (see page 119) and suggests Baudelaire's obscurity and madness.

mean, the killer line? He blew up. Who killed whom, young man? Who killed whom? It was Gide who was killed by that witticism. The other, the visionary, is, as poets are, invulnerable. What about his spiritualism? I insisted. Those stories of turning tables and spirit channelers in Guernsey, which allowed him to converse, across the grave, with Dante, Shakespeare, and other geniuses? Why not! he said. And he went one better, with such bad faith that I couldn't help laughing. Turning tables—why not? Conversations with dead people from one end of hell to another—why not? You're surely not going to hold it against someone if they prefer speaking to dead great minds than small living ones . . .

Finally, we also spoke of the question that had obsessed him since that book, which was and would remain unfinished, which had appeared as a sketch almost twenty years earlier, called *J'abats mon jeu*,* and for which I'd always felt a special affection: poetry and novel, poetry *or* novel, politics, literature, short tracts, great organ music, autobiographical narratives and historical frescoes . . . *Hourra l'Oural* and *Les Cloches de Bâle, Mouscou la gâteuse,* and *Vive le Guépéou* . . . the homage to Matisse, the insult to Picasso, the journalism (for *Commune*, then *Ce Soir*, then *Les Lettres françaises*), the academies and the avant-garde, Thorez and Rimbaud, the homage to Barrès and the discovery of Sollers, the bulimia of that man, who wanted until the very end to be both the prince of youth and also the great literary pontiff, the coherence of all that, the unity of that work and that life, whether there is, as you say, a "major genre" from which the rest originates and that gives some order to this bric-a-brac . . . Or whether there

---

*Louis Aragon, *J'abats mon jeu* (1959): texts dealing with "socialist realism" and Aragon's political involvement in the 1950s.

is, as they themselves, the "Erostrates"* of the 1920s and '30s used to say, in terms not that dissimilar from those used by the Surrealists, "a certain mental point in which life and death, the real and the imaginary, the past and the future, the communicable and the incommunicable, high and low are no longer perceived as contradictory . . ."

Aragon's argument that night was that there is indeed a unity . . .

I saw that he would never give up on the theory of that certain point, giving coherence to his thousand lives . . .

But his argument was also that this coherence does not derive from the existence of one presiding genre cementing all the rest of the work.

And that's the point I want to make.

Let's go back to the beginning.

I understand the reasons, all the reasons, for which poetry may be said to be, as you stated, "the" major genre par excellence. There's Heidegger's argument when he sees it as a magic wand allowing direct access to the living sources of being, Aristotle's argument cited by Heidegger, on poetic experience being "more true," more "precise," than the "methodical exploration of Being" or the thesis put forward by Mal-

---

*Herostratus was an ancient Greek figure who set fire to the Temple of Artemis at Ephesus in his quest for fame. His aim was to immortalize his name in history. Not only was he executed, but it was forbidden to mention his name under pain of death, so that he was punished by being consigned to obscurity. Here, "Erostrates" seems to refer to a group in the 1920s and '30s with some affinities with the Surrealists. The lack of information available about them suggests that they were successful in embracing obscurity. It does not appear to refer directly to Sartre's story "Erostrate," a satire on Surrealism; Sartre dismissed the Surrealists and probably saw them as an adolescent, flash-in-the-pan movement similar to the Erostrates.

larmé in his essay "La Musique et les lettres," according to which poetry is a later form than believed, which consumed, digested, and fundamentally ousted even the musical form, being the only form of language—he claimed—that is our master as much as our instrument, the only lexical structure that Being inhabits and in which it reveals itself. Who can put it better?

I also see the reasons for objecting to this and claiming that the novel is the major genre, that it can only be the novel, that nothing apart from the novel can incorporate, absorb, reproduce, and even improve on the double thrill offered by music and poetry with the bonus of thought, philosophy, knowledge: Kundera, for example, Cervantes as well, Proust, the great Austro-Hungarians, Dostoyevsky. There's this idea everyone has about the novel being this "great form" that gobbles up all the others, demoting them to cantons within its empire, the idea that Mallarmé was right in essence and simply got the genre wrong and that this power he recognized in poetry should be attributed to the novel, Joyce and his paper Babel, Borges and his dream of one great book that would contain all the other books in the world and the world itself, my friend Danilo Kiš, who by the way has been quite forgotten and yet his conception of the novel as an encyclopedia of the dead and library digest is highly convincing . . .

I can also imagine a filmmaker, Antonioni for example, or Lubitsch or Renoir for their part, objecting that no, you're wrong once again about the genre; it's the cinema that swallows everything up, absorbing music, painting, theater, philosophy; it's cinema that's the total artwork, the major definitive art form, having the power to attract the other arts and melt them in its cauldron, to reduce them to the status of components of its language in gold and bronze. Look at Godard's first films, see in *Pierrot le fou* and *Breathless*, which incidentally Aragon reviewed, the use made of literary quotations and philosophical aphorisms, and then try to tell that wild metaphysician, leaping from theorem to matheme, that he's practicing a minor art!

I could even demonstrate to you that if the major genre is the one that colonizes and cannibalizes the other genres, reducing them to provinces in its empire, there is yet another art form that could make that claim: the theater. Not only could I do this, I have done it strenuously, quite a long time ago, in my first year at the École Normale, in an essay for Jacques Derrida's seminar, in which my task was to relate Artaud's *Théâtre et son double* and Nietzsche's *Birth of Tragedy*. If, I argued, the theater is this scene of cruelty, this "shattered mound" on which embryonic man, yet to be born, is moving about, if this operation of "transubstantiation" in which the psychology of actors, characters, and even the author yields to a "metaphysics of gesture and trance," if it is the sacred ceremony that Artaud saw in it—Antonin Artaud, that martyr, that great, radiant figure, that man "suicided" by society (who for me at that time had a colossal shadow and was a totem, an evangelist, whose first name I would later give to my son)—then it was absolute, peerless, the art of arts.

At the very limit, others could argue for fashion—and I'm not just saying this because I'm coming from the funeral at L'Église Saint-Roch, said to be the artists' church, of the great designer Yves Saint Laurent, a man who couldn't design a dress without incorporating a page of Proust, a color lifted from Ingres, a design inspired by Matisse or Picasso, a gesture he'd seen made by Giacometti or Germaine Richier; a man who could justifiably have not only lived like an artist but described his work as an unrivaled art. He didn't do so, being too modest and too charming. But ultimately, the law of the cauldron, the great melting pot of genres, does it not apply equally in a case like that? On what basis can we deny him or anyone else admission to the rank of the artist who melts and boils, absorbs, ingests, crystallizes, and transforms?

As you can see, there's a problem.

If you can claim both one thing and its opposite and cannot decide between them; if to the same question you can give replies that are so different, so contradictory and equally well founded; if you can still say (since I didn't finish the list and the possibilities are almost endless), like Rousseau, that it's the confession that is the genre of genres or, more precisely and following St. Augustine, that it's the confession of conversion that is the great book blessed by God, this implies that the question itself has been badly formulated.

So, following from the remarks I made above and my experience of Aragon's case, I've going to offer you my own personal response to the problem you posed, avoiding an aporia.

There is no major genre: that's the principle of my reply.

Any genre will become major once an artist takes possession of it and decrees it to be such; that's the practical law.

If you prefer, art is like the Messiah, of whom the Maharal of Prague* said that he would never be such-and-such a special person coming at a special moment in time to perform a particular miracle in a particular place. The Maharal said, he's you, he's me, he's any of us at any time in history and no matter where, as long as he's faithful to the Torah and animated by the will to carry out the commandments. In the same way, art is this verse, a page of prose, Praxiteles wielding his chisel or Uccello his paintbrush, it's a wonderful cin-

*Name given to Judah Loew ben Bezalel, Talmudic scholar, mystic, and scholar, best known for creating the legend of the Golem of Prague.

ema shot, the "and" at the head of the sentence in *Madame Bovary*, the added knowledge you get from a novel by Philip Roth, a photograph by Richard Avedon, an autobiographical page by Gombrowicz,* a scene from Aeschylus or Racine. Yes, all that is major, locally and definitively, and may occur even in a single work by the same artist, who, according to his mood, the time, the dead end in which he finds himself, his regular or unsettled breathing, the woman he loves, digs for the materials he needs for his great work under the headings of the genres in turn.

Not to choose—that's the rule.

To be more opportunistic, more of a pirate than the guardians of the temple of genres would allow—that's the secret.

A poet one day.

A novelist the next.

And back to being a poet again on another day when you feel that the art of the novel has exhausted you or that you have temporarily exhausted its resources and its remit.

At least, that's the way I work.

I take the "genres" the way I take a taxi: *Here, this is where I get out . . . thanks and good-bye . . . how much do I owe you?*

I borrow them, the way in the old times you would leave an exhausted horse at a coaching inn and get on another one to take you for the next stage (Michel Foucault and Gilles Deleuze said something of the sort in a discussion published forty years ago in the journal *L'Arc*).[†]

Therefore, in reply to the famous question of the "mental point" from which life and death, the real and the imaginary,

---

*Witold Marian Gombrowicz, Polish novelist and dramatist.

[†]"Intellectuals and Power: A Conversation Between Michel Foucault and Gilles Deleuze," 1972.

the past and the present, etc., would no longer be perceived as contradictory, etc., I take it for granted that for a writer the reply is never rhetorical (verse or prose, poetry or novel . . .) but is a question of diet (what is good at this moment for this body who writes and the body of the writing, which is also a living, growing body?) or even metaphysical (since truth is a being in movement and not only has the right but the obligation to switch from one genre to another according to the needs of its trajectory).

There is no "mental point" other than the mind.

No other light for a work than that of which Proust said, in relation to Vinteuil and his sonata, that even if it were refracted through different surroundings, it would remain the same monotone light.

The literary odyssey has no center other than the ego that surrenders to it, gets drunk on it, and naturally often loses itself in it.

When I say the "ego," clearly I don't mean His Royal Highness with its narcissism, its mirror, its store of stratagems and secrets. I'm thinking of this highly unstable, improbable, fragile, sometimes tiny ego that is nothing more than the subject of the literary adventure, its real "cruel theater," the agent of its construction and deconstruction. I'm thinking of an ego that has become a mere place, sometimes a point, which inflates, empties, swells in time with the work and disappears when the work is finished. Didn't I tell you that I hardly retain anything about Baudelaire, Piero, Angola's cities, Sartre since I wrote of them? And haven't we both had the experience of books that changed us and whose only interest lies in that?

Dear Michel, that's what I think.

That's why I believe that you will write more poetry and I'll write another novel.

That's why you made a film, a very good film, very poetic and metaphysical (bless Arte for having managed in the end to screen it!), which is first and foremost—I must say it again—another zigzag on the road where you scatter and snare your pursuers.

I also wanted to reply to what you said about actresses: one, in any case, for whom I can do no better than to apply Baudelaire's dictum: "my great, my single, my original passion."

I wanted to reply too about Gary, that other writer/filmmaker and master, if ever there was one, in the art of snares and hooks: what an odd idea, that concept of the duties we supposedly have toward our readers getting in the way of Operation Ajar!*

Maybe next time.

For the moment, I'll send you this.

*Émile Ajar was one of Romain Gary's pseudonyms (see page 33).

Maybe I expressed myself badly, dear Bernard-Henri; I think maybe I should start off by dealing with the unnecessarily pompous phrase "major art." But before dealing with this issue, which is almost dearer to my heart than anything else, I'd like to catch my breath and share something I remember, something I've always found funny, about the director of an arts festival in Göttingen, an aging jittery punk who explained to me that he *insisted* that, at his festival, the writers be treated *exactly* the same as the musicians—including the planetary rock stars—and who concluded his diatribe with this phrase, which I could not but agree with, "*Literature is one of the fucking major arts of the Western world!*"

Rather than talk about major art, I should have said *simple art* (in the sense in which we talk about the chemistry of simple bodies) or maybe *profound art*. That is to say, almost the antithesis of what Wagner (whose work I rather like) meant by *total art*. Something that might be thought of as a more generalized version of *cante jondo*.

Obviously, there is not simply poetry. There are the moments when a musician finds, almost in spite of himself, a melody creating itself. There is the gesture, perhaps the most primitive of all (though we can never actually know), where a man dips his fingers into colored mud and traces lines on the wall of a cave.

For me, there are moments when words come, with no purpose, no coherence, no judgment, and then I need a piece of paper because I realize that something is happening. It lasts for a certain time—well, it lasts as long as it lasts—but it lasts long enough for me to write a poem, deep down, that's all I ask for. One morning I will never forget, while I was waiting for and then taking a taxi, I managed to write eight poems, the last of them being "The Possibility of an Island."

But this could never work when writing a novel. What's my maximum? Between five and ten pages, I'd say. After that you have to get blind drunk, calm the machine, wait for tomorrow, when it all starts up again.

And the problems appear only gradually. I'll take a basic example, that will be easier: in *The Possibility of an Island* (the novel), at the point when Daniel and Isabelle meet Fox on a piece of waste ground off a motorway in Spain, I initially wrote that Daniel stepped out of his Bentley. A few months later, my Dutch translator (a guy of incredible precision and rigor, and a nice guy too) pointed out to me that the Bentley had been sold fifty pages earlier; Daniel should have stepped out of his Mercedes. No one at my French publisher had noticed a thing. When I'd visualized him pulling up by the motorway, I'd visualized the Bentley; being a good boy I changed it to the Mercedes. Did I do the right thing?

And this kind of thing happens all the time, because poetry says one thing and coherence, structure, logic tend, with depressing regularity, to say the opposite. If you abide by the poetry, you're not far from becoming unreadable. If you don't, you're all set for a *run-of-the-mill* career as a *storyteller*.

The conflict between these two is my everyday routine when I'm writing books (or, to be exact, when writing novels), this negotiation with lucid consciousness. And with a film it's worse, you need to be entirely aware of what you want because you have to explain it to your collaborators—and to make yourself understood, you have to spell things out. Not to mention the worst of the worst, the *clashes of power*, which require not only lucid consciousness but tactical intelligence, as Patrick Bauchau* warned me early on, with the overused expression "Directing is politics." All of these things—lucidity, politics, tactical intelligence, war—are the antithesis of rapture. So you will understand my joy when I have the opportunity to return to the source, the deep source.

Deep, yes, but I don't want to give the impression of its being overly mysterious. It's easy to laugh at Joseph Beuys's naïve idealism, his crazy projects for social revolution, but it doesn't change the fact that his assertion "every man is an artist" contains a great truth. Because every man experiences moments when he is capable of creating magnificent artistic works, in which his reason plays no part. He experiences them every day, or rather, every night. Put simply, every man *dreams*.

(And even certain animals dream.)

The Surrealists did not invent this deep relationship between art and dream; the first Romantics said exactly the same thing. And all those who have worked in an artistic field throughout human history have known it, even if the Romantics were the first to be forced to defiantly say as much because they came after an eighteenth century of suffocating elegance and rationalism: there comes a moment when things write themselves, beyond the control of reason. This moment may be prolonged, though certainly not by the use of

---

*Patrick Bauchau (born 1938) is a Belgian actor who first came to fame in 1967 in Eric Rohmer's *La Collectionneuse*. He starred in Houellebecq's film of his own novel *The Possibility of an Island*.

drugs (here I can only confirm what Baudelaire says on the subject). All you need do is put off the moment of true wakefulness. When critical consciousness, rational judgment intervene, it is time to stop; to go take a shower. In short, it is time to face the day. You can deal with administrative matters, talk about business, go clubbing, whatever you like; or you can get drunk to get back, as quickly as possible, to sleep; this is the option I have chosen.

Since we began writing to each other, you've talked to me a lot about the writer's body and I confess I have not said much on the subject. But the only thing I can say with certainty, when I think about it, is that for me, it always means a body only half awake. Which of course does not exclude the possibility of having a hard-on. In fact, the point when I've always preferred to fuck is in the early hours, half asleep (*PERSONAL INFORMATION!!!*). Perhaps certain people have made love in a state of complete lucidity; I don't envy them. The only thing I have ever managed to do in a state of complete lucidity is balance my checkbook or pack my suitcase.

That said, I do not adhere to Flaubert's injunction, his sort of phallic maxim: "You have to have erections! You have to have erections!,"* combined with his Stakhanovist corollary: "But your vagina must remain the inkwell."† Shit, you do what you like. There are dreams that are not erotic. Of all the

---

*Flaubert's maxim (from a letter to Louise Colet) is "La vie! la vie! bander, tout est là! C'est pour cela que j'aime tant le lyrisme!" (Life! Life! To have erections! That is everything, the only thing that counts. That is why I so love lyricism!) From *The Letters of Gustave Flaubert, 1830–1857*, translated by Francis Steegmüller (Cambridge, Mass.: Harvard University Press, 1980).

†Flaubert, in a letter to Ernest Feydeau: "Mais, misérable, si tu répands ainsi toujours ton foutre, il ne t'en restera plus pour mettre dans ton encrier. C'est là le vrai vagin des gens de lettres." (Poor wretch, if you sow your wild oats [spill your come] in such a way you will have none to put in your inkwell. That is the true vagina of men of letters.)

criticisms leveled at me, the one that I have put *too much sex* in my books is the most serious, the most universal; it is also the most curious. This is 2008 and it seems to me that Western societies have decided to brush the subject of sex under the rug; and they do not want, really do not want, anyone lifting up a corner of the rug. In 1994, with *Whatever,* I benefited from the element of surprise; since then, people have had time to get organized.

I have a number of honest adversaries, and amid the concert of horrified reactions that greets the publication of each of my books I have a certain fondness for the editorials of Marie-Françoise Colombani.* I remember that when *Platform* was published she wrote, substantially, "You have to keep telling yourself it isn't true, life isn't like this, that it's like some horrid story you might tell children, you have to read this book the way we play at scaring ourselves." I understand that a world in which some men her age go halfway around the world in search of a few minutes of sexual pleasure is hardly likely to delight her; and the fact that some women her age do the same thing is not likely to improve her mood. I understand that this is not the world as she would wish it, I understand all that, I am not writing in order to upset her (and yet, I manage to do so).

After all, her interpretation holds up; because it is true, this is fiction, I've never said that it wasn't. Maybe, like Lovecraft, all I have ever written are *materialist horror stories;* and given them a dangerous credibility into the bargain. I could have chosen to portray senior citizens involved in humanitarian works, fighting racism by surfing the Net, living in the bosom of a loving blended family but still capable

*Marie-Françoise Colombani is a French journalist with *Elle*.

of having a weekend away with their lover in the Lubéron thanks to their two-for-one senior citizen rail pass. I might well do so, if I've got five minutes to spare.

One of the readers' e-mails that gave me the most pleasure in my life was one where some guy started relating (not without talent) different anecdotes from his personal life; then he realized that that wasn't enough, that he should have sketched out his main themes, set out his principal characters, marked out the social boundaries, a whole bunch of things that he was happy for me to do in his place, and concluded with this sentence, which was exactly what I had wanted to hear for a long time: "Thanks for all the hard work."

This man's life was very different from Marie-Françoise Colombani's; but both of them, deep down, reacted as *readers*. I have considerably less respect, in fact I have a serious contempt, for those who give themselves over to some sort of *reductio biographica* and there is little chance that I will forgive their accomplices in the media. The conflict here is simple and brutal. I hold a mirror up to the world, but the world does not find its reflection beautiful; it turns the mirror around and argues, "It's not the world you're describing, it's yourself." I turn it back again and state, "The pitiful articles you write are not about me or about my books; all you are doing is revealing your shortcomings and your lies." The real front line here is not intellectual but moral. Aude Lancelin,* for example, whatever else one might think of her, is capable

---

*Aude Lancelin (born 1973) is a French journalist and literary critic with *Le Nouvel Observateur*; in 2008 she co-wrote *Les Philosophes et l'amour*.

of admiration, whereas Marie-Dominique Lelièvre* is not, and all she sees of the world, her "vitriolic portraits" in *Libération*, bear in every word the colors of her inadequate soul. I could give more examples, but what I am trying to say is that all mirrors distort, and that this distortion still makes it possible for an image to form. Some are also dirty, pockmarked, and here it is more serious because at that point they no longer reflect much of anything. In your last letter, you quote a stupid remark of Gide's; there is another one, even more well known; the famous "fine literature is not made with fine sentiments,"† which is immediately interpreted as a call to use vulgar sentiments. The truth, of course, is that fine literature can be made with any sentiments you like, the finest and the worst, and that one is entirely free to choose the dosage. The problem, I believe, is not resentment, nor sad passions, since what man can entirely avoid them? The problem is the absence of elevation, of enthusiasm, of joyous passions. When all these things coexist in a single soul, it is—from a literary point of view—saved. Or, to put it in more concrete, more immediate terms: I think the point when I really have to worry is the day I stop being bipolar—the day the surface of the mirror starts to tarnish. Or—the other danger—the day it begins to crack, then shatters into pieces.

In this war of mirrors, you were right to note, my victory is guaranteed. Historically, it's a rout. There will inevitably come a moment when the reaction to my books is considered

---

*Marie-Dominique Lelièvre is a French journalist and novelist who is perhaps most famous for her biographies of François Sagan, Serge Gainsbourg, and Yves Saint-Laurent.

†Gide, in his letter to François Mauriac, is actually more damning: "C'est avec les bons sentiments qu'on fait la mauvaise litterature." (It is with fine sentiments that bad literature is made)

to be a *symptom*. Some have already chosen to speak of me in a fictional mode. I have never had a problem with appearing as a character in a novel; I have no choice given that I have become a sort of *public figure;* but the decision still surprises me. And actually, it's only been done by mediocre writers, with the exception of Philippe Djian (in *Vers chez les blancs*). But to make the novel more interesting, Djian had to deviate quite a bit from his model—and the episode with Madonna is very funny, but really has nothing whatever to do with me. The obvious conclusion: as a fictional character, I'm not very interesting.

It is probably a pity, on the other hand, that no one has had the idea of writing a book about the critical reception of my books. I've just spent a week in Poland during which there were exceptionally heated debates, mostly focusing on sexual morality between Catholic conservatives and liberal progressives. One of the most interesting moments was a long conversation I had with a young girl in which she explained how both camps were trying to use me. Interesting to me, I mean; for her, meeting me in person was entertaining, nothing more. Her real subject was not me, nor even books; it was Poland. She managed to shed on the subject the detached, composed light that sociology brings to bear when it succeeds in dissociating itself from immediate ideological issues.

This vaguely Christlike turn my destiny has taken ("I have not come to bring peace, but war";* "they will tear one another apart in my name," etc., etc.) does not exactly plunge me into the depths of joy. All this is distressing, gloomy, tiresome. But what can I do? The die is cast.

*Houellebecq is referring to Matthew 10:34, "I have not come to bring peace, but a sword."

The official version, therefore, is that everything is fine, that things are getting better and better and that the only people who·deny this are a bunch of neurotic nihilists. Whose existence can easily be explained away by some painful family history (raped by his father, abandoned by his mother . . . you get the picture, heavy shit). From this point of view, my mother's reappearance was quite a coup, I have to admit. Visually, she was perfect—a complete nightmare. As soon as she opened her mouth, things went downhill. Her "conversion to Islam," which had given secret agent Assouline food for interpretation, quickly turned out to be a farce; moreover, it soon became obvious that she and I barely knew each other; that we had run into each other once or twice, no more.

When Nietzsche uses Schopenhauer's poor relationship with his mother to explain away his misogyny, he is committing an intellectually terrible act, one that prefigures many others; but at least he has the excuse of plausibility. It is possible to imagine that someone who spent his childhood and adolescence in daily contact with a mother he despised would be unlikely, later in life, to appreciate a woman's qualities. But what about someone who barely knew his mother? One might imagine he would be particularly determined to seek out the company of women; that he would try with all his might to be reunited with this thing that, to him, will forever remain a mystery.

Does this mean I should be a *sex maniac*? Looking back over my life, I have my doubts. I have certainly been one at times, but at other times I find I have been inexcusably offhand. I think that in this, as in everything, I have been bipolar.

And if I am an author (because I am; on that it is too late to have doubts, in fact it would be a little ridiculous to affect *false modesty* at my age), it is, I believe, for a number of fundamental reasons that on the surface seem slight: my way of being half-present, a capacity for stupor, perceptions that are organized in such a way that they can easily crystallize into rigid forms; a neotenic weakness that makes it necessary for me, every morning, more than for others, to relearn how to live.

It is with no pleasure, dear Bernard-Henri, that I see our correspondence coming to an end (but that's how it must be, it is to be published and time is needed to create the object). I have discovered many things that I have not even reevaluated while we were discussing them because they settled in with the serenity of obvious facts. I now think I understand why I have always felt, though nothing in my life story could explain it, that I was "on the side of the Jews." I have also accepted philosophy as a genre of literature, and have come to realize that I like it like that; I have given up classifying it alongside rational certainty and placed it next to interpretations and narratives. Mathematical signs have their domain, textual signs have theirs, I accept that. On balance, I am happy now to see Schopenhauer and Plato not as masters but as *colleagues*.

I have sidestepped certain issues that might have caused conflict: Nicolas Sarkozy, for example, because I have rather a good impression of him. I don't get the impression he's a cynic, he's doing what he thinks is best for France; more important, he is implementing the program on which he was elected. It's curious that, in a democracy, this simple fact can provoke astonishment; clearly, before him we must have been governed by real crooks.

If I avoided the subject of Sarkozy, it certainly wasn't to

avoid confrontation. It's mostly because, among my friends, those I have left, a lot of them despise Nicolas Sarkozy much more than you do and I confess that, when I can talk about something else, it's restful. And on that subject, you can have the last word.

For the most part, we have talked about literature. It's not a bad thing, from time to time, to get things clear in one's mind on the subject. And never before these letters have I felt as strongly how viscerally, primitively, I am attached to poetry. Never had I realized so clearly why I was so proud of having, in the third part of *The Possibility of an Island*, to quote the words used by Sylvain Bourmeau in his review, "brought victory to poetry in the heart of the novel."

We have also talked a little about ourselves. On several occasions in these letters, I have recounted personal memories; I enjoyed doing so in the course of the conversation. Three years ago I made a more systematic attempt at auto-biography, the first fragments of which I published on the Internet; the fact is, I gave up quite quickly. For certain authors, the self, the miserable everyday self, is a privileged means of accessing the universal: I am not one of them. I will never have the serene indecency of Montaigne (nor the less serene one of Gide). I will never write *Les Confessions*, or *Mémoires d'outre-tombe*, or even *Un pedigree*. This is neither because of nor in spite of my esteem for these books and for their authors. It's simply that my natural bent does not tend that way. Rather than dig within myself for some hypothetical truth, I prefer to feel characters being born, developing inside me; I like to feel, between them and between me and them, admiration, hatred, jealousy, fascination, desire. I don't know why, but I need this other life.

You, I believe, are in much the same boat. One can sense your attraction to characters—it comes through clearly in *Le*

*Lys et le cendre**—characters that are immediately ambiguous, beyond redemption, utterly out of place in a book whose aim is to persuade.

So I believe you will write other novels. I think it is desirable and probable; and probable because you desire it. At least these letters will have reminded you of the pleasure of secrets indispensable to the success of such an enterprise. I only say probably, because with you one is never safe from the nightmare scenario. For example, you manage as best you can to free yourself of your most pressing responsibilities; Ségolène Royal is elected president of the Republic and asks you to be her minister of culture, and you accept.

You would be an excellent minister of culture, probably the only thing that might salvage a Ségolène Royal administration; but you would likely be too conscientious to write novels while you were doing it.

We all need role models, at least at the beginning and usually right to the end; but I think that, for you, it is time to break away completely from the *Malraux model*. I know it's difficult; I've talked about how difficult it is for me to break with the *Baudelaire model*, which at my age is tantamount to suicide. It's difficult, but you have to do it.

I feel strange, suddenly, playing the role of adviser, but it's true that when it comes to fiction I'm still pretty hot. And I can well imagine the flak you'll get when you start writing again. I can see them now, the vile little creeps with their evil

---

*Le Lys et la cendre: Journal d'un écrivain au temps de la guerre de Bosnie", (Lillies and Ashes, a writer's diary during the war in Bosnia; untranslated), published by Grasset, 1996.

grins looking at the novels in Grasset's autumn schedule. Oh yes, it could give you pause.

So, what about the *Romain Gary ruse*? Feel free to talk to me about it if you like, I can tell you're tempted by it; personally, I've got something else. Something simple, dead simple, but it has always worked for me.

You simply have to visualize your own death. And imagine that it will occur shortly before publication. After the book has been printed, of course, so you have the pleasure of touching it, smelling it. But a couple of days before publication or, at the extreme, on the publication date itself. Imagine that, as a result, the *critical reception* doesn't affect you at all.

To achieve this, all you need do is summon up some medical crisis, we all have them once we get to a certain age. I've had several of them, specifically, a bout of pericarditis in Rouen I recount in *Whatever:* for an hour or two I really thought I was about to kick the bucket, it was pretty intense. It served me well later, that pericarditis. Whenever I think of that night, I can feel the symptoms. I usually close my eyes, I lie down, and it all comes back with ample precision.

I perform this exercise for a few minutes and afterward, I'm not afraid anymore, I can go for it. I can really go for it.

So go for it, Bernard-Henri. I've lifted a corner of the rug, but there are others; there are as many as you want. It's a circular rug.

I'm also feeling funny about our correspondence nearing its end.

How long has it been? Five months ... six months ... It's been almost six months that we've been writing to each other like this, from a distance, without speaking—just our first phone call the day before yesterday, when I mentioned that I had gone to the country and you asked if the country was Esbly ...*

Good God, Esbly!

I hadn't heard or said the name in twenty years.

Nobody in the world, almost none of my friends, knows or remembers that my parents used to have a house there, sold when that pretty village on the banks of the Marne was poisoned by Disneyland.

And it took you, my secret correspondent, who knows about it from God knows where (I didn't have the presence of mind to ask you), to throw out this name all of a sudden, to draw it back from the semi-oblivion to which I had consigned it and at the same time to inform me that a little later you

---

*Esbly is a commune in the Seine-et-Marne department in the Île-de-France region of north-central France.

spent your adolescence at Crécy, the neighboring village, a mere ten miles away. I used to cycle there or go there by boat on the Ourcq Canal. I recall the smell of the first picnics and of forbidden cigarettes, of blackberries and hawthorn. Guermantes was just down the road . . . a sort of Vivonne . . . my Combray . . . maybe yours.* How strange.

By the way, I mentioned on the phone that I had one of my first flirtations with the daughter of the notary in Esbly. I got that wrong. The notary's daughter was at your place, Crécy. In Esbly there was the butcher's wife. There were two butchers. One of them was called "the dead one" because the real butcher had been found dead in his cold room and his assistant, who was also his wife's lover, had immediately taken over. The other was known as the "cuckold" because his wife, who was also his sales assistant, liked young boys and consumed them in great quantities. She sat enthroned on a high stool, with her Louis XIV hairstyle, attractive chin, and enormous bust just at the level of your eyes, a sort of trunk of a woman, the rest of whose body disappeared into the half-shadow of what you guessed was a small apartment. There was only a gap at the bottom of the pane of glass that divided her from the customers through which she handed people their change. If she liked a boy, she would give him back one franc more than he was owed and that was the signal to meet her at 7 p.m. exactly, under the Marne bridge at the entry to Isles-lès-Villenoy. She would bring her few things—a blanket, a folding chair for putting the clothes on, an empty bottle of aftershave that she had filled with brandy, and in winter a thermos flask with coffee.

In short, we've been corresponding for six months.

---

*Guermantes (meaning "le Côté de Guermantes" or "the Guermantes Way"), Vivonne, Combray: all places with an emotional resonance in Proust.

And it's true that in the course of these six months something has happened.

As a rule I don't really believe in dialogue.

As a philosopher I should—see Plato, Berkeley, Hume, Leibniz, and so many others.

But the truth is, I don't believe in it, and in real life I've never understood the theory according to which it is enough to oppose each other, confront arguments and counterarguments, for the shadows of ignorance to lift as if by magic. In most discussions people arrive with their convictions and leave with the same ones. The idea of dialectics that would allow them to refine their point of view, to enrich or change it, has always struck me as highly unlikely. (Almost as unlikely as that other, Hegelian, idea, or to be more precise so-called Hegelian, which tells us that the dialectics between thesis and antithesis will always ultimately give rise to a synthesis— fortunately, the great Hegel never thought or wrote anything so silly!)

Let me say it again: undeniably something has happened here.

A real effort at dialogue has occurred through which, against expectation, we have moved forward a little.

We didn't convince each other, although, in what you've just said about your relationship with being Jewish and the noun "Jew," and through the story about your mother, I too have understood the impasses of a certain "materialism."

But we are further ahead, I think, as regards what characterizes and is specific to our visions of the world. Do you remember your first letter? "We have nothing in common, as the saying goes, except for one fundamental point we share— our contemptibleness..." etc. You opened fire back then, groping your way through the fog. But the truth is that we knew nothing about each other and certainly about what we did or didn't have in common, whereas today . . . today, there's this correspondence through which we've learned more.

What unites us: the animosity we inspire, that's true; the intuition that allows us immediately to pick up the evil smell of a manhunt. But also (to stick to your last letter, which I believe sums things up nicely): the certainty that we will nevertheless triumph eventually; a joyous love of reading; the love of writers who are also readers of other people's books; pessimism without rancor; the idea that happiness is the utopia of men who don't believe in the unconscious; our liking for cinema; for literature turned up to the temperature of a God, as Nizan* said, and which is in any case primarily a continuation of speech through other means; Esbly (before); Baudelaire (forever).

What separates us: animals (I don't like them); Nietzsche (whom I prefer to Schopenhauer, while the opposite appears to be the case for you); the matter of the Bentley (which I would have left as it was in the novel, because that's how life is, absurd, contradictory, you forget that you sold the Bentley, you believe that you always were who you are now until you wake up one fine morning and notice that time has changed you); your concern, as you said, about sometimes "cooling down" the engine (there too I take the opposite view; the machine will cool down soon enough so in the meantime my advice is rather not to touch anything, to let it do its thing, roar, bolt away—isn't it at these moments of overheating when you have the impression that it's going too fast, too hard, that it's in danger of exploding, isn't that when the literary tool becomes like a hammer with a white-hot shaft hitting the finest sparks?); the use of drugs (I'm in favor); torpor

*Paul Nizan, French philosopher and writer who died in 1940 at age thirty-five.

(I'm against); our lovemaking preferences (I've no objection to doing it half asleep but, to return one confidence for another, I'm one of those people who prefer having their eyes open, their senses alert, being in that state of complete lucidity that you say is good only for balancing your checkbook and packing suitcases); literary technique (we're in agreement of course on waiting for the moment when the book will pour out and almost write itself—except that for me that moment is not one where reason is eclipsed and dreams or thoughts from the depths take over but rather the opposite, where language and therefore, whether you like it or not, logic, meaning, once again lucidity, triumph over vagueness); the theory of the mirror (I did understand the image and I like your way of sending the imbeciles back to the empty two-way mirror they think they can hand you, but allow me to put forward another, loosely inspired by *Spirit [of] the Life*, a book by Chaim of Volozhin, a Lithuanian rabbi of the nineteenth century, which states in substance: What is the point of not exactly books but the Book? What is the point of the centuries spent in schools in the hairsplitting interpretation of the Law when nobody can have the last word? It is what prevents the world from collapsing, from falling into ruins and dust, because God created the world but immediately withdrew from it, abandoning it to itself and its self-destructive forces, so that only study, only letters of fire projected in columns toward the sky, can prevent it from undoing itself and keep it standing. In other words, the commentaries are not reflections but columns, in a world that without them would return to nothingness. Books are not a mirror but the girders of the universe, and that's why it's so important that there should continue to be writers.

There you are.

This list of what we do and don't have in common may interest no one apart from ourselves.

But that's how it is.

It's been established.

The second thing I've enjoyed is that in the course of and because of this exchange, I've said things that I would have otherwise probably never said in the same way.

I've already explained about my pathological taste for secrecy.

And when I say pathological, I mean that because of the partitions, compartmentalizing, lies that are false and false clues that are true, through—as in my novels earlier—multiplying the diversions whose aim is to send the voyeurs to see whether I am somewhere else, I myself, as you put it, sometimes slip up. In such cases, I remind myself of a secret agent who knows that he's on a mission but doesn't know which one or for whom, or of an excessively wily actor losing himself in the panoply of his masks and ruses.

That's just to say that it would never occur to me either to take up my pen to write my memoirs or still less my confessions.

Even around my journal I've built up a truly paranoid protection system, allowing my legal heirs to destroy it immediately should I die without having had time to use it or destroy it myself.

By the way, that's a colorful story.

One night two years ago I was at the bar in the Hotel Excelsior in Venice with Olivier Corpet, the director of IMEC, the Institute of Contemporary Publishing Archives, who is thus a professional, an expert in and fanatic about the archives of writers.

We were accompanying Alain Robbe-Grillet, who had come to present *C'est Gradiva qui vous appelle* to the festival, and we were therefore surrounded by the usual fauna of starlets, fly-by-night producers, and gossip columnists. While waiting for the man of the moment to appear and in order to kill some time, we began to chat about one thing and another.

Corpet put pressure on me, as he does whenever we meet, to start thinking about storing my archives with him.

I teased him, as I also always do, about the twenty thousand and something pages of this fantastic journal full of secrets, one more explosive than the next, which he will never get to hold in his hands because, if I die suddenly and without having been able to use it as I would like to (e.g., as material for a real and lengthy novel), my secretary has been given an order to shred them.

Then he looked at me in a way he'd never done before, with a steady gaze, a Buddhist stillness, and said in a soft voice, almost too soft, each word seeming loaded, "I don't want to upset you but archives are my thing, and I know all about these journals, correspondences, papers kept under lock and key while a writer's alive. There's a law, which, as an expert and fanatic, I can tell you brooks no exception. There is no example—do you understand, not a one—of a document of that kind that really was destroyed and escaped from literary curiosity. Let's save time. I'm sure you've organized everything, I'm not questioning the loyalty of those close to you, but I also know that in one way or another—don't ask me how, the number of scenarios is infinite—a chink will appear in the armor. A betrayal? An emotion? Someone who loves you too much and at the last instant will not have the heart, on top of the sorrow of your death, to burn your papers? An

indiscretion? An error on the part of the bank where I imagine you store the document? Anything's possible, literally
anything, as history has more imagination than man. Whatever measures you take, there will be a bug, a failure, a ruse, a
grimace on the part of history, and your journal, like everybody else's, will end up in IMEC . . ."

I slept badly that night.

That conversation haunted me for weeks.

If I'd been to the Delphic oracle and had learned the hour
of my death, I could hardly have been more agitated.

I used those weeks to set up a complicated system, which
in my opinion is one of a kind, whose function was to thwart
Corpet's theorem and prediction.

From Kafka and Max Brod to Henry Miller's *Crazy Cock*
or the affair of Nabokov's last novel, *The Original of Laura*,
which I heard about thanks to a friend, I studied all the great
cases recorded.

I consulted legal specialists, notaries, attorneys, capable not
only of examining alongside myself the letter and spirit of the
law but also of helping me to make an exhaustive inventory of
accidents, unforeseen and possible events, and to deflect them.

I appointed—without their always being aware of it—chief
inspectors instructed to monitor the executors to my will
when the time came and also to monitor one another.

Like a computer specialist who tries to protect himself
from hackers by increasing the number of barriers, firewalls,
sophisticated and encrypted access codes, and stepped-up
security and alerts, I made a device with double, triple,
indeed quadruple backup, which goes so far as to anticipate
the death of one, the descent into madness of another, the
posthumously revealed stupidity or hatred of the third; and
in case these misfortunes and others should occur all at

the same time, a last-defense lock that in principle will make the system inviolable and inevitably bring about the self-destruction of my capsule of words.

I don't know if I have succeeded. Those who survive me will find out.

I've told you this story to show once more that I'm a real neurotic when it comes to secrecy.

I opened and now close this other parenthesis to let you know that I've always believed that this secrecy was as indispensable to me as the air I breathe.

And I'm going to tell you something rather awful, but when we've come this far, why not? When I was in the thick of Operation Corpet, at the height of my imaginary duel with this charming friend who, through no fault on his part, had become the real incarnation of the devil in my nocturnal and other dreams, in which I heard him, frozen in his stonelike immobility, repeating, "Whatever measures you take . . . whatever measures you take," I saw myself like those tyrants immured in their silence, of whom it is said that a milligram of truth, freedom, or transparency would be enough to kill them, or even those poor American Indians dying like flies from being infected with a pinch not of truth but of unknown microbes.

Now, something extraordinary has happened.

I've spoken to you about my father, my mother, my body.

I've told you some of the reasons why I write, why I'm an activist, why I'm committed, why I keep traveling from one of the world's most rotten wars to the next, why I lay myself open.

In order to tell you this, I've given up my advantageous pose of the friend to humanity, the good man, disinterested and pure.

Not only am I still here, not only has the sky not fallen in on top of me but as a matter of fact I feel rather well.

That may not last.

The opposition, mine I mean, may turn things to their advantage, swarm into the gap I've opened up and see these confessions as confirming their worst suspicions.

They're bound to harp on in this way: "Didn't we tell you . . . no sincerity . . . waited till he was nearly sixty to discover that a writer's foremost virtue is to be authentic . . . au-then-tic . . . but it's too late . . . far too late . . . statue of salt . . . early grave . . . hot air . . . will he ever be quiet . . ."

But that's too bad for them, isn't it?

They're free, if they wish, to mix up the freedom of a writer who as far as he can fights his unequal struggle with the angel or the beast, and this murky "authenticity" that in their mouths means nothing but the absence of style and talent.

I'm emerging from this dialogue serene, happy with the same sort of relief, I imagine, that the criminal feels after his confession.

My impression is that instead of endangering myself, I've been liberated and that I'm ready to reengage with that adventure of the novel that I tasted twenty years ago and which since then, as you understood, I've been afraid to return to.

I can hardly believe it myself, but that's how it is.

It's the best effect our correspondence could have had on me.

There are also all the subjects we didn't speak of, which you seem to regret.

We haven't talked about Sarkozy, you said. Frankly, that's no harm. And I propose that we continue to keep him out of it, a book without Sarkozy being something of a miracle these days.

Nor have we mentioned his opponents on the left, and

that's no loss either. As for my becoming minister of culture, frankly, the post would be so opposed to my lifestyle, to my most pressing literary and philosophical needs, and also to my taste for independence, I think we'd better forget about that.

Among the list of the omissions you regret, there are only two names that I'm also sorry we didn't get to talk about more, and I don't want to finish up without saying at least a word or two about them.

First, Malraux. That giant. Along with Malaparte, perhaps, the most underestimated writer of the twentieth century. Except that in my case I wouldn't describe him as a "model," for the simple reason that I am too torn, fractured, divided, and my taste for multiple, parallel, and contradictory lives is too strong for me to have one single model, no matter how immense, radiant, incontestable he might be . . .

I told you how, when I was a child, I fixed up a hut at the bottom of the garden, among the trees, where I used to hide in order to imagine my funeral and declaim my future oration.

What I didn't mention is that I regularly changed the speech I made, as in the meantime I'd changed my biography and destiny.

I might be a writer whose premature death was lamented.

Or an explorer to whom the word owed the discovery of a city that had been engulfed, an Atlantis.

Or a revolutionary, as incorruptible as Robespierre, as angelic as Saint-Just, as surrounded by women as Danton or Mirabeau.

Or the John the Baptist of a religion whose liturgy and rites I imagined in detail.

Another time, in my musical period, I was a virtuoso who, like Glenn Gould, dropped dead onto his piano.

Another time I was a hero of the Resistance and in a

trembling voice I conjured up the tortures he had been forced to endure in order to make him give up his network, before dying without having said a word.

I can't even say that I was always a hero, a great this or that, lamented by the community of honest folk. My appetite for trying out destinies was so strong, the spectrum of the lives that seemed to me to be worth living seemed so vast, that sometimes I also slipped into the roles of the bad guys, bastards, or official scum, into whose eulogies I put just as much effort: Tony Camonte in *Scarface,* whose execution I considered shameful for the police but rather glorious for himself . . . Cody Jarrett in the final scene, apocalyptic but beautiful and also worth a eulogy in *White Heat* by Raoul Walsh, or, of course, Michel Poiccard, alias Jean-Paul Belmondo, killed by Inspector Vital in the last scene of the great *À bout de souffle,* which contributed no less than the *Comédie humaine* or *Phenomenology of Spirit* to make me the man I am. Jean Seberg was there before me in my garden, in the front row, choking with emotion, grief, and remorse when she heard my oration . . .

And the worst thing is that at those moments when, at the summing-up, the tears came to my eyes as well, it was less my death that I was lamenting than the concentration of merit that I had just been praising, with which Plutarch's *Lives* or Marcel Schwob's *Imaginary Lives* could hardly keep up, and I also mourned all those other lives, the ones the men I buried had renounced and that I didn't have enough of my childhood or—what am I saying—enough of my life left to fit in also.

Fifty years later, I'm still in the same place.

Les vies—Lévy* . . . the lives of my infinite number of models.

---

*Lévy puns on his name to suggest his plurality of lives/identities.

Malraux, of course, without whom there would have been no Bangladesh and no Bosnia.

But Sartre also, the man of the century. And Camus—I dream of writing an equally extensive book about him one day. And Baudelaire, to whom I've already devoted a book containing some of my real secrets. Hemingway because of Spain. Ovid because of the art of loving. And my rabbis. My criminals from Sarajevo. Leibniz of the thousand lives. And those who, like Proust, were able to give themselves to one work only. And the scholars of my adolescence who, while others chased after more conventional ambitions, could risk damnation for an elegy by Tibullus, a rediscovered verse by Ennius, or an ode to Cynthia by Propertius. Others . . . so many others . . . A menagerie of saints and monsters. My uncompounded models. Mine.

And then, there's Gary . . .*

It's true that he's really engraved into me.

First of all, I knew him, unlike Malraux, whom I saw only once, at Verrières, the day before I left for Calcutta. I met Gary quite regularly in the last years of his life, while he was losing himself—the worst thing possible for him and with almost no one suspecting it—in the threads of his Ajar tapestry: long lunches at Lipp where I followed his example, ordering my unchangeable "*entrecôte* steak"; late afternoons at the rue du Bac where we drank tea made in dented samovars, which, as he reminded me each time, he had brought back from Majorca. He had that side to him that was a magnificent loser, a fake firebrand, a comedy cowboy with his Stetsons and his boots with their fussy stitching, that made a change from my teachers in the rue d'Ulm.

---

*Lévy comments again on his affinity with Romain Gary, one further point being that, like Lévy, Gary was married to an actress (Jean Seberg).

Then, there was the principle itself of that Ajar adventure, its premises. Here was a writer who was famous but enraged by his lack of recognition, someone who saw the sparkle of his books dulled by his life, his love story with an actress, his films failing or being regarded as failures. His life and work were engaged in a ferocious competition, in which the first overshadowed the second and the second got into a terrible rage with the first. Here was a man who had been celebrated, won awards, become a member of the Academy, fulfilled, a truly glorious person enjoying all the things you could wish for but suffocating in an identity that choked the very things he cared for most, his novels. I don't need to draw you a picture. With my personality and in my situation, it would be hard for me to be insensitive to that story.

But watch out—I believe that all this was more than a matter of a pseudonym and an oeuvre started up again under a different banner. I believe you cannot understand what a peculiar adventure this was if you see it only as a farce, a ruse, or even a leap made by a writer who considered himself unloved and threw down the gauntlet to his contemporaries: "So you didn't recognize me with my first face? Well, you're going to celebrate me with the mask I'll wear and you'll be taken in." If you prefer, you could describe this as an entire metaphysical dimension, which has nothing to do with those questions of literary vanity or even with my fantasies of a double or triple life, a new birth within the same existence, secrets. It is this dimension that gives the whole business its air of disaster and tragedy and is the reason why this highly fissile material should be handled with care . . .

Unlike what he had already done when he hid behind the pseudonyms of Fosco Sinibaldi or Shatan Bogat, Gary did not content himself with assuming a borrowed name; he gave a body to that name and that was the body of Paul Pavlowitch.*

He didn't even content himself with this body and the biography that went with it (after all, Pessoa had already done that using fifty-something names, each endowed with its own life, imagination, a catalogue of opinions and disputes). He delegated, subcontracted to that body the entire public part of the life of the new writer he was becoming.

In other words, he underwent a unique chemical operation in literary terms, which, by the way, is not unrelated to what you described in your film: between him and Paul, between the real writer he was and the fictional writer he sent in his place to stir things up on the literary scene, one identity was substituted for another, a transfusion of sensibilities and memory occurred, a relocation to a parallel brain, cloning.

And the result of this alchemy, the fruit of this pathetic—and very soon unbearable—duplication, the conclusion of this more than Faustian pact, since he really lost his soul, was a descent into hell. It was the snare that caught him, the lie like an acid that corroded even his zest for life with, at the end of the road, death looming as the only exit. This was not practicing dying, "visualizing" one's own death after the production but before the critical reception of the book; alas, this meant really dying, with a red sheet around his head so that his young son wouldn't be too frightened by the sight of the blood and the pistol shot as the last cadence, the orchestral climax, the logical epilogue to those years he had spent taking himself for another and from another, removing his

---

*Gary's nephew. At this point Gary went beyond using pseudonyms and used a real person, his cousin, to pose as the author of his work published under the name Émile Ajar. Here, Lévy sees this as leading to the dissolution of his personality.

self from himself, the way you would take off a wig or a pair of suspenders.

I saw Gary go mad.

Without understanding, of course, what was going on, I saw him, a number of us saw him, lose his head and die under our noses.

We understand it better today.

I know, we all know, that there was a diabolical undercurrent to this enterprise.

I can see that this is an infinitely seductive temptation but one to which—beyond some pleasant mystification—we must not succumb. It's the very worst there is. I know that I at least have been cured of this unhealthy fascination, not, as you said in your previous letter, out of consideration owed to the reader (we owe them nothing) but because of my appetite for life (and the last images I have of Gary, staggering along the boulevard Saint-Germain, frenzied, his mind elsewhere, death in his step).

Poor Gary, poor "lyrical clown," who believed that you could play with all that with impunity—the art of fleeing, masks, the Oedipal refusal of the patronymic, the zest for a life that he never stopped starting anew. He needed to start anew, of course. He certainly needed to attempt a rebirth. But he needed it in the same life; it had to be in the same life. He needed to stir up a revolution, not only in a single country but within a single identity, a single soul, a single body. My program was his lesson, the real lesson, a mixture of darkness and light, that he reluctantly bequeathed me.

One more word, dear Bernard-Henri, a last word because I think it interesting to dispel the mystery: it was you yourself, in one of your books, who mentioned Esbly. Oh, it's only a brief passing mention, I think you'd have to have lived there to notice it; but you do mention it . . .

One of the things Schopenhauer wrote that I never tire of—it is not one of the major pillars of his philosophy, not the grandiose intellectual reconstruction of the world as Will and Representation, but is one of his disconnected, late remarks, where he expresses doubt about the notion of being, where he envisages the possibility of giving a sense to something analogous to destiny, to the extent that he wonders whether, if his life had been a little longer, he might not have undermined the foundation of his earlier work. Anyway, it is this: "We remember our lives a little better than a novel we once read."

To which I would add that we remember our lives a little less well than a novel we once wrote.

But even that eventually fades. And though I am (a little) younger than you are, I already find it happening with my own books. In general, I'm quite happy with myself; I tell myself, "Hey, I did that . . . it's not bad . . ." But sometimes it's not like that and then I try, desperately, to change the subject.

Just the same, the fact is, in the end we forget even our own books. And I don't know why, but this morning, I find that really comforting.

Really? I don't know. I see what you mean. But I'm not sure I find the idea that comforting. Maybe because of what I have told you on several occasions about my fanatical passion for lucidity. Maybe also because I once experienced for a few hours, I mean really experienced what it is for anyone— and it's even worse for a writer—to have their own memory clinically erased. Salpêtrière* ... the whole accident and emergency drill ... stupidity ... stupor, suddenly hardly remembering your own name, being able only to repeat in a loop before the group of doctors, all aghast, "Baudelaire's illness ... Baudelaire's illness ..."

So maybe you're right and perhaps it's inevitable that one day or another the moment will come when those great chapters of life, of books, grow to resemble pale shadows or mirages or billowing clouds of warmth dissipated by the end of a wonderful, vivid now. But unlike for you, there's nothing that terrifies me more than that prospect. And faced with that fear, that loss, that enforced coming apart, that leaching, I for my part tend to train myself to become an athlete of memory, a puny

*Historical hospital in Paris, previously focused on neurology, now a general and teaching hospital covering most major medical areas.

but tenacious Hercules who either carries his precious images in his arm or pushes them ahead of him, without rest, like a heavy, compact, reassuring boulder that's always head-on.

Sometimes it's exhausting. Nietzsche, like Schopenhauer, even believed that we die of this and that it's the most precise definition of that morbid state par excellence that he called *ressentiment*. No matter. It's what helps me move forward. It's what gives me a sense of time that is not dead time, time that slips through your fingers, or, which comes to the same thing, an eternal present. And to return one last time to the only one of our debates that left me with a taste of insincerity, it's the most serious reason I know for bolstering up one's desire to write and, come what may, to go on.

I don't like all my books equally, of course. Or all the moments of my life. But I like the idea of being answerable for them. And I particularly like the thought that each new sequence is a mute but imperious and joyful interrogation of the preceding ones. Contrary to the famous theory, I don't believe that it's at the last moment, the last breath, that you rediscover the total memory, fully available to itself, that life has dispersed. I believe it's here and now, at every moment of life, as long as it is really lived. On each page of each book, as long as it is intensely desired. And my premonition, if I had one, would be rather that it's time to start worrying when in reply to the question "What is living?" too many of those books, moments in life, or the faces that accompanied them stop answering the roll call. There's a feeling in return for a feeling, a wager for a wager.

Let's wait and see.

Glossary of Letters

Letter of January 26, 2008

In which Michel Houellebecq opens hostilities: "Together, we perfectly exemplify the shocking dumbing-down of French culture and intellect."

Letter of January 27, 2008

In which Bernard-Henri Lévy responds and brings up the lynching, by their contemporaries, of Sartre, Cocteau, Pound, Camus, and Baudelaire.

Letter of February 2, 2008

In which Michel Houellebecq examines Schopenhauer to divide a writer's motives into the desires to please, to irritate, and to conquer.

Letter of February 4, 2008

In which Bernard-Henri Lévy, immersing himself in memories of childhood, resuscitates the ghost of a little scapegoat whose destiny was to illustrate and continue the theories of Girard and Clausewitz.

Letter of February 8, 2008

Social self? Innermost self? Some rules to follow in case of prolonged exposure to *postpolitical society* as Michel Houellebecq invites Bernard-Henri Lévy to follow him along the (perilous) path of "confessional literature."

Letter of February 16, 2008

In praise of cold, nonconfessional literature (Flaubert); in praise of self-interest, of war, and of maximum dissimulation (Pessoa); this is Bernard-Henri Lévy's response.

Letter of February 20, 2008

In which Michel Houellebecq talks about his father and the relationship between his father and his mother and in so doing lifts a corner of the veil.

Letter of February 22, 2008

In which Bernard-Henri Lévy talks about his own father, who, it is revealed, practiced the same profession as one of the celebrated heroes of a novel by Robbe-Grillet.

Letter of March 1, 2008

In which Michel Houellebecq talks about Céline and Proust and recounts how his father, an alpine guide, went skiing with Valéry Giscard d'Estaing and Antoine Riboud. How he himself has developed a passion for post-Soviet Russia—the girls, the music, the energy.

Letter of March 12, 2008

In which Bernard-Henri Lévy vehemently denounces the crimes of "Putinism" and begins his confession, revealing some of the true reasons (honorable and shameful) why writers have to worry about the world and being politically committed.

Letter of March 16, 2008

In which Michel Houellebecq talks about his reasons (honorable, shameful) for not being politically committed—and in passing discusses the reasons for his exile in Ireland. Inaptness for obedience. Mistrust of heroic posturing.

Letter of March 21, 2008

Bernard-Henri Lévy picks up on a remark by Michel Houellebecq (in between a quote from Goethe and commentary on a text by Dürrenmatt) about Houellebecq's inability to distinguish between just wars and those that are not just. Rimbaud and the Paris Commune. Mallarmé and the suffering of the working classes.

Letter of March 24, 2008

Michel Houellebecq does not like chaos: "disorder results in the greatest injustices." Philippe Muray is mentioned; the pressing imperative to distinguish between "reactionaries" and "conservatives"; what might persuade Michel Houellebecq to return someday to France.

Letter of April 4, 2008

Bernard-Henri Lévy is terrified by the void, but likes secret agents. *De natura rerum* or Genesis? Lucretian materialism or the hodgepodge of the Prophets, of Spinoza or Emmanuel Levinas? Bernard-Henri Lévy believes one must choose. Humanity does not have many great books and, alas, one must choose.

Letter of April 10, 2008

First trip to Germany as a teenager. First dazzling encounter with Pascal. In which we learn much about the Christian temptations of Michel Houellebecq.

Letter of April 17, 2008

Memories of uncles Moïse, Hyamine, Maclouf, and Messaoud. The infamy of Jean-Edern Hallier. In which we realize that a child born, like Bernard-Henri Lévy, in the aftermath of the Shoah could not be Christian nor truly Jewish.

Letter of April 26, 2008

In which Michel Houellebecq rejoices to see that the Jews are prepared to face down the new pantheism, which is the true religion of our times. There is talk of Comte, of Chateaubriand, of the Bible, and of Schopenhauer (again).

Letter of May 1, 2008

In which Bernard-Henri Lévy, horrified, refuses to discuss the madness of Kant, the chess games of Marcel Duchamp, or the secret kinship between Comte and Althusser to solicit Michel Houellebecq's reaction to his mother's book.

Letter of May 8, 2008

Michel Houellebecq's response, in which he talks about his mother, a little about his sister, and about the hateful pack which, he believes, will hound him until death and a little beyond.

Letter of May 12, 2008

Bernard-Henri Lévy responds, relying on Spinoza's theory of *sad passions*, predicting the rout of the pack.

Letter of May 20, 2008

One must "carry on writing." But what is the writer's Achilles' heel? Money? Fame?

Letter of May 27, 2008

On the fact that one writes as one makes love and vice versa. That Baudelaire is categorically a better poet than Rimbaud. Who is right, the Lithuanian rabbis, disciples of Vilna Gaon, or Sartre in the *Critique of Dialectical Reason*?

Letter of June 3, 2008

In which we learn that Michel Houellebecq considers the novel to be a "minor genre" compared to poetry. The "radioactive halo" of poetry; the "power of words." There is also some mention of Jean Cohen and Victor Hugo.

Letter of June 8, 2008

In which Bernard-Henri Lévy relates a tale of an evening spent with Louis Aragon in a Paris long since vanished.

Letter of June 26, 2008

Whether it is best to make love in the wee small hours or when completely conscious. Flaubert and Michel Houellebecq respond. Whether Schopenhauer and Plato are masters or colleagues? Michel Houellebecq responds.

Letter of June 30, 2008

On whether Malraux is a model. The truth about the Gary affair? What, at the end of the days, truly separates and unites Michel Houellebecq and Bernard-Henri Lévy? Bernard-Henri Lévy responds.

Letter of July 3, 2008

What one forgets most quickly, of life and of one's books.

Letter of July 11, 2008

Why it is important to try not to forget—and why Nietzsche was wrong in his theory of resentment.